Culture of Class

CULTURE OF CLASS

Radio and Cinema in
the Making of a Divided
Argentina, 1920–1946

MATTHEW B. KARUSH

DUKE UNIVERSITY PRESS
Durham & London 2012

© 2012 Duke University Press
All rights reserved.

Designed by Jennifer Hill
Typeset in Chaparral Pro by Keystone Typesetting, Inc.

Library of Congress Cataloging-in-Publication Data appear on the last printed page of this book.

For Eli and Leah, with love

CONTENTS

ix Acknowledgments

1 Introduction

1
19 Class Formation in the Barrios

2
43 Competing in the Transnational Marketplace

3
85 Repackaging Popular Melodrama

4
133 Mass-Cultural Nation Building

5
177 Politicizing Populism

215 Epilogue
The Rise of the Middle Class, 1955–1976

225 Notes
251 Bibliography
269 Index

ACKNOWLEDGMENTS

I would like to express my gratitude to the various institutions and individuals whose financial, intellectual, and moral support enabled me to complete this book.

Both the National Endowment for the Humanities and George Mason University provided crucial research funding for the project, enabling me to make several trips to Argentina over the years. In Buenos Aires, the staffs of the Archivo General de la Nación, the Biblioteca Nacional, and the Museo del Cine Pablo Ducrós Hicken provided useful guidance to their collections. Fabián Sancho, the director of the library at the Museo del Cine, was particularly helpful in securing images for the book. Julia Choclin of Arte Video helped me assess the availability of Argentine films from the 1930s. Valerie Millholland, Gisela Fosado, and Fred Kameny at Duke University Press have been a perfect editorial team: encouraging, responsive, and constructive at every turn.

Parts of chapters 2, 3, and 5 were published in different form as "The Melodramatic Nation: Integration and Polarization in the Argentine Cinema of the 1930s," *Hispanic American Historical Review* 87, no. 2 (2007), 293–326, and as "Populism, Melodrama, and the Market: The Mass Cultural Origins of Peronism," in Karush and Chamosa, eds., *The New Cultural History of Peronism* (Durham: Duke University Press, 2010). I am grateful for permission to republish.

At George Mason University, I have benefited enormously from being around a group of talented and supportive colleagues. In particular, I would like to thank Joan Bristol, Jack Censer, Michele Greet, Deborah Kaplan, and Mike O'Malley. The late Larry Levine and Roy Rosenzweig were both models of scholarly collegiality. Over the course of many memorable conversations, they taught me more than I can say about doing social and cultural history. This book is better for having been conceived in their presence, but it would be better still had they been around to read the many drafts that I certainly would have sent them.

Over the years, many people read or heard sections of this work and made insightful criticisms and suggestions. Oscar Chamosa, Christine Ehrick, Eduardo Elena, Florencia Garramuño, Mark Healey, Joel Horowitz, Andrea Matallana, Natalia Milanesio, Mariano Plotkin, Mary Kay Vaughan, and Barbara Weinstein were particularly helpful. I also benefited from research assistance from Patricia Inés Conway, Ludy Grandas, and Damián Dolcera. Federico Finchelstein and an anonymous reviewer, both assigned by Duke University Press, gave the manuscript an exceptionally close reading. Their numerous suggestions substantially improved the final product.

Having been trained in labor and political history, I embarked on the study of mass culture with trepidation. The brilliant Alison Landsberg inspired me to pursue this topic despite my utter lack of preparation. Luckily for me, she did not then abandon me to sink or swim on my own. Instead, she patiently guided me through the enormous scholarship on Classical Hollywood cinema and on film melodrama, and she graciously consented to read draft after draft. I am afraid that I still "write about film like a historian," as she once gently observed. Yet insofar as I have managed to avoid an entirely reductive approach to mass culture, she deserves most of the credit.

An inexplicable case of filial insecurity led me to neglect my parents in the acknowledgments section of my first book. To their credit, they never complained about the oversight, but let me set the record straight here:

I am deeply grateful to Drs. Ruth and Nathaniel Karush for their love and support as well as for setting such a high standard of intellectual integrity.

Finally, even though they probably do not realize it, my children, Eli and Leah, have made a substantial contribution to my scholarship. Not only are they tons of fun to be around, but they also ask great questions. Their curiosity is an inspiration, and it is to them that I dedicate this book.

INTRODUCTION

In 1932 the writer Roberto Arlt described the challenge facing Communist organizers in Argentina: "Out of 100 proletarians, 90 have never heard of Karl Marx, but 90 can tell you how Rudolph Valentino used to kiss and what kind of mustache [the Hollywood actor] José Mojica wears."[1] Arlt's pessimism regarding the revolutionary potential of the nation's workers was prescient. To the immense disappointment of a generation of leftist intellectuals, the large majority of the Argentine working class would reject Socialist and Communist parties, embracing instead the populist movement built by Juan and Eva Perón in the mid-1940s. But more illuminating than Arlt's assessment of working-class consciousness is his reference to the movies. Arlt recognized not only that workers made up a substantial proportion of the audience for mass culture in Argentina, but also that the mass culture they consumed must have had a significant impact on their consciousness, one potentially as decisive as their experience of exploitation or their participation in class struggle. That Arlt used two Hollywood stars to make his point is also revealing. By invoking Valentino and Mojica, he drew attention to the powerful influence of North American commercial culture in Argentina.

Arlt's suggestion that mass culture tended to dilute class consciousness anticipated the arguments of contemporary historians who have described the 1920s and 1930s as a period in which the militant working-class consciousness of earlier years gave way to a less class-based identity. For these scholars, Argentina's expanding economy effected a kind of national integration, in which radical ideologies were replaced by the pursuit of upward mobility. At the start of the twentieth century, politicians and intellectuals were haunted by the specter of a largely immigrant working class enthralled by anarchism and syndicalism. Yet within a few decades these fears had been dispelled. The new "popular sectors," largely the Argentine-born children of immigrants, were focused on self-improvement and were far less hostile to the state and the nation than their parents had been; they embraced integration into Argentine society as the means to a more comfortable life.[2] The radio and the cinema are typically seen as contributors to this process. Through film distributors and radio networks based in Buenos Aires, Argentines throughout the country were increasingly exposed to a common national culture. Moreover, this new mass culture allegedly encouraged consumerism and middle-class aspirations, thereby reinforcing the trend away from working-class militancy.

Yet despite these dynamics, Argentina was, if anything, more divided in 1950 than it had been in 1910. Although a generation of workers had turned away from orthodox leftist ideologies, their enthusiasm for Peronism revealed that they were still inclined to embrace a working-class identity. The Peróns mobilized the nation's workers behind a project of state-led industrialization and corporatist social organization. They addressed their followers as workers, celebrating their proletarian status. Peronism polarized the country along class lines, creating a fragmented national identity that would persist for decades. Somehow, a society characterized by ethnic integration and the decline of orthodox left-wing ideologies also contained the seeds of this populist explosion and of the intense, class-based polarization that followed. This book argues that the key to understanding this paradox lies in a reassessment of the mass culture of the 1920s and 1930s.

Arlt was right to emphasize workers' enthusiasm for the movies, but he was wrong to assume that this pastime came at the expense of class consciousness. The films, music, and radio programs produced in Argentina during the 1920s and 1930s trafficked in conformism, escapism, and the fantasy of upward mobility. But they also disseminated versions of national identity that reproduced and intensified class divisions. Facing stiff competition from jazz music and Hollywood films, Argentine cultural producers tried to elevate their offerings in order to appeal to consumers seduced by North American modernity. At the same time, the transnational marketplace encouraged these cultural producers to compete by delivering what foreign mass culture could not: Argentine authenticity. Domestic filmmakers, radio and recording entrepreneurs, lyricists, musicians, actors, and screenwriters borrowed heavily from earlier forms of popular culture such as tango music and the short, comic play known as the *sainete*. The result was a deeply melodramatic mass culture that extolled the dignity and solidarity of the working poor, while denigrating the rich as selfish and immoral. Despite myriad efforts to modernize and improve domestic mass culture, the Argentine media tended to generate images and narratives in which national identity was prototypically associated with the poor. The profound classism of this mass culture has been overlooked by historians who have depicted the radio and the cinema as instruments of national integration and middle-class formation. Instead of unifying national myths, the Argentine culture industries generated polarizing images and narratives that helped provide much of the discursive raw material from which the Peróns built their mass movement.

THE SIGNIFICANCE OF MASS CULTURE

The primary objects of analysis in this book are mass cultural commodities: movies, recordings, and radio programs produced by capitalists seeking to attract an audience in order to turn a profit. As such, these sources pose a particular challenge to the historian. Most basically, they cannot be seen as a direct reflection of popular consciousness. Pop songs and movies are made by artists who are unlikely to be in any way typical of the larger population. More important, the relationship between these artists and the people who consume the products they make is anything but simple or direct. Recording companies, film studios, radio stations, and advertisers intervene, as do the state, intellectuals, fan magazines, and critics. As a result of these multiple layers of mediation, the mass cultural market does not simply give people what they want. Through marketing strategies, audience segmentation, genre definition, and in many other ways, the capitalist media, themselves under complex and competing outside pressures, help shape audience preferences.[3] Most of these effects vary unpredictably across time and place, but some are more universal. As Stuart Hall pointed out long ago, the mass media tend to direct attention toward consumption and away from production, thereby fragmenting social groups into individual consumers and forging new groupings designed to facilitate capital accumulation.[4] In short, mass culture is not so much a reflection of its audience's attitudes, values, and worldviews as it is one of the forces that work to shape them.

Within the Marxist tradition, the line of argument that depicts mass culture as fundamentally manipulative descends from the work of Theodor Adorno and Max Horkheimer. In their attack on the "culture industry," published in 1947, Adorno and Horkheimer emphasized the predictability and homogeneity of mass culture. They argued that movies and commercial music encouraged a passive response, leaving no room for the audience's imagination. The result was a depoliticized working class, incapable of thinking for itself or of generating any critique of the status quo.[5] This view goes far beyond the assertion that mass culture helps shape popular consciousness to assert that it is always and inevitably an instrument of social control and top-down manipulation. Since the 1970s, scholars in both cultural studies and cultural history have tended to reject this pessimistic—and, some would say, condescending—view. Within cultural studies, scholars have reconceptualized consumption as an active process in which consumers make their own meanings out of the commodities supplied by the culture industries. From this perspective, culture is a contested space; ordinary people are shaped by the images and meanings disseminated by mass culture even as they reshape those meanings for their own purposes.[6] Cultural historians like Lawrence Levine have agreed, insisting on the agency of the mass cultural consumer: "What people *can* do and *do* do is to refashion the objects created for them to fit their own values, needs, and expectations."[7]

Far from the all-powerful, monolithic products that Adorno and Horkheimer imagined, mass cultural commodities enable oppositional readings in particular ways. For Jürgen Habermas, the mass media help modern capitalism overcome its perpetual "legitimation crisis," but not without generating a series of contradictions. Capitalism, according to Habermas, seeks to spread consumer consciousness by elevating private consumer choice over social and civic responsibility, but since this new form of consciousness threatens established values and cultural practices, it requires validation. Mass culture invokes the moral authority of older patterns of family and community life in order to legitimize a society characterized by consumerism and commodified leisure. Yet by continually reintroducing those older values, the media provide consumers with the means to criticize capitalism.[8] Following Habermas, George Lipsitz has shown how North American television programs of the 1950s featured ethnic, working-class families in order to encourage viewers to embrace consumerism. These families reminded viewers of a cherished past rooted in community and working-class solidarity, while at the same time suggesting that all individual needs could be satisfied through the purchase of commodities. Still, if this reconciliation of past and present was useful to advertisers, it was inherently unstable.[9] The film scholar Miriam Hansen reaches similar conclusions in her study of North American silent cinema. The early cinema, she argues, appropriated earlier cultural traditions and popular entertainments as its raw material, depoliticizing them in the process. But this depoliticization was never total. The persistence of these earlier traditions meant that the cinema contained the potential for "alternative public spheres." Subordinate groups like women and working-class immigrants could, at times, find in the cinema a space from which to elaborate their own autonomous points of view.[10]

The work of Lipsitz, Hansen, and others suggests that mass cultural commodities are inherently polysemic. The subordination of cultural production to capitalism does not obliterate alternative or oppositional meanings. On the contrary, the profit motive impels the recycling and repackaging of elements that push against the privatizing thrust of consumer capitalism. As a result, mass culture, like culture more broadly, both enables and constrains, providing a limited but varied set of discursive raw materials from which consumers can build their own meanings. Analysis of this meaning-making process needs to attend to the context of reception—how and where consumers interact with mass culture—as well as to the points of tension or latent contradiction that exist in the texts themselves. Finally, the best scholarship in cultural studies and cultural history reminds us of the political significance of mass culture. The cinema and the radio constitute important sites for the elaboration of identities, values, and aspirations which can and do become the basis for political action.

THE TRANSNATIONAL CONTEXT: ARGENTINA'S PERIPHERAL MODERNITY

Both the production and the consumption of mass culture typically occur in transnational contexts. Even though people throughout the world attend local movie theaters and listen to radios in their own living rooms, much of what they consume is imported, and even domestically produced mass culture is created in dialogue with foreign styles and practices. The Argentine audiences described in this book enjoyed imported films and music alongside domestic products, and that context shaped the way they interpreted what they saw and heard. For their part, Argentine mass cultural producers self-consciously competed against foreign imports that enjoyed significant technical, economic, and cultural advantages. In short, this was a mass culture decisively shaped by what Beatriz Sarlo has referred to as Argentina's "peripheral modernity." Examining the intellectual and literary circles of Buenos Aires in the 1920s and 1930s, Sarlo describes a "culture of mixture, where defensive and residual elements coexist with programs of renovation; cultural traits of native formation at the same time as an enormous importation of goods, discourses and symbolic practices."[11] Extending Sarlo's concept to Latin America as a whole, Nicola Miller emphasizes the "uneven and dependent" character of Latin American modernity, in which formal political sovereignty combined with economic dependence.[12] In the 1920s and 1930s, Argentines were fully engaged in modernity, enthusiastically adopting the latest technology, tastes, and styles. Yet their nation's visibly subordinate position in global economic, political, and cultural circuits also produced ambivalence, nationalist defensiveness, and localist nostalgia. Something very much like the "culture of mixture" that Sarlo finds in vanguardist novels is also visible on the level of mass consumption.

As Benjamin Orlove and Arnold Bauer have argued, Latin America's distinctive postcolonial identity crises produced a nearly insatiable demand for imported goods.[13] After achieving independence from European empires in the early nineteenth century, elites redefined their relationship to Europe even as they sought new justifications for racial hierarchies rooted in the colonial experience. Consumption was a key site for this process of national identity formation. In consuming European imports, Latin Americans were engaged in an effort to create local versions of modernity, which they understood to be centered in Europe. By the twentieth century, the locus of modernity was increasingly shifting to the United States, even as an active culture of consumerism was extending far beyond the elite classes. Corporations in the United States, penetrating Latin American markets to an unprecedented extent, launched an ambitious effort to disseminate North American "corporate culture" abroad. Along with North American goods came a fascination with newness, an ethos of individualism, and the ideal of the self-made man.[14] Yet as Julio Moreno demonstrates for the case of Mexico, the arrival of goods, retailers, and advertising agencies from the United States did not produce a one-way process of Americanization. On the contrary, North American businesses were only successful when they adapted their message to Mexican nationalism, producing a "middle ground" in which cosmopolitan modernity could be reconciled with Mexican tradition.[15] The rising commercial influence of the United States had profound but complex consequences for Latin America, producing hybrid discourses, rather than straightforward cultural domination.

Recent scholarship on the influence of mass culture from the United States in Latin America has reached similar conclusions. Bryan McCann has shown that the introduction of jazz in Brazil in the 1930s, as well as the domination of the local recording industry by the multinationals Columbia and RCA Victor, did not Americanize Brazilian popular music. Instead, these corporations appealed to Brazilian fans with new hybrids that mixed local rhythms with cosmopolitan arrangements.[16] Like other North American businesses trying to succeed in Latin American markets, mass cultural producers had to adapt their products to the local context. However, Latin America also received a flood of imported mass cultural goods that were originally designed for the North American market. Here, too, historians have uncovered complex outcomes. Eric Zolov argues convincingly that the adoption of rock music by Mexican youth in the 1960s and 1970s ought not to be considered an instance of cultural imperialism. A generation of middle-class Mexican kids appropriated a set of North American cultural practices and preferences in order to forge an alternative, countercultural national identity.[17] Similarly, jazz music and Hollywood movies held an irresistible appeal in Latin America as symbols of modernity. But Latin Americans did not simply capitulate to foreign cultural domination. On the contrary, they appropriated imported cultural forms for their own purposes, while generating domestic alternatives that aimed to reconcile the local with the cosmopolitan.

By the 1920s several decades of rapid economic growth in Argentina had made a range of both domestic and imported goods available to an ever-growing segment of society. Alongside increases in the demand for foodstuffs, cigarettes, and clothing, Argentina also imported rising numbers of typewriters, bicycles, and telephones. Local advertising agencies imitated the techniques of their North American counterparts, using market research and sophisticated designs to expand the market. At the same time, the introduction of the radio and the cinema extended the democratization of consumption to the cultural sphere. Seemingly overnight, the new technologies transformed daily life for many Argentines, particularly those who lived in Buenos Aires and other cities. In 1930 there were eighteen radio stations broadcasting in the capital, and movies were shown in more than 150 theaters located in all the neighborhoods of the city. Alongside domestic productions, these radios and theaters offered patrons a steady diet of jazz music and Hollywood movies. By 1927 Argentina had become the second biggest market for film from the United States, far surpassing its much larger neighbor, Brazil.[18]

As in other parts of Latin America, the enthusiastic adoption of technology and mass cultural content from the United States did not obliterate local cultural practices, but it did exert a powerful influence. Argentine representatives of multinational recording companies produced a steady stream of tango records that betrayed the influence of jazz instrumentation and arrangement. But despite this influence, these records continued to offer consumers a clear alternative to imported and domestic jazz. Argentine-owned radio stations developed a programming formula that emphasized both tango and jazz, alongside a growing menu of radio theater, modeled partly on Hollywood plots and partly on local theatrical and literary traditions. Similarly, Argentine film studios elaborated a cinematic style that combined Hollywood elements with a self-conscious localism. In all these ways, mass cultural industries produced what I will call, paraphrasing Miriam Hansen, "alternative modernisms" that reconciled cosmopolitan modernity with local tradition.[19] In other words, Argentine mass cultural producers competed for domestic audiences by emulating the technical and stylistic standards set by North

American imports, even as they distinguished their own products by highlighting their *Argentinidad*.

This self-conscious effort to represent the nation was visible in the refusal of many tango bands to incorporate the drum set; in tango lyrics that featured *lunfardo*, the popular Buenos Aires slang; in film plots and characters drawn from an established, local tradition of popular melodrama; and in countless other ways. All of these gestures amounted to efforts to construct and to market authenticity. As Michelle Bigenho points out, any claim of "cultural-historical authenticity . . . purports a continuity with an imagined point of origin, situated in a historical or mythical past."[20] By invoking an allegedly unchanging essence, representations of authenticity offer a consoling experience of rootedness for people facing a world of rapid and uncontrollable change. Invoking authenticity was the only strategy available to Argentina's small mass cultural entrepreneurs. Lacking the resources of their competitors from the North, they could strive for, but never quite achieve, modern style and technique. Yet their global marginality gave them preferential access to local tradition.

Latin American alternative modernisms have been most visible to scholars as elements in intellectual and official programs of cultural nationalism. As the ethnomusicologist Thomas Turino describes the process, "Cultural nationalists typically express that a new national culture will be forged from the best of local 'traditional' culture combined with the best of foreign and 'modern,' that is, cosmopolitan, culture. The localist elements (e.g., gauchos, 'folk' music) in the reformist mix are for emblematic distinction and also function as signs of unity or inclusion; the cosmopolitan features (e.g., national anthems and 'folk' music) create iconicity with other nation-states, and are also due to the fact that the designers of state-cultural nationalism are cosmopolitans themselves."[21] This sort of cultural nationalism was certainly present in Argentina, where the writings of intellectuals like Ricardo Rojas inspired a program of folklore research in the early twentieth century. After Perón came to power in 1946, several influential cultural nationalists joined the government, helping it to elaborate a cultural policy built on the principle of harmonizing Argentine folk culture with the best of the modern world.[22] Nevertheless, I will argue that Argentina's local-cosmopolitan hybrids were chiefly the result of forces unleashed by mass cultural capitalism, rather than the inventions of intellectuals or politicians.[23] During the period studied in this book, the radio and cinema, while not completely free from state intervention, were shaped primarily by the contradictory pressures of the market. Alternative modernisms resulted from attempts to appeal to consumers who were accustomed to North American standards of modernity but who also demanded authentic Argentine products.

Since they were the result not of top-down projects but of the messy functioning of a capitalist marketplace, Argentine music, radio programs, and movies disseminated unintended and even contradictory messages. They were polysemic in the ways described by scholars of North American mass culture: built by repackaging elements drawn from existing popular culture, they contained the basis for oppositional readings. But Argentina's peripheral modernity—its subordinate position within transnational cultural networks—deepened this potential by necessitating the turn to authenticity. Lacking the means to replicate Hollywood or jazz modernity, Argentine cultural producers needed to stress their national distinctiveness. And the Argentine images and narratives available to them were distinctly populist in tone. As in the rest of Latin America, elites had embraced European products and cultural practices throughout the nineteenth century; Argentine "high culture" offered little that was distinctive. The only cultural practices that could be packaged as authentically Argentine were those of the poor.[24] Borrowing heavily from a highly developed tradition of popular melodrama, mass culture tended not only to celebrate the poor as the true representatives of the nation, but also to denigrate the rich.

As I will argue in more detail in the chapters that follow, comparison with the United States throws into relief the centrality of class in Argentine mass culture. In a series of groundbreaking essays, the historian Warren Susman described the essentially conservative role played by consumer culture in the United States during the 1930s and 1940s. In this view, a culture of material abundance provided the basis for the construction of a powerful sense of national belonging. Historians have modified Susman's conclusions, pointing out that the impact of mass consumerism was not necessarily conservative; for example, the rise in labor militancy during the Depression may well have represented an effort by workers to realize the promise of consumer culture. Nevertheless, in the long term, mass consumption does appear to have led to a more unified nation.[25] And within that process, the mass-culture industries played a salient role. According to the film historian Lary May, Hollywood films of the 1930s imagined a more diverse, pluralistic, and just nation, providing a language for a new national consensus even before the New Deal began to make it a reality.[26] Likewise, in the realm of popular music, Lewis Erenberg stresses the inclusiveness of the swing era in jazz.[27] Not all historians are as sanguine, but most do call attention to mass culture's capacity for national mythmaking. Robert Sklar, for example, argues that in the context of the Depression and the rise of Nazism, American filmmakers "saw the necessity, almost as a patriotic duty, to revitalize and refashion a cultural mythology." In Sklar's account, filmmakers like Frank Capra and Walt Disney avoided critiques of American society in favor of national myths that audiences could easily embrace.[28]

The national myths packaged in North American mass culture, whether essentially progressive or conservative, were not easily transposable to the Argentine context. Despite the enthusiasm with which local cultural producers imitated styles popular in the United States, their products tended to reproduce an image of an Argentine society deeply divided by class. Like their North American counterparts, Argentine filmmakers celebrated hard work, yet this trait was usually insufficient to overcome class prejudice. Argentine films appealed to their audience's dreams of attaining wealth and living a good life, yet they delivered these consumerist fantasies alongside explicit denunciations of the selfishness and greediness of the rich. Tango stars performed in black tie and were celebrated as modernizers and innovators, yet they were only deemed authentic to the extent that they had roots in the gritty world of lower-class slums. Tango lyrics endlessly revisited the story of the pure, humble girl from the barrios seduced and ruined by an evil *niño bien*, or rich kid, and by the luxurious, immoral world of downtown cabarets. In short, Argentine mass culture encouraged consumers to identify the nation with the humble. Both the cinema and the radio celebrated poor people's capacity for solidarity, generosity, and honesty while attacking the egotism, frivolity, and insincerity of the rich.

INTERDISCIPLINARY CULTURAL HISTORY

Methodologically, this book belongs to a large and growing body of literature within Latin American history dedicated to exploring the connections between culture and power. Inspired by the Gramscian tradition, this scholarship views culture both as shaped by social, political, and economic processes *and* as a key factor in shaping those processes. It situates culture explicitly within the process of state formation, exploring how commitments, alliances, and identities are constructed simultaneously from above and below. Attentive to the unequal distribution of power, it nonetheless refuses to impose the reductive framework of domination and resistance. According to one formulation, "popular and elite (or local and foreign) cultures are produced in relation to each other through a dialectic of encounter that takes place in arenas and contexts of unequal power and entails reciprocal borrowings, expropriations, translations, misunderstandings, negotiations, and transformations."[29] In this spirit, this book offers a cultural history that explores how meaning is produced in a complex interaction between the state, capitalist entrepreneurs, intellectuals, critics, artists, and consumers.

Such a cultural history requires interdisciplinarity. More specifically, it requires borrowing from social history on the one hand and from a wide range of "culture studies" on the other. This book relies heavily on the extensive literature on Argentine social history, particularly in the subfields of immigration studies, labor history, and urban history. This literature provides the basis on which I can contextualize the production and consumption of mass culture. The changing physical geography of Buenos Aires, the development of neighborhood and working-class institutions, the interactions between immigrant groups and "natives," the ebb and flow of the economy, and the transformations of the political system all helped determine the meanings that mass culture disseminated, even as mass cultural messages shaped the way people experienced these social, economic, and political phenomena. Yet a purely social-historical approach to mass culture would be insufficient. Social historians often note the existence of mass culture while avoiding any examination of its content. Vexed by the difficulty of ascertaining how mass cultural messages were decoded by audiences of the past, they often limit themselves to examining the conditions of production and reception: Who produced the movies and radio programs and under what constraints? Who owned a radio? Who went to the movie theater? When, how, and with whom did they engage in these activities? These questions are all vital, but cultural history must also directly explore the content of the mass culture that Argentines consumed.

Toward that end, I have benefited from a large and sophisticated body of literature in a variety of disciplines, including film studies, musicology, literary studies, and cultural studies. Tango lyrics and music, pulp fiction, newspapers, sports, movies, and theater have all been the object of sustained analysis by scholars in these fields. In addition to a wealth of insights about particular mass cultural products, this scholarship underscores the importance of paying attention to genre and form. When we treat songs as if they were poems meant to be read, when we analyze the plot of a film without attending to the mechanics of the cinematic apparatus, when we ignore the process of genre formation and how it constructs meaning, our analysis suffers.

Nevertheless, cultural history has its own contributions to make. For one thing, cultural history can avoid putting mass cultural forms into hermetically sealed interpretive boxes. Quite understandably, film scholars tend not to consider the music industry, while musicologists have little to say about film. Yet in practice, these two cultural fields were inextricably entwined at every level. Radio station owners were often involved in film production, popular singers became movie stars, film plots and tango lyrics developed in tandem, and, most important, the audiences for these entertainments obviously overlapped extensively. The "generalist" approach of the cultural historian may amount, in some contexts, to a lack of expertise, but it also enables him or her to identify larger trends and tendencies that may be misread as specific to one medium or another. Even more important, cultural history asks different questions than do other disciplines. The best cultural history, focused on questions of power, treats movies or pop songs much the same way it treats political speeches or manifestos. Of course, going to a movie is not the same thing as attending a political rally or going on strike. Yet neither do people shut down their political consciousness when they walk into the theater. Commodified mass culture disseminates the ideological and discursive building blocks with which individuals construct their identities and points of view. By exploring mass culture, and in particular by attending to the points of tension or contradiction that structure the possibilities for oppositional or alternative readings, cultural history can illuminate key issues in political, social, and economic history.

This book examines a wide range of sources in order to chart the central dynamics of mass culture in the 1920s and 1930s. My primary focus is on the texts themselves: films, radio plays, tango, and folk songs. But my reading of these texts is informed by an analysis of the production process and a consideration of mass cultural consumption practices. Rather than divide the process of meaning-making into analytically distinct moments of production and reception—what Stuart Hall described as "encoding" and "decoding"[30]—I have tried to attend to the ways these levels of meaning-making are intertwined. Argentine filmmakers, for example, were consumers of Hollywood products and local theatrical traditions, even as they were producing their own alternatives. In the transnational marketplace, there was no moment of production that was not also a moment of reception. Needless to say, this analytic approach cannot overcome the paucity of sources available to study the appropriation of mass culture at the grassroots. Since oral history is no longer a viable option for this period and in the absence of surveys or other similar material, I have relied extensively on the entertainment press to inform my readings of mass cultural texts, as well as to chart the debates that swirled around mass culture. Fortunately, vibrant "letters-to-the-editor" sections do enable the voices of ordinary consumers to come through, even though these voices are heavily mediated. Finally, this book does not offer a cultural history of the entire nation. The production of mass culture in this period was almost entirely dominated by Buenos Aires: Argentina's film studios were located in or just outside the capital, and the nation's radio networks were based there as well. Just as important, the primary market for Argentine mass culture was composed of the residents of *porteño* (or Buenos Aires) barrios. The reception of these products in the Argentine interior is an important object of study, but it lies outside the scope of this book.

THE MASS CULTURAL ORIGINS OF POPULISM

The populism of Juan and Eva Perón was more than an instrumental appeal to workers' material interests; it was an identity and worldview that resonated with their experiences and attitudes. More than thirty years ago, Ernesto Laclau argued that the power of Peronism lay in its ability to mobilize already existing cultural elements and rearticulate them in defense of the class interests of Argentine workers. For Laclau, "populism starts at the point where popular-democratic elements are presented as an antagonistic option against the dominant bloc."[31] Laclau's examination of these "popular-democratic elements" focused primarily on the formal political realm: he explored the capacity of Hipólito Yrigoyen's

Radical Party to articulate liberalism with democracy and then argued that this synthesis fell apart in the 1930s. Yet the two decades before the advent of Peronism saw the transformation of the radio and the cinema from novel curiosities into a major part of everyday life. As Roberto Arlt recognized, this new mass culture must have had an impact on popular consciousness. In the chapters that follow, I argue that consideration of the films, music, and radio programs of the period can help resolve some of the persistent puzzles about this period in Argentine history and shed important new light on the origins of Peronism.

The 1920s and 1930s appear in Argentine historiography as a crucial transitional period, but the nature of the transition has remained mysterious. With the onset of the international economic crisis in 1930, Argentina experienced several key changes: The massive immigration of the previous period came to an end as did the experiment in electoral democracy on the national level begun in 1912. The Depression also catalyzed a major economic and demographic transformation, deepening a process of import substitution industrialization and, by the late 1930s, spurring large-scale migration from the provinces of the interior to greater Buenos Aires. In other ways, though, these decades reveal important continuities. Economic growth had produced the rapid urbanization and expansion of barrios in the outlying zones of Buenos Aires, neighborhoods characterized by a heterogeneous population and significant levels of homeownership. The 1920s and 1930s saw the spread of advertising and consumer culture, the growing importance of neighborhood associations promoting self-improvement and upward mobility, and the rise of a much more inclusive public sphere, with the emergence of popular tabloid newspapers like *Crítica*. Partly thanks to the increased demographic weight of the children of immigrants, anarchism and syndicalism lost their appeal, and the labor movement lost members and militancy at least until the Communist-led resurgence of the late 1930s. But if this period is characterized by the decline of unions, the rise of consumerism, and the pursuit of upward mobility, then where did the Peronist explosion come from? If the 1920s and 1930s were marked by national integration, then how can we explain the profound, class-based polarization of the 1940s?

Much of the literature on the origins of Peronism has focused on the process of industrialization, internal migration, and the rise of industrial unions.[32] But the majority of Perón's followers did not belong to any union before 1946, and even unionists enjoyed a life away from the shop floor and the union hall. By examining the content of mass culture in this period, this book offers a new perspective on the roots of Peronism. My contention is that the spread of consumerism and mass culture in the 1920s and 1930s did not promote a decline in class consciousness. Historians have too easily assumed that upward mobility, self-improvement, material abundance, and homeownership represent "middle-class" aspirations, and that the rise of these values must coincide with a decline in working-class consciousness and, indeed, in the significance of class itself. These assumptions leave scholars struggling to account for the apparently sudden reemergence of class in the popular imagination after the advent of Peronism. What the cinema and radio reveal is that class was not, in fact, disappearing during the 1920s and 1930s; it was instead being refigured. Mass culture embraced the deeply classist, Manichean moral vision of popular melodrama, disseminating versions of national identity that privileged the poor and rejected the rich. On movie screens and over radio waves, this classism was combined with consumerist titillation, conformism, the celebration of individual upward mobility, misogyny, and other conservative messages. The result was a deeply contradictory discourse, but one in which class loyalties still resonated powerfully. In other words, many of Arlt's proletarians were proud of being proletarians, even if they also dreamed either of kissing or of being Valentino. When Juan Perón emerged after the military coup of 1943, he spoke a language that was built to a significant extent from mass cultural elements. These discursive borrowings help explain his appeal for workers who, as Arlt recognized, were unlikely to embrace Communism. By charting the emergence of populism within the commercial mass culture of the 1920s and 1930s, this book illuminates both the power and the internal contradictions of Peronism.

Chapter 1 examines the fluid process of class formation under way in the expanding barrios of Buenos Aires, where the primary audience for the new mass culture was forged. In these areas, uneven economic growth and a series of contradictory discourses from advertisers, neighborhood associations, labor unions, and political parties meant that class identity was very much in flux. Upward mobility was the dream for many, but it coexisted with expressions of class consciousness. As cultural producers sought to attract consumers, these competing discourses inevitably found expression in the movies and on the radio. Yet the fluidity and indeterminacy of class identities in the barrios also meant that the new mass culture would exert a profound influence on the consciousness of its consumers.

Chapter 2 explores the introduction of the phonograph, the radio and the cinema in Argentina and assesses the strategies through which small, undercapitalized firms sought to compete against their wealthier rivals from the North. The entrepreneurs who came to dominate the new culture industries tended to be immigrants who were open to exploiting the commercial potential of popular cultural forms disdained by elite Argentines. Although they emulated North American standards of mass cultural modernity, they were unable to replicate them. Instead, they offered consumers an alternative modernism that repackaged existing popular culture, offering fans a distinctly populist vision of Argentine authenticity. While this sort of populism came to dominate radio programming, the nascent film industry was forced to accept a segmented market in which domestic films were screened in "popular" theaters and ignored by many of the well-to-do. These consumption patterns reinforced the classism of the new mass culture.

Chapter 3 examines the meanings of Argentine melodrama. More than a genre, melodrama was a language that shaped virtually all mass cultural products in this period. Melodrama was premised on a profoundly fatalistic view of the world, in which individuals were victimized by fate, and resistance was futile. Yet at the same time, by positing a Manichean world in which poverty functioned as a guarantor of virtue and authenticity, melodrama presented Argentina as a nation irreconcilably divided between rich and poor. In this way, melodramatic mass culture disseminated the ingredients for a profound critique of the values that supported the status quo. Even the heavily gendered aspects of Argentine popular melodrama—its tendency, for example, to punish women for the "sin" of pursuing a better life—reinforced a subversive class message by celebrating working-class solidarity.

Chapter 4 explores the contradictory results of the many attempts to sanitize and improve mass culture. Despite efforts to purge music, film, and radio theater of their associations with plebeian culture and violence, the commercial viability of these commodities depended on their capacity to satisfy nostalgia for an authentic past defined by just these troubling associations. Unable to reconcile modernity and authenticity, Argentine mass culture swung between an insistence on middle-class respectability and a defense of plebeian grit, between the pursuit of upward mobility and the celebration of working-class solidarity. Despite the proliferation of efforts at mass-cultural nation building—attempts, for example, to identify an untainted folk culture in the countryside or to elaborate a high art based on Argentine folk traditions—cultural producers failed to generate national myths capable of integrating the nation across class lines.

Finally, chapter 5 examines the political appropriations of mass cultural images and narratives of national identity after the military coup of 1943. By reading Juan and Eva Perón's rhetoric of 1943–46 in light of the preceding analysis, this chapter will reveal the mass cultural origins of Peronism's essentially moralistic view of class conflict, its critique of the egotism of the wealthy, and its celebration of the humility, solidarity, and national authenticity of working people. Likewise, I will argue that Peronism inherited many of its contradictions—such as its tendency to attack elite greed while legitimizing working-class envy and to embrace both anti-elitism and conformism—from the cinema and radio of the preceding period. Peronism's debt to mass culture helps account for the movement's explosive appeal. It also helps explain how such a polarizing political movement seemed to appear so suddenly. The deep social divisions that characterized Argentina after the rise of Peronism were incubated and reinforced on movie screens, on radio waves, and in fan magazines during the 1920s and 1930s.

CLASS FORMATION IN THE BARRIOS

Los tres berretines (1933), one of Argentina's earliest feature-length sound films, is a comic meditation on modernization, consumerism, and mass culture. An opening montage of congested downtown streets set to jazz music establishes the film's setting in cosmopolitan, chaotic, ultra-modern Buenos Aires.[1] The camera then leaves the city center and enters one of the quieter outlying barrios. Here, the hubbub is created not by cars and pedestrians but by a group of kids playing soccer in the street. The camera settles on the exterior of a hardware store and then moves inside, where the owner, the Spanish immigrant Manuel Sequeiro, is helping two women interested in purchasing an electric bed warmer. The women are dissatisfied with the model the store owner shows them. It seems this apparatus is "vulgar," not at all like the ones they have seen in the movies and in magazines. Manuel declares that he doesn't sell "cinematic bed warmers" and angrily shoos the women out of his store. His bad mood worsens when the soccer ball the kids are playing with flies through the front door, smashing into the merchandise. Cinema and soccer are, along with tango, the three *berretines*, or "popular passions," of the film's title. And like his store, Manuel's value system has been upended by these new mass cultural practices and the desires they have awakened. As we soon learn, his wife and daughter have abandoned their domestic responsibilities in favor of frequent trips to the cinema with a male friend of dubious sexuality. One of his three sons wastes his days fantasizing about making it as a tango composer despite his complete lack of musical education, while another dreams of becoming a star soccer player. Meanwhile, the economic crisis of the period has dampened the prospects of his one worthy son, an unemployed architect whose financial difficulties are about to cost him his upper-class girlfriend. Manuel's traditional values—hard work, patriarchy, education—seem suddenly useless, replaced by the consumerist titillation offered by movies, tango, and soccer. Yet the film offers a happy ending. Although denounced as "bums" by their father, both the tango composer and the soccer player find success. The latter becomes a star forward and convinces the management of his club to hire his architect brother to design the new stadium, thereby rescuing him from poverty and allowing him to marry his girlfriend. In the end, Manuel himself embraces the new mass culture, climbing a telephone pole in order to join thousands of fans cheering on his soccer-playing son.

Most obviously, *Los tres berretines* is about the quest for upward mobility: both Manuel's commitment to work and education and his sons' pursuit of success on the stage or in the stadium are strategies for improving one's class position. But between these two paths from rags to riches, the film clearly sides with the pursuit of stardom, poking fun at both the immigrant's faith in hard work and his pursuit of middle-class respectability. Lorenzo, the soccer-playing son, saves the day and Eduardo, the architect, gets the girl, but the star is unmistakably Luis Sandrini, who plays Eusebio, the would-be tango composer.[2] Spending the day hanging out in cafés, happily whistling his tango and being victimized by swindlers who promise to help him get it transcribed, Eusebio poses a clear alternative to the gospel of hard work and personifies mass culture's promise of an escape from drudgery (see figure 1).[3] Moreover, Eusebio's success as a composer depends upon his rejecting pretentiousness and embracing plebeian tastes: when he pays a café poet to write lyrics for his tango, he rejects the first draft as too fancy and holds out for what the poet disdains as "pedestrian verses." The result is "Araca la cana"

| Luis Sandrini dreams of tango stardom as Eusebio in *Los tres berretines*. Courtesy of Museo del Cine Pablo Ducrós Hicken.

("Look Out for the Cops"), a tale of frustrated love told almost entirely in lunfardo, the famously disreputable porteño slang. Similarly, the final, carnivalesque image of Don Manuel perched on the telephone pole outside the soccer stadium underscores the defeat of his apparently old-fashioned notions of respectability. Manuel has overcome his condescension toward Argentine mass culture; he has recognized the value and the beauty of both tango and soccer. If the third berretín is excluded from this happy resolution—Lorenzo's soccer success "cures" his sister and mother of their unhealthy cinema addiction—it might well be because the movies being shown in Buenos Aires theaters in 1933 were overwhelmingly foreign productions. Like the cinematic bed warmer of the opening scene, these imports are merely the occasion for frivolous, unproductive consumption. By contrast, Argentina's domestically produced mass culture is productive; it has reunited the Sequeiro family and enabled its immigrant patriarch both to reconcile himself to the modern world and to assimilate into the nation.

Los tres berretines must be understood in the context of a complex process of class formation under way in the Buenos Aires of 1933. During the preceding decade, dynamic economic growth and industrial development produced significant social mobility, a mushrooming consumer culture, and the rapid expansion of new barrios that were home to a heterogeneous population of blue- and white-collar workers as well as small business owners and professionals. But if these developments encouraged a blurring of class distinctions, Los tres berretines reveals forces pushing in the opposite direction. While Eduardo's commitment to hard work and education leaves him unemployed, his brothers succeed precisely by rejecting those values. This film, like so many other mass cultural products in these years, celebrates the cultural practices of Argentina's poor, not the diligence of its upwardly mobile architects. The movie's rags-to-riches narrative reads as escapist fantasy, a fantasy that spoke not to typical, middle-class values like hard work, education, and respectability, but to a sense of pride in Argentina's plebeian popular culture. The resonance and power of such populist messages in the mass culture of this period suggest that class-based identities persisted in these years.

This chapter will situate the emergence of Argentina's new mass cultural technologies and commodities within the context of the rapidly changing economic, political, and social conditions in Buenos Aires. Although the radio and cinema reached a massive audience throughout the country, both media targeted the capital city first and foremost. And in the rapidly growing barrios of Buenos Aires, class identity was very much in flux. Residents of these neighborhoods were the targets of various competing and contradictory messages: from commercial advertising's promises of upward mobility to the barrio improvement associations' paeans to progress and "culture," from the appeals to national unity favored by politicians to the labor movement's insistence on working-class solidarity. This was not a population that had sorted itself into rigid, class segments. Since mass cultural entrepreneurs needed to build an audience within this milieu, their radio programs and movies were influenced by existing discourses. Nevertheless, the fluidity of class identities in this period meant that the new mass culture would exert a profound influence of its own on the consciousness of porteños. During the 1920s and 1930s, many porteños would follow the Sequeiro family in embracing a nation constructed in large part by mass culture.

MOBILITY AND ETHNIC INTEGRATION IN A TIME OF GROWTH

Beginning in the last quarter of the nineteenth century, Argentina experienced a vertiginous process of economic growth, demographic expansion, and modernization. The nation's insertion into an increasingly globalized economy as a major producer of wool, beef, and wheat led to impressive growth rates and massive immigration. Between 1875 and 1930, Argentina's population exploded from two million to twelve million, and its gross domestic product increased by a factor of 20. And despite its long-standing image as an essentially agrarian country, Argentina also achieved significant levels of industrialization in this period, both in sectors connected to the export business as well as in the production of consumer goods for the growing domestic market.[4] By 1914, in fact, the industrial sector was the nation's largest employer, and 58 percent of the population lived in cities. The social and cultural transformations that accompanied these processes were dramatic to say the least, and nowhere were they more evident than in the city of Buenos Aires. Although the export boom of the late nineteenth century led to the rapid growth of several provincial cities, Buenos Aires dominated the nation's banking system, its import and export trade, and its nascent industrial sector.[5] The political and economic primacy of the capital city imposed a severe limit on development elsewhere: by 1914 Greater Buenos Aires was home to 25 percent of the nation's population, a proportion that would continue to rise in subsequent decades.

Paradoxically, the massive scale of immigration to Argentina in this period may have facilitated a relatively rapid process of national integration. Historians have long questioned the popular image of the country as a melting pot, in which a national culture emerged magically from the blending of various European strains. Immigrants often preferred to marry people of the same ethnic and even regional background, and this preference likely slowed the process of assimilation.[6] Moreover, regional and ethnic identities flourished in the host country, nurtured in part by an extensive network of ethnic mutual aid associations, clubs, newspapers, and other institutions. By 1925, for example, the Spanish community in Buenos Aires enjoyed a total of 237 voluntary associations.[7] Italians, the largest immigrant group in Argentina, did not lag far behind. In 1908 there were seventy-four Italian mutual aid societies in Buenos Aires with a total membership of more than fifty thousand.[8] Nevertheless, these ethnic affiliations did not prevent the rapid Argentinization of the immigrant population. The fact that men always outnumbered women within the immigrant communities forced a great many Italians and Spaniards to marry Argentine women. And fragmentary evidence indicates that the Argentine-born children of immigrants tended not to take ethnicity into account when choosing a spouse.[9]

More important, immigrants in Argentina were not marginalized to the extent that they were in other host societies. This is not to deny that Argentine elites and intellectuals were often extremely xenophobic. During the early twentieth century, anarchist mobilization helped inspire a profound anxiety about the effects of immigration, and the state responded with repressive deportation measures and an intensely patriotic curriculum in the schools. Still, other, less coercive forces were at work. Unlike, say, New York City, Buenos Aires was never a city of ghettos. In fact, in 1910 the Argentine capital had one of the lowest average indices of ethnic segregation in the world, a pattern that continued as the city expanded.[10] Similarly, immigrants in Argentina were far less likely to be relegated to certain occupations at the bottom of the social structure. The major immigrant groups were well represented among property owners and within the Argentine elite.[11]

Even if the notion of a melting pot is too simplistic, the pioneering Argentine sociologist Gino Germani was probably right to argue that what might be seen as the assimilation of immigrants into a dominant culture is more accurately described as a process of cultural "fusion."[12] Given the small size of the pre-immigration population, immigrants enjoyed a demographic dominance in Argentina that they lacked anywhere else. By 1914 foreign-born men outnumbered native-born men in Buenos Aires and several other cities. That same year, 80 percent of the Argentine population was composed of immigrants and the descendants of people who had immigrated since 1850.[13] Although the country was home to significant communities of Russians, Poles, and Ottoman Turks, the majority of immigrants came from Italy and Spain. As a result, the religious, cultural, and even linguistic differences between immigrant and native populations were minimized. Immigrants could not, of course, reproduce

Old World societies in America, but they did fundamentally remake Argentine culture. This impact is partly visible in the many Italian and Spanish customs adopted as Argentine: the opera and the zarzuela, which dominated popular entertainment offerings in the early decades of the twentieth century, or the pasta, pizza, and *puchero* that continue to be staples of the local diet. But ethnic integration is perhaps even more obvious in what might be called cases of "invisible ethnicity." The Podestá brothers, Uruguayan-born sons of Genoese immigrants, virtually invented the *circo criollo*, an enormously popular turn-of-the-century entertainment that celebrated the rustic talents and culture of the Pampas. Their ethnic origin posed no obstacle to their ability to play the role of quintessentially Argentine gaucho heroes like Juan Moreira. Similarly, when Argentine soccer teams played rivals from abroad, sports columnists saw the local players as representatives of a *criollo*, or native, style, regardless of their actual ethnicity. The Argentine club Provincia that faced a visiting Scottish team in 1928 included such surnames on its starting roster as Bearzotti, Talenti, Tornatti, and Lunghi, yet they were described by one reporter as "a team of native boys (*muchachos criollos*)."[14]

In truth, ethnic identity had not disappeared, so much as it had been relativized. Immigrants continued to be the butt of jokes as they had been since the late nineteenth century, when the character of Cocoliche was created in order to ridicule Italian newcomers for their broken Spanish and their desperate efforts to assimilate. But by the turn of the century, cocoliches were clowns whose participation was required in any enactment of criollo or native culture; the presence of an Italian immigrant now lent authenticity to representations of the nation.[15] Similarly, making fun of immigrants was the central comic ploy of the sainete, the short play that dominated porteño theater in the early decades of the twentieth century. Increasingly, though, this humor had a gentle, lighthearted tone. By the 1920s many sainetes depicted the embarrassment that the children of immigrants felt for the awkward and old-fashioned customs of their parents.[16] By laughing at these jokes, audiences were not only teasing immigrants; they were also endorsing the assimilationist project of the second generation. *Los tres berretines*, which originated as a sainete, reveals the same attitude: Manuel Sequeiro is comically out of touch with current Argentine popular culture, but successful assimilation requires only that he learn to love the soccer and tango music of his sons. In the 1920s immigrants continued to be targets for xenophobic, nationalist intellectuals as well as for playwrights pursuing an easy laugh, but their children were widely seen as Argentine. Ethnic affiliations persisted, as the vitality of Italian and Spanish mutual aid associations attests, but they did not block the emergence of more inclusive, hybrid forms of national identity.

Immigration came to an abrupt halt in 1930, when the international Depression began to take a significant toll on the Argentine economy. The end of the era of massive immigration reinforced the declining significance of ethnic division, as the proportion of foreigners in the Argentine population fell from 40 percent in 1930 to 26 percent in 1947.[17] But economic developments continued to reshape the population of Buenos Aires. Although the interruption of international trade reversed nearly a decade of strong economic growth, the Argentine economy recovered more quickly than most of the more developed world. By 1934 grain exports had resumed, and economic recovery was in full swing. Meanwhile, the Depression had provoked a deepening of the process of import substitution industrialization under way since the 1890s. Led by growth in textiles, the manufacturing sector boomed. As David Rock notes, "In 1935, the value of industrial production was still 40 percent below that of the agrarian sector; in 1943 industry surpassed agriculture for the first time."[18] Beginning in the late 1930s, this industrial growth produced a significant flow of migrants from country to city. Between 1937 and 1947, 750,000 migrants, mostly from the neighboring provinces of Buenos Aires, Santa Fe, Entre Ríos, Corrientes, and Córdoba, arrived in Greater Buenos Aires, where they now represented a significant proportion of the growing industrial workforce.[19]

The 1920s and 1930s, then, were decades of economic convulsion, as prosperity gave way to crisis and then recovery and transformation. Unsurprisingly, this economic history exerted a profound impact on the geography and social organization of Buenos Aires. The rapid growth rates of the 1920s produced significant levels of social mobility. Needless to say, the poor did not benefit equally from the boom; inflation produced a dramatic increase in the cost of living at the beginning of the decade, and unemployment remained a significant problem.[20] Still, real wages climbed steadily, if moderately, from 1923 to 1928.[21] In Buenos Aires, this economic growth was accompanied by a dramatic transformation in the spatial distribution of the population, deepening the urbanization of outlying areas that had begun earlier in the century. With the construction of an extensive public transportation system—by 1910 the city already had over four hundred miles of electric streetcar track—and the availability of parcels of land that could be purchased in monthly installments, new barrios grew rapidly, especially in the northern and western zones of the city, and increasing numbers of porteños relocated from the congested city center. The barrios of Almagro, Caballito, Flores, Belgrano, Palermo, and Villa Crespo all emerged around 1910, and the process continued throughout the 1920s and 1930s. In 1914 the outlying census districts of Vélez Sarsfield, San Bernardo, and Belgrano were home to 300,000 people, or 20 percent of the city's population. By 1936 the population of these areas had mushroomed to 1,000,000, or 40 percent of the total.[22]

As we have already seen, Buenos Aires had never been a city of ghettos. With the exception of Barrio Norte, the city's exclusive, upper-class district, and a handful of working-class neighborhoods such as the Italian portside community of La Boca, residential areas were not segregated by ethnicity or class. Nevertheless, housing conditions at the turn of the century tended to underscore class differences. As Argentina's economy took off, Buenos Aires was unprepared for the massive numbers of immigrants who poured into the city. As a result, workers endured precarious housing arrangements and severe overcrowding. In the absence of a large-scale transportation network, most people needed to live near their workplaces downtown. In 1887, 26.5 percent of the population lived in centrally located *conventillos*, formerly elite residences transformed into dilapidated tenements housing multiple working-class families.[23] Others lived in small apartments, hotels, and various types of improvised shacks in what was then the outskirts of the city. But conditions changed dramatically with the growth of the barrios. As early as 1919, the proportion of the population living in conventillos had dropped to 9 percent, replaced in large measure by single-family houses, which sprang up with impressive speed throughout the new barrios. By 1930 the three outlying districts contained more than 50 percent of the city's buildings, the majority of them single-family residences.[24]

The journey from a downtown conventillo to a single-family, owner-occupied home in the barrios is something of an Argentine cliché, symbolizing the social mobility that characterized the period. To be sure, historians have qualified the image, pointing out that only the most privileged workers were able to afford the monthly payments, and even they needed the extra income of family members. Many would-be homeowners were victimized by speculators selling unlivable lots. Rental housing, often of quite poor quality, remained common throughout the city in the 1920s and 1930s. Moreover, even those who did manage to purchase land and build their own homes often faced extremely difficult conditions, in the form of a lack of basic services and shoddy construction.[25] Nevertheless, the general picture of relatively high levels of social mobility in these years does seem supported by the evidence. With the transition to an open and competitive electoral system on the national level in 1912 and in the municipality of Buenos Aires in 1917, patronage jobs in the rapidly growing public sector became an important avenue for advancement into the white-collar workforce.[26] But the expansion of the state was hardly the only factor at work. As scholars of immigration have shown, Argentina's middling level of development created many opportunities for newcomers beyond manual labor, enabling them to achieve more occupational mobility than either more or less developed destinations. Even as industrialization spread and large factories became more common, proletarianization proceeded far more slowly in Buenos Aires than in cities like New York. Not only was there a greater proportion of skilled labor in the workforce, but also it was far more common in Buenos Aires for immigrants like Manuel Sequeiro to become their own bosses.[27]

Like the shop owner in *Los tres berretines*, most immigrants dreamed of a better life for their children, and here also, evidence suggests a high degree of success. Crucial in this regard was Argentina's system of public education, which made white-collar work as well as the professions accessible to many children from humble families. Examining the records of the largest Spanish mutual-aid society, José Moya has demonstrated that while 43 percent of Spanish-born women worked as servants in 1920, only 13 percent of their Argentine-born daughters did. By 1930 the proportion of Spanish women servants had remained roughly constant, but the daughters were doing even better: only 9 percent were servants, while 30 percent had achieved "professional" status, mostly as teachers.[28] Studies of Italian immigrants and their descendants reveal similar patterns.[29] Overnight, rags-to-riches success remained a rarity, but the economic expansion of these years made significant upward mobility from one generation to the next a realistic goal. As the case of the Spanish servants and their daughters suggests, economic growth expanded women's participation in the workforce. And women were not only domestics and teachers; they were also present in meatpacking plants and textile mills. As early as 1895, women represented 22 percent of the economically active population, and nearly one-third of those employed by the capital city's largest factories.[30] As the industrial sector grew over the next few decades, so too did the numbers of women working outside the home.

The barrios that grew with such speed in the 1920s and 1930s, products of economic growth and social mobility, were extremely heterogeneous. Professionals, merchants, and small business owners lived alongside public employees, white-collar workers, skilled artisans, and industrial laborers. At the turn of the century, large factories had been mainly confined to the city's southern districts, a tendency that was reinforced by a municipal regulation in 1914 that created specific industrial zones. As a result, many residents of the new northern and western barrios lived far from their workplaces, a tendency that likely encouraged patterns of social interaction that did not revolve around work. Nevertheless, this trend ought not to be overemphasized. Despite the zoning ordinance, the 1920s and 1930s saw significant industrial expansion in Buenos Aires's three outlying districts, which by the mid-1940s housed 38 percent of the city's industrial establishments. Both domestic manufacturing and construction work were widespread in the barrios. Still, Buenos Aires had hardly become a factory town; alongside industrial development, the city also experienced a major expansion in both the commercial sector and the government, both of which continued to be major sources of employment in the city.[31]

CLASS IDENTITIES IN FORMATION

The rapid growth of the barrios as well as the diversity of the population that lived there made for an extremely fluid process of identity formation. Barrio residents were the targets of multiple, competing appeals, which sought to constitute their identities in diverse ways. Among the most salient of these appeals were those that emanated from a host of new associations and institutions, including political party committees, soccer clubs, libraries, newspapers, and the omnipresent *sociedades de fomento*, or development societies. These latter organizations tended to dominate the burgeoning public sphere of the barrios, and if they originated as vehicles for making concrete demands on the state, they soon took on more explicitly ideological roles, actively disseminating a set of values that included progress, education, culture, and morality. In 1926 *Labor*, the newspaper of the Corporación Mitre, the sociedad de fomento of Barrio Nazca, described the institutions' evolution this way: "The sociedades de fomento of the Federal Capital have left aside their primitive modalities as groups of enthusiastic residents who, acting in hostile climates, combined their efforts toward the simple goal of getting one or another street paved and drained. . . . Their action is [no longer] limited to the physical improvement of the zones in which they operate, but rather they also work on the diffusion of primary and secondary education, on the creation of libraries and popular culture centers where the mentality of the people is forged."[32] As *Labor* proudly proclaimed, these new barrio associations aimed to shape the consciousness and identity of the heterogeneous residents of the barrios they represented. The sociedad de fomento was an ideological instrument wielded by an emerging elite that hoped to impose its own vision on the barrio. Central to this hegemonic project were the many popular libraries created either by the sociedades themselves or by outside institutions such as the municipal government or the Socialist Party, which by 1932 had organized fifty-six of them throughout Buenos Aires. The barrio library served, as local leaders in the barrio of Barracas put it, as an instrument for disseminating "culture" to the "popular classes."[33] This project was visible both in the collections of books housed by the libraries, which emphasized the classics of the Western literary canon, and in the principal activity that took place there: the *conferencia*, in which visiting speakers addressed heterogeneous audiences on such topics as public health, education, literature, or art. As several historians have argued, these well-attended events offered barrio residents the opportunity to acquire "culture." What mattered was not so much the particular knowledge one could gain from a public lecture, but rather the performance of a certain "desirable lifestyle" that emphasized respectability, formality, and education. The goal was self-improvement as a means to achieve upward mobility.[34]

Many of these values were, in fact, visible in the origins of the barrios. As Adrián Gorelik has argued, the municipal government played an active role in shaping the new barrios, particularly those that emerged in the southern and southwestern parts of the city. Concerned about the potentially negative effects of industrial development, authorities embarked on the project of moralizing the working-class population of this part of the city through urban reform, including especially the construction of parks and plazas. The Industrial Regulation of 1914, which lent juridical force to the de facto segregation of industry in the southern districts, also aimed to ensure the creation of the *suburbio obrero decente*, or decent working-class suburb. The model for this type of community, according to Gorelik, was Parque Patricios, a barrio created in 1902 when the municipal government dismantled the old slaughterhouse in the southern district of San Cristóbal and replaced it with a park. Similarly, when working-class housing developments were built nearby, each was oriented around a green plaza. The idea was that these green spaces could impose a certain moral order on the leisure time of workers and thereby help build a decent, respectable community. By the 1920s Parque Patricios's reputation as a model, working-class barrio was enshrined in works of literature, and the suburbio obrero decente had become, in Gorelik's words, a "cultural paradigm."[35] The sociedades de fomento and popular libraries run by barrio elites embodied the same moralizing impulse visible in official urban reform. These institutions were instruments for imposing a particular model of respectability and decency. Even as they promised to deliver progress for the community and upward mobility for the individual resident, they also represented an effort to discipline the barrio population.

The image of barrio society that local elites disseminated via their associations, their libraries, and their newspapers was strongly inclusive. Social division and conflict were virtually absent from the lectures held at the popular libraries, even those run by the Socialist Party. Instead of class struggle, this discourse suggested that cooperation across class lines, as embodied by the sociedades de fomento themselves, was the most effective means of achieving social reform.[36] Local newspapers defined the barrio in opposition to the city center: whereas life downtown was dominated by money and selfish individualism, healthy family life and communal cooperation in the barrios eliminated, in the words of one community newspaper, "hateful social differences." In this discourse, as Luciano de Privitellio has pointed out, the barrios were both modern and capable of ameliorating the worst consequences of modernization. In the barrios, progress was open to anyone who was willing to embrace the values of hard work, morality, and culture.[37] This spirit of inclusiveness was visible as well in another characteristic of the discourse: barrio associations vehemently insisted on and celebrated their apolitical character. The identity they sought to impose on the barrio was supposed to unite residents across petty distinctions of class or political faction.

Yet egalitarian rhetoric could mask or even facilitate elitist practice. In addition to serving communal interests, barrio organizations also provided positions of leadership for more "distinguished" residents.[38] In particular, the sociedades de fomento, despite insisting on their apolitical character, played an important role in politics both by presenting specific barrio demands to the authorities, and by occasionally aligning explicitly with one or another political party in order to affect policy more generally. In the mid-1930s, for example, a large group of sociedades de fomento seeking to protest the high rates charged by CHADE, one of the city's electric companies, lent their support to the Socialist Party. In response to this threat, the conservative *intendente*, Mariano De Vedia y Mitre, was able to put together a competing coalition of barrio organizations.[39] For barrio leaders to attain this sort of political relevance and power, they needed to appear both as advocates of modernization and progress and as the legitimate representatives of their communities. Their commitment to an inclusive, egalitarian vision of progress was, thus, a key component of their hegemonic practice. Barrio leaders, who were most often doctors, merchants, or public employees, were involved simultaneously in the construction of an egalitarian, inclusive image of the barrio and in the pursuit of an elite status that would allow them to speak for the community. In fact, residents were encouraged to participate in community organizations as a means of achieving distinction: even if entry into the Argentine political or economic elite remained far out of reach, a white-collar worker or small shop owner could realistically aspire to becoming a *vecino notable* in his barrio.[40] At times, the tension between inclusiveness and elitism could produce conflict, as, for example, when barrio elites criticized the preference of many residents for soccer over other, more "serious" cultural pursuits.[41] Clearly, the efforts of barrio elites to dress their institutions in egalitarian clothing did not convince everyone. The left-leaning tango poet Dante Linyera offered a more cynical, class-conscious interpretation: "In every barrio there is a sociedad de fomento for the rich and a police station for the poor."[42]

The competing tendencies toward egalitarianism and distinction were visible beyond the public sphere of the barrios; they were apparent as well in the changing consumption practices of porteños. As Fernando Rocchi has argued, rapid economic growth, urbanization, and rising industrial production in turn-of-the-century Argentina laid the groundwork for the emergence of a "consumer society."⁴³ As market culture spread, demand for domestically mass-produced goods like cigarettes, beer, and ready-to-wear clothes skyrocketed, and advertising gained new significance. Beginning in the early twentieth century, Argentine newspapers and magazines were filled with colorful announcements seeking to attract potential consumers and encourage brand loyalty. The target audience for much of this advertising, and the bulk of the market for the new products of domestic industry, was composed of the same heterogeneous population moving into the new barrios: workers and white-collar employees seeking, in part, to emulate the tastes and fashions of their social superiors. As Argentine industrialists recognized, elites bought imported goods; demand for the products of domestic industry came entirely from workers in pursuit of upward mobility and "the social classes of middle pecuniary position."⁴⁴ This new consumer society helped produce a blurring of class distinctions in public life. Industrialists happily noted the tendency of porteño workers to spend a lot of money on proper shirts, ties, and even gold watches, while well-to-do porteños bemoaned the presence of plebeian families in the formerly aristocratic Palermo Park. As Rocchi has shown, denunciations of the nouveaux riches were common in the literature of the 1920s and 1930s. In 1932, for example, the writer Enrique Loncán declared that Argentina was the land of the *guarango*, a crude, poorly educated, and pretentious striver who failed to appreciate true elegance.⁴⁵

While these critiques testified to the democratizing impact of the new consumerism, they also revealed a desire to resist the trend and to reassert class distinction. And the world of consumption still provided the means to achieve this distinction, as the elite preference for foreign products reveals. If workers and others of modest means were increasingly able to emulate the rich through consumption, huge disparities in quality still separated the goods purchased by the poor from those available to the rich. In any case, even as advertisers appealed to the desire for upward mobility, the pitfalls of consumption as a means of attaining status were well known. The comic strip *Timoteo Puertonuevo* featured a poor bumbler intent on making it as an elegant radio star. In one strip from 1933, Timoteo sees an advertisement for a suit promising that "for just 50 pesos, you can become a Jhon [sic] Barrymore." He rushes to the shop and purchases the suit, reminding the tailor to leave off the epaulets that Socialists wear. He then impresses the object of his affection, a chorus girl, who declares him "elegant" and, using the English word, a true "gentleman." But alas, when it begins to rain and his date asks for his jacket, Timoteo hesitates. When she declares that a real gentleman (this time, she uses the Spanish *caballero*) would gladly give her the shirt off his back, he pulls off the suit jacket revealing that he has no shirt.[46] Like all such attempts, Timoteo's effort to purchase respectability and higher class status is doomed to fail. The strip criticizes social striving but from a different perspective than Loncán's attack on the guarango. Here, it is not Timoteo's poor taste we are laughing at; it is his gullibility. The comic strip depicts the widespread desire for upward mobility and the tendency of advertisers to appeal to it, even as it reveals a common-sensical skepticism toward the utopian promises of advertising. The social leveling that characterized the new consumer society had clear limits.

Both barrio elites and advertisers tended to encourage the pursuit of upward mobility and the erasure of class differences. Whether by acquiring culture and respectability at the local library or by purchasing a proper suit, porteños could aspire to overcome the increasingly invisible barriers that separated them from their socioeconomic superiors. The tendency to play down class differences was visible as well in the sphere of electoral politics. After electoral reforms in 1912 and 1917, the expansion of the electorate and the implementation of the secret ballot created a competitive environment in which political parties could no longer rely exclusively on fraud and patronage, and campaign rhetoric took on a new importance.[47] Throughout these years—and it is worth noting that universal male suffrage and competitive elections continued to function on the municipal level even after the military coup of 1930—the parties tended to avoid appeals to particular social classes and to emphasize instead their capacity to represent *el pueblo*. The Unión Cívica Radical, which dominated national elections in the years before 1930, was particularly insistent on this point. In the words of the Radical leader Hipólito Yrigoyen, elected president in 1916 and again in 1928, "we are the nation itself."[48] In general, though, the aversion to class politics characterized most politicians regardless of party. Even the Socialists, who were the Radicals' principal challengers in the capital city, were as likely to appeal to consumers, merchants, employees, or residents of suburban barrios, as they were to address themselves directly to workers. Despite their commitment to Marxist orthodoxy, the Socialists' rhetoric shared many features with that of the Radicals. Both claimed to be the only party capable of representing the interests of the pueblo, and both tried to identify themselves with progress, modernization, and upward mobility. Direct appeals to working-class interests were not entirely absent from the political arena in this period: the Socialists did promise to pursue social reforms aimed at workers; some Radical factions outside of Buenos Aires were explicit in their promises to help the laboring classes; and even Yrigoyen himself engaged in *obrerismo*, expressing a vague commitment to attend to workers' needs. Still, political competition was for the most part conducted within the parameters of a non-pluralist vision of democracy, in which appeals to the people or to the nation as a whole enjoyed more legitimacy than class-based interpellations.[49]

The inauguration of a competitive political system contributed to the emergence of a more inclusive and integrated society in 1920s and 1930s Buenos Aires. Although immigration rates remained high until the crisis of 1929, by the 1920s the Argentine-born children of immigrants made up a substantial proportion of the city's population. Unlike their parents, these porteños enjoyed full citizenship and effective suffrage. As we have seen, they also lived in a society in which economic opportunities existed and upward mobility, including the possibility of homeownership and a good education for their children, was a real possibility. They often lived far from their places of employment, in heterogeneous barrios where they were encouraged to participate in a rich network of local clubs, associations, and libraries. And they lived in a consumer society in which an increasing number of domestically manufactured goods were available at affordable prices, and in which advertisers frequently appealed to their desire for status. For Luis Alberto Romero and other historians, these developments produced a new set of values, as the working-class identity of earlier decades gave way to a "spontaneous ideology of social mobility." According to this view, the barrios in this period were filled not with members of the working class but with a diverse population better understood as the "popular sectors." For Romero and others, the widespread pursuit of self-improvement, higher status, and a better life was essentially middle-class. In other words, even though many individuals failed to realize the dream of middle-class respectability for themselves or their children, the aspiration was nearly universal; this was a "mass society of middle classes."[50]

This description certainly does capture certain aspects of the period. It is undeniable that Buenos Aires had a large and growing number of small business owners, white-collar and public employees, teachers, and other middling groups. Many porteños, in other words, were neither poor nor rich. According to one recent estimate based on annual income statistics for 1914, the lower classes made up 55 percent of the population, while the rich constituted a tiny elite of less than half of 1 percent. In between these two extremes was a huge group—nearly 45 percent of Argentines—who might be called middle class.[51] Though imprecise, these numbers are suggestive. They help demonstrate that the economic growth of these years did provide important economic opportunities for ordinary people. In this sense, they seem to substantiate both the image of this period as one characterized by high rates of social mobility and the widespread view of Argentina as the country with the largest middle class in Latin America. Moreover, in certain arenas, "middle-class" affiliations were increasingly visible in the 1920s and 1930s. The leaders of barrio associations, for example, did occasionally embrace their "middleness." Barrio elites in Boedo stressed the importance of modesty, criticizing those who disdained the local shops in favor of more expensive and pretentious stores downtown.[52] In celebrating their own upward mobility even as they distinguished themselves from the rich, they were beginning to craft a middle-class identity.

Nevertheless, as Ezequiel Adamovsky demonstrates in his recent history of the subject, middle-class identity was not widespread in Argentina during the 1920s and 1930s. Although some politicians and intellectuals hoped that something called the "middle class" might serve as a counterbalance to a radicalized proletariat, no political party or trade union presented itself as the defender of that sector. On the contrary, the organizations that represented retail clerks, public employees, and telephone workers adopted an explicitly working-class identity, while even the teachers' and bank workers' unions typically expressed solidarity with the labor movement. Unlike their counterparts in some Latin American countries, these white-collar workers did not embrace an explicit middle-class identity. In other words, the 45 percent of Argentines with middling income levels do not seem to have perceived themselves as members of a distinct class with a particular set of interests that distinguished them from those above and below them on the social spectrum.[53]

This is not to deny that many values often associated with the middle class were indeed on the rise, including not only self-improvement as a path to upward mobility, but also modesty, thriftiness, respectability, and patriarchy. An idealized image of the respectable family, with a hardworking father who provides for the education of his children and a nonworking mother who nurtures their moral development, became prominent in this period.[54] Advertisers reinforced this gendered message by focusing their efforts on housewives who, they believed, controlled the family budget. By sponsoring daytime radio programs designed to appeal to stay-at-home mothers, manufacturers of food and medicines helped to construct a powerful image of respectable domesticity.[55] Yet these allegedly middle-class values were not incompatible with working-class identity, as the notion of a "decent working-class suburb" suggests. Moreover, these values did not cohere into a unified ideology or identity. On the contrary, tensions and ambivalence persisted. For example, barrio elites and politicians emphasized their commitment to modernization, but they also worried that the increasing presence of women in the modern workplace threatened the traditional respectability of the family.[56] *Los tres berretines* features an almost stereotypical, middle-class family ruled by a patriarch who seeks to inculcate an ethos of hard work in his sons while hoping for a good marriage partner for his daughter. But modern mass culture undermines Manuel Sequeiro's patriarchal control over his wife and children as well as his idea of respectability. In the end, education and self-improvement are not so much the means to achieve upward mobility as quaint relics of a bygone era. Of course, the promise of transgressive mass culture is clearly limited by gender: unlike Manuel's sons, his daughter remains confined by notions of respectability and agrees to stop attending the cinema. Yet for young men, *Los tres berretines* offers a choice between old-fashioned respectability and affiliation with the cultural practices of the poor; a modern, middle-class identity is not even an option.

Further complicating the idea that middle-class identity was on the rise is the fact that working-class militancy persisted and even expanded throughout the period. Extensive labor mobilization in Argentina dates to the first decade of the twentieth century. This first wave of labor struggle was led principally by anarchists, whose message seemed perfectly tailored to a society in which rampant fraud made the constitutional guarantee of universal male suffrage an empty promise.[57] With little reason to pursue Argentine citizenship, immigrant workers were often receptive to anarchism's anti-political message. Nevertheless, even during the heyday of anarchist militancy in the first decade of the twentieth century, the growth of the labor movement owed a great deal to the ability of the unions to press workers' wage demands.[58] The pragmatism of the labor movement became even more evident after 1915 with the ascendancy of syndicalist organizers, who were more willing than the anarchists to seek the mediation of the state. The bread-and-butter orientation of Argentine unions reflected the consciousness of the immigrant rank and file. These immigrants combined working-class identity with a deep desire to achieve the upward mobility that had motivated their transatlantic journeys.[59]

This combination produced an aggressive militancy that culminated in a massive strike wave during the 1916–21 period. Although the Bolshevik Revolution certainly inspired a new radicalism among many in the labor movement, working-class pragmatism persisted. Led by syndicalists, the unions openly sought the support of the Radical government of Hipólito Yrigoyen, a strategy that initially met with success as the administration backed workers' demands in order to keep exports flowing and to curry favor with working-class voters.[60] But labor mobilization eventually provoked repression: the government encouraged strikebreakers to crush the ongoing port conflict, allowed right-wing nationalists to attack unions and leftists, and unleashed the army on strikers during the infamous "Tragic Week" of January 1919. In the wake of this repression and facing a new surge in immigration, the labor movement entered a protracted period of decline. In 1920 the syndicalist labor federation had mobilized more than 100,000 workers in more than 598 unions, but just two years later, a newly formed federation could claim only 22,000 members in 161 unions.[61] Strikes continued throughout the 1920s, but with the exception of a massive strike wave in and around the city of Rosario in 1928, they never came close in scope or intensity to the conflicts of 1916–21.[62] This decline had many causes. While repression hampered the efforts of union organizers, ideological divisions weakened the labor movement from within. In all likelihood, the dynamism of the economy in these years also played a role. With wages rising, homeownership expanding in multiclass barrios, and the explosion of advertising exalting the promises of consumerism, it is not surprising that the labor movement lost ground and that many porteños chose the pursuit of upward mobility over the defense of class interests.

But the weakening of the labor movement was a temporary phenomenon. Although the military coup of 1930 unleashed a new wave of repression and the high unemployment of the next few years served to dampen labor militancy, the unions began to recover by the middle of the decade. After only 60 strikes in Argentina in 1934, there were 180 in 1935, 215 the next year, and an annual average of 118 for the rest of the decade.[63] This new aggressiveness accompanied rapid growth in union membership and a shift in the characteristics and strategy of the labor movement. Before 1930 the movement had been composed primarily of skilled workers organized in small craft unions; only the railroad and port workers had begun to create national organizations. But now, with the Socialists, syndicalists, and anarchists weakened and with industrialization producing a rapid increase in the ranks of the proletariat, the Communists—relative newcomers to the Argentine labor movement—were able to achieve significant growth in industrial unions. Between 1936 and 1941, the number of union members in the industrial sector doubled under the leadership of Communist unions. With thousands of unskilled and semi-skilled workers in their ranks, these organizations could not rely on their strategic position in the production process, as the old craft unions and railroad and port unions had done. Instead, the Communists built national organizations with highly centralized bureaucracies and forged political alliances to benefit their members.[64]

The resurgence of the labor movement in the 1930s demonstrates that working-class affiliations and loyalties remained widespread in this period. If the growth of multiclass barrios and the advent of a consumer society served to blur class distinctions, industrialization and the efforts of Communist organizers pushed in the opposite direction. Moreover, working-class solidarity was not confined to discrete industrial zones; by the second half of the 1930s, it was widespread even in the new barrios. The three outlying census districts that were home to 40 percent of the porteño population in 1936 also housed some 22 percent of the city's industrial workers. Even if they lived in multiclass barrios, these workers had not simply exchanged their class consciousness for the pursuit of upward mobility. At key moments, many residents of these neighborhoods proved willing to express their solidarity with striking workers. In late 1935, sixty thousand construction workers walked off the job demanding wage increases, improved workplace safety, the reduction of hours, and the recognition of their union. As the conflict dragged on into

January, the principal labor unions launched a general strike. The result was a massive two-day protest, the largest and most violent since the Tragic Week of 1919. The epicenter of this conflict and the site of virtually all of the clashes between strikers and police was the zone of most recent urbanization, the booming neighborhoods of northern and western Buenos Aires.[65] Furthermore, class solidarity was not limited to industrial workers. During the 1930s, many white-collar workers embraced the labor movement.[66] Particularly influential were unionized retail clerks, who used their connections to the Socialist Party to secure the passage of protective legislation. By the end of the decade, some 15 percent of the city's clerks were organized, and the commercial employees' union threw its support to the Communists.[67] Both the intensity of the general strike in January 1936 and the strength of the retail clerks' union suggest that the expansion of working-class affiliations had a significant impact beyond factory walls.

Despite this upsurge in labor militancy, union members remained a minority among the working population in Buenos Aires. Nevertheless, working-class solidarity had an appeal and an influence beyond the unions. It was visible, for example, in the mainstream press and particularly in *Crítica*, the city's most popular evening newspaper. During the 1920s, *Crítica*'s owner, the Uruguayan businessman Natalio Botana, embraced the sensationalist techniques of Hearst and Pulitzer, including attention-grabbing headlines, extensive crime reporting, and detailed coverage of the city's nightlife. By October 1924, *Crítica*'s average circulation was 166,385, putting it in third place among Buenos Aires's many dailies; by the end of the decade, the paper was selling more than 300,000 copies per day.[68] Sylvia Saítta argues that the newspaper built its audience through two complementary strategies. On the one hand, the paper pursued "expansion through specialization," continually generating new sections in order to appeal to distinct groups of potential readers.[69] On the other hand, *Crítica* adopted a consistent editorial pose as "the voice of the people."[70] The paper often employed this language in an inclusive manner, using its circulation figures as evidence of its status as the true representative of popular interests. But *Crítica*'s populism also pushed it into an explicit alliance with the working class and the poor. In 1923 *Crítica* led a high-profile campaign in support of Kurt Wilckens, an anarchist who had assassinated an army colonel in retribution for the latter's role in the brutal repression of striking workers in Patagonia. Throughout the remainder of the decade, *Crítica* supported Argentina's labor unions, organized charity drives on behalf of the needy, and repeatedly presented itself as a defender of the poor.[71] Although Botana's paper would never be confused with an orthodox, leftist publication, the defense of workers' interests was central to its appeal. That this strategy proved so successful reveals the continuing relevance of working-class identity for many porteños.

In the 1920s and 1930s, the barrios of Buenos Aires were not home to a self-conscious middle class. Instead, these areas experienced a fluid, ambiguous process in which a diverse population was addressed in various competing and contradictory ways. Political parties, barrio associations, and advertisers tended to emphasize modernity, upward mobility, and respectability, while downplaying class differences, but working-class solidarities persisted. These were most obvious in the revival of the labor movement, but they were also visible in the populist stance of *Crítica*, in the conflicts between the leaders and rank-and-file members of ethnic associations, in the recurring conflict in barrio associations between the "culture" promoted by barrio elites and the sports embraced by more plebeian residents, as well as in the sporadic but noteworthy appearance of appeals to workers in electoral politics. The audiences for all these discourses overlapped significantly. A member of a Communist-led labor union, for example, might well live in a multiclass barrio, participate in the local sociedad de fomento, and vote for Radical Party politicians.

The ambiguity of class formation in this period is visible in the memoir of Edmundo Rivero, a major tango singer of the 1940s, 1950s, and 1960s.[72] Born in 1911, Rivero grew up in Saavedra, a recently urbanized barrio in the northwest corner of Buenos Aires. His father had been a railroad station chief and later worked as a police officer, while his mother was a housewife. The family lived in a large house with Edmundo's grandparents. Here, then, was a model of the home-owning, ostensibly middle-class family of the Buenos Aires barrios. As a child, Rivero made extensive use of Saavedra's municipal library, where he read the novels of Dumas and the poetry of Dante. Moreover, a certain expectation of respectability structured his youth. Rivero initially kept his musical pursuits a secret from his parents, since he feared they would not approve, and although he sang with his sister at home, she, as a young woman, was not allowed into the bars. Nevertheless, this was by no means a uniformly middle-class world. In addition to the library, Saavedra also had a bar frequented by tough guys and petty criminals, where the young Rivero would listen to the musicians who came to perform. Rivero remembered the sadness that reigned in his neighborhood in the aftermath of the labor conflicts of January 1919. Moreover, he grew up speaking lunfardo and was enamored of *payadores,* or itinerant singers, like Juan Pedro López and Martín Castro, whose verses denounced poverty and social injustice. Rivero did not finish his secondary education and became a professional tango singer after completing his military service in 1929. His upbringing in the barrio had provided him with a desire for upward mobility but also with a strong affiliation with the popular culture of poor Argentines.

The entrepreneurs and artists who developed the music, radio programs, and films of the 1920s and 1930s sought to build an audience among the residents of these Buenos Aires barrios. The mass culture they created bore the traces of this ideological milieu: it combined a progressive commitment to upward mobility with populist, even class-conscious discourses. Ostensibly middle-class values, like respectability, hard work, and the pursuit of upward mobility, found expression in the new media, but so did nostalgic critiques of modernity, populist denunciations of the rich, and celebrations of the virtues and national authenticity of the working poor. Nevertheless, mass culture did not simply hold up a mirror to its consumers. In fact, the mass culture of this period refashioned local cultural elements into an image of Argentine society that differed sharply from the heterogeneous and ambiguous world of the porteño barrios. The positive depiction of plebeian culture in *Los tres berretines* was typical of local mass culture, but the film's focus on a respectable middle-class family was less so.[73] Most domestic movies, songs, and radio programs in this period depicted Argentina as a society hopelessly divided between the poor and the rich. To understand why, we need to recognize that Argentina was not a hermetically sealed cultural world. Argentine producers faced intense competition from a flood of imported mass culture. As I will argue, this transnational marketplace encouraged a reliance on melodrama and an emphasis on populism, expanding the distance between Argentine reality and its mass cultural representation.

2 COMPETING IN THE TRANSNATIONAL MARKETPLACE

Mass cultural technology arrived in Argentina, as it did in most of the world, as an import. The invention of the phonograph, the radio, and the cinema, and the growth of industries in the United States and Europe dedicated to commercializing these entertainments, had a globalizing impact, as these nascent industries energetically pursued overseas markets. Nevertheless, the result was not a simple process of cultural imperialism. In his analysis of globalization in the contemporary world, Arjun Appadurai emphasizes the "tension between cultural homogenization and cultural heterogenization. . . . At least as rapidly as forces from various metropolises are brought into new societies they tend to become indigenized in one or another way."[1] This was no less true at the dawn of the mass cultural era. Throughout the world, the new technologies disseminated the cultural products and ideological messages of the developed world, but at the same time, they were quickly put to use in packaging local popular culture for the domestic market. The result was the elaboration of national cultural products in dialogue with those imported from abroad. The film scholar Miriam Hansen argues that Hollywood movies "offered something like the first global vernacular," a discourse through which people around the world made sense of the dislocations of modernity. In Buenos Aires, as elsewhere, local filmmakers responded by elaborating what Hansen calls an "alternative vernacular modernism," a reconfiguration of North American models of genre, cinematography, and style capable of articulating the fantasies and anxieties of the Argentine mass public.[2] And this creative reworking of imported culture was not limited to the cinema; similar processes shaped the local recording and radio industries.

The rapid adoption of mass cultural technologies in the 1920s and 1930s inserted ordinary Argentines into global cultural circuits to an unprecedented extent. When local entrepreneurs and artists began to produce and distribute cultural commodities for the new media, they faced a marketplace already saturated with imported culture.[3] The expectations and aesthetic preferences of Argentine audiences were shaped by extensive exposure to jazz music and Hollywood films, among other imported products. In this transnational marketplace, Argentine mass culture succeeded commercially to the extent that it offered an alternative modernism capable of reconciling local traditions with cosmopolitan modernity. Given the enormous prestige of mass cultural products from the United States, as well as the cachet of modernity that attached to them, local producers needed both to emulate those products as well as to distinguish their own offerings. They strove simultaneously to reproduce North American style and technical achievement and to emphasize their own distinct, national authenticity.

The transnational marketplace thus had contradictory effects, creating enormous demand for both the foreign and the national. Argentines danced the fox trot and watched the latest Hollywood releases, but their thriving mass cultural industries produced music, radio shows, and movies that repackaged and celebrated Argentine popular culture. And these commodities were themselves shaped by transnational pressures. Tango music took on many of the sonic characteristics of jazz, even as it asserted its claim to represent Argentine national identity. Radio programmers developed an increasingly standardized menu of offerings that set tango music and gaucho melodramas alongside cosmopolitan genres. Filmmakers sought to combine Hollywood style and technique with thematic material drawn from Argentine popular culture. These efforts attracted large audiences but yielded persistent ideological contradictions. In particular, the new mass culture tended to celebrate the cultural practices of poor Argentines, an affiliation that often undermined the attempt to emulate modernity.

THE RECORDING INDUSTRY, JAZZ, AND THE RISE OF THE TANGO

Some twelve years after the German American Emile Berliner invented the gramophone in 1888, the new machines arrived in Buenos Aires, and shortly thereafter local companies began recording music onto discs. During these early years, many local record labels competed in Buenos Aires, but the economic convulsions precipitated by the First World War forced smaller enterprises out of business. Beginning in the 1920s, four foreign companies dominated the Argentine market: Victor, Columbia, and Brunswick, all based in the United States, and the German conglomerate Odeon. These companies sold North American and European recordings to Argentine consumers, but they also invested considerable resources in recording local artists. The fact that the recording of Argentine music was largely the work of foreign companies undoubtedly shaped Argentine music history. Nevertheless, it is important to recognize that the influence of foreign standards and preferences was highly mediated. Both the selection of material and the actual recording process were typically in the hands of local producers. Each of the major recording companies had a local representative who enjoyed the exclusive right to distribute its catalogue and to record local acts.

Easily the most important of these local mediators was Max Glücksmann, an Austrian Jew who emigrated to Argentina at the age of fourteen in 1890. Shortly after his arrival in Buenos Aires, Glücksmann went to work at the Casa Lepage, a small photography shop. Very early on, Glücksmann foresaw the commercial potential of new technology in both cinema and audio recording. With the French-born cinematographer Eugenio Py, Glücksmann began making short silent films and eventually became a prolific producer of newsreels. He was also active in distributing foreign films to local movie theaters. In 1908 Glücksmann was able to purchase the Casa Lepage and that same year, he built his first movie theater, the Buckingham Palace. Around the same time, he became the

Argentine agent for the German Odeon record label. In addition to selling the company's international catalogue, Glücksmann dedicated himself to recording local acts for his own label, Discos Nacional-Odeon (later, Discos Dobles Nacional). He signed an exclusive contract with the tango bandleader Roberto Firpo, and in 1912 he succeeded in overcoming the technical obstacles involved in recording a band that included piano. In 1917 he signed the singing duo of Carlos Gardel and José Razzano, who until that point had specialized in folk songs. Gardel's recording of the tango "Mi noche triste" that year would later be credited with inaugurating the golden era of tango song. Glücksmann retained popular artists like Gardel by offering generous contracts that guaranteed royalty payments. Seeking to reduce the price of phonograph records in order to reach a broader audience, Glücksmann opened the first record factory in Argentina in 1919 so that he would no longer need to ship the masters to Germany for pressing. In 1926 Glücksmann's studio adopted the electric microphones invented by Bell Laboratories the previous year, keeping pace with international technology and his local competitors, Victor and Columbia. Throughout these years, he built an extensive catalogue, recording most of the major tango singers and musicians of the period. By the early 1930s, Glücksmann was an impresario; he owned seventy movie theaters, and his company employed some fifteen hundred workers.[4]

Entrepreneurs like Glücksmann, as well as the talent scouts and engineers who worked for them, had a far more direct influence on Argentine popular music than the foreign record companies. Glücksmann himself seems to have been more interested in making a profit than in advancing any particular musical preference. Lacking any background in music, he drew on local expertise when it came to deciding which acts to record. He pursued Carlos Gardel, for example, after being encouraged to do so by José González Castillo, a playwright and prolific tango lyricist who was employed by Glücksmann's firm as a translator of subtitles for imported films.[5] Glücksmann worked hard to respond to the preferences of his audience. Beginning in 1924, Discos Nacional hosted an annual contest in which audience members would select their favorite tangos. The first contest was held in Glücksmann's luxurious Teatro Grand Splendid in downtown Buenos Aires and broadcast on the recently founded Radio Grand Splendid. The competing tangos were performed by Roberto Firpo's orchestra, which immediately recorded the prizewinners for Glücksmann's label.[6] These contests enabled fans to hear their favorite musicians, provided Glücksmann with a sort of "focus group" to test the market potential of new compositions, and also served as a clever marketing device. By prominently featuring the results of the contests in its advertising, Discos Nacional could assure the public of the popularity of its records even before they went on sale. These and other strategies made Glücksmann's company the most important player in the Argentine recording business; Victor, Columbia, and other companies competed with Nacional to sign the most popular local acts. Thus, the key decisions about how to build a domestic market for recorded music were made not in North American or European boardrooms but in Buenos Aires by entrepreneurs assessing local tastes. The introduction of recording technology and the penetration of foreign companies into the Argentine market did not result in the Americanization of Argentine popular music. On the contrary, through the mediation of local entrepreneurs like Glücksmann, these powerful cultural forces were, to borrow Appadurai's term, "indigenized."

Nevertheless, the appropriation of foreign technology was inevitably shaped by the unequal distribution of economic and cultural capital. The economic power of recording companies based in the United States meant that North American musical styles were disseminated widely in Argentina, while the image of the United States as the locus of all things modern lent those styles an undeniable prestige. Jazz, in particular, began to attract the attention of the most cosmopolitan porteños during the 1920s. Many records that were hits in the American market sold well in Buenos Aires, especially the symphonic jazz of Paul Whiteman, the so-called King of Jazz, and the "sweet" sounds of the Benson Orchestra of Chicago. As was the case in other locales, the "hotter" jazz played by African American bands was less influential, at least at first.[7] Since porteño dancers demanded to hear "fox trots," as the songs played by jazz bands were known in Argentina, local bands made it their business to play and even record them. In the early 1920s, tango bandleaders like Roberto Firpo, Francisco Canaro, and Francisco Lomuto, as well as singers like Gardel, included fox trots and "shimmies" in their repertoire, and bandleaders like Pedro Maffia, Francisco Pracánico, and Juan Carlos Bazán offered both jazz and tango.[8] Composers got into the act as well: in 1928 the tango lyricist Luis Rubistein published the fox trot "¡Oh! Girl! (¡Oh, Muchacha!)."[9]

For many of these musicians and composers, offering an occasional fox trot was a way of cashing in on the latest fad. But by the 1930s, the increasing popularity of both jazz and tango encouraged a process of specialization. Most tango bands now left jazz to local outfits like the Dixie Pals and the Santa Paula Serenaders. At this point, the two genres confronted each other as competitors, and devotees of tango increasingly saw the popularity of jazz as a threat to national prestige. In 1933 a cartoon in the fan magazine *La Canción Moderna* announced Roberto Firpo's decision to stop performing jazz. Playing on the fact that Firpo had the same last name as the great Argentine heavyweight Luis Firpo, the cartoon depicted the bandleader as a boxer and proclaimed that he had launched "a bloody struggle against the American fox-trot."[10] And Firpo was not alone in his desire to see tango triumph over jazz. One letter writer to the magazine *Sintonía* urged Osvaldo Fresedo's *orquesta típica* to stop playing fox trots and concentrate instead on "those rhythmic and beautiful tangos to which we are accustomed,"[11] while others bemoaned the omnipresence of jazz on the radio: "I cannot conceive how eight of the ten stations currently broadcasting can simultaneously be playing fox-trots."[12]

Not all porteños saw jazz and tango as implacable antagonists, and the two musics coexisted in the same record catalogues and magazines and on the same radio stations and bandstands throughout the period. Nevertheless, the competition with jazz had a profound effect on the tango. Many tango musicians were inspired by the jazz records they heard, from which they freely borrowed musical ideas. Adolfo Carabelli, a classically trained pianist, became a devotee of the new music in the late 1910s, formed a jazz band, and began recording, at first for the small Electra label and then for Victor. In 1925 when Victor decided it needed a house band in order to compete with Nacional-Odeon for the tango market, the label hired Carabelli to form the now legendary Orquesta Típica Victor. The next year, Victor named Carabelli its artistic director in Argentina, and he oversaw the label's growing offerings in both jazz and tango. Carabelli's own band included the *bandoneón* and violins typical of tango bands, but also a tuba and a drum kit; his was a hybrid music.[13] Similarly, Osvaldo Fresedo's influential brand of tango was deeply influenced by American jazz, notwithstanding the objections of Fresedo's more orthodox fans. Fresedo was one of three Argentine tango musicians sent by Victor to record in the company's studio in Camden, New Jersey, in 1920. Although the so-called Orquesta Típica Select had little impact, Fresedo seems to have returned with new ideas. He would go on to a long and extremely productive career, during which he was not afraid to experiment, incorporating both the vibraphone and the drum set into his band.[14]

The influence of jazz on Argentine popular music went beyond the adoption of brass and percussion instruments. The cachet of American mass culture, its aura of modernity, exerted an irresistible appeal, one that is apparent, for example, in the English name of Glücksmann's Grand Splendid Theater and radio station. The prestige of jazz undoubtedly helped shape audience expectations and preferences. Having been exposed to the latest hits from the United States, Argentine audiences expected recordings of local music to live up to North American production standards. But more than that, they responded to tangos that shared certain musical affinities with jazz. In this way, musical styles that had been developed in order to sell records in the United States exerted an indirect, but important influence on Argentine music. During the 1920s, record companies like Victor achieved success by promoting what the historian William Howland Kenney has described as "a synthesis of jazz with late Victorian sentiment and propriety."[15] Victor's biggest star was Whiteman, a white bandleader who offered listeners a refined, technically sophisticated version of jazz that seemed appropriate for the homes of the middle-class consumers Victor sought to attract. In Argentina, Whiteman's "concert-hall sound" epitomized modernity. In order to compete with records like these, Argentine musicians needed to offer music that emulated their orchestral sophistication and danceability, which in this context functioned as aural signifiers of modernity.

During the 1910s and 1920s tango bands replaced the Cuban habanera, which had provided the basic beat for early tango, with a reliance on four equal quarter notes—"the four," as tango musicians call it. Robert Farris Thompson compares this rhythmic evolution to the rise of a "four-to-the-bar" feel in big-band jazz. However, for Thompson, this similarity is evidence of a common origin: in both cases, he argues, musicians of African descent gave the music a certain "black swing."[16] Yet he does not say what makes the four "blacker" than the habanera, nor explain why this innovation happened when it did. Without discounting the important role played by Afro-Argentine tango musicians such as the bassist Leopoldo Thompson, I would argue that the rise of the four probably reflects the influence of jazz. If jazz was the sound of modernity, then the adoption of 4/4 time certainly made tango sound more convincingly modern.

The transformation of tango into a sophisticated, modern dance music took a big step forward in the 1920s with the emergence of the New Guard, a generation of bandleaders committed to innovation.[17] The New Guard included Osvaldo Fresedo, Juan Carlos Cobián, and others, but it was most clearly associated with the violinist and bandleader Julio de Caro. Among tango historians, de Caro is best known for having enriched tango's musicality by broadening its use of harmony and counterpoint and for having sought to elevate the genre by creating a symphonic tango. But de Caro's image as an innovator and modernizer was also informed by jazz. Beginning in the mid-1920s, de Caro played a "violin-cornet" specially designed for him by the technicians of the Victor Company. The look of the instrument, which used the bell of a cornet in order to amplify de Caro's solos, offended traditionalists with its obvious allusion to jazz instrumentation.[18] Moreover, de Caro's attempts to improve the musical quality of tango were a self-conscious response to what he saw as the "serious threat" posed by jazz.[19] He intended to demonstrate that the tango, "like waltzes or jazz," could be the basis for a sophisticated music.[20] In light of his effort to modernize tango orchestration in order to help the genre survive in the face of competition from American jazz, de Caro was described as the "porteño Paul Whiteman."[21] By putting de Caro and Whiteman on equal footing, the comparison affirmed de Caro's modernity as well as his commitment to refining and improving popular music.

Thanks in part to the efforts of de Caro and other New Guard bandleaders, the tango proved capable of holding its own in competition with jazz. An advertisement that appeared in 1935 reveals the extent to which tango had been reconciled with modernity (see figure 2).[22] The ad, which promotes radio programs sponsored by Brasso polish, features two drawings of dancers. Under the caption "Do you like tango?" an elegantly dressed couple moves while a musician plays a bandoneón. Under the caption "Do you like jazz?" an equally elegant couple dances while a trumpeter performs. Aside from the choice of instrument, subtle differences distinguish the drawings. The lowered heads of the tango dancers give them an air of seriousness, while the upturned faces of the jazz couple, which mirror the position of the trumpet, suggest frivolity. The dark hair and mustache of the male dancer in the tango drawing contrast with the lighter coloring of the jazz dancers. But notwithstanding these differences, the drawings suggest a larger similarity; jazz and tango are

2 Radio advertisement, *Sintonía*, July 6, 1935.

here depicted as two of a kind, even mirror images. Not only are the dancers similarly attired and positioned, but the curves of the drawings also echo each other. In this image, tango and jazz are equivalent, if not identical. Tango here is just as modern as jazz; it is an alternative modernism.

Competing in the mass cultural marketplace encouraged tango artists to emulate jazz modernity, but it had contradictory effects as well. Entrepreneurs hoping to create a niche for tango needed to distinguish the music from what jazz bands could offer. Tango artists could strive to be modern, but they could not hope to outdo North American jazz musicians on that score. De Caro might be the "porteño Paul Whiteman," but Whiteman would remain the measuring stick. On the other hand, tango was well positioned to offer something jazz could not: Argentine authenticity. Responding to the mass cultural marketplace, the recording industry reinforced tango's traditionalism and helped turn it into a symbol of Argentine national identity. The nationalization of tango is visible in some of the earliest tango recording sessions. José Tagini, the Argentine agent for Columbia Records, made the label's first tango recordings in

1911, when he brought Vicente Greco's band into the studio. Until that moment, Argentine bands did not specialize exclusively in tango; in addition to tango, they played music suitable for a host of dances of foreign origin, including polkas, mazurkas, and *pasadobles*. But for marketing purposes, Columbia wanted to give Greco's group a name that would signal its expertise in tango; what they came up with was orquesta típica criolla, a somewhat redundant name meaning "traditional, native band."[23] While the last adjective was soon dropped, orquesta típica survived for decades as the generic term for a tango band. The name was ironic, for it stressed tango's traditionalism and its rootedness in Argentine culture. In reality, tango was a new musical form and one that was constantly evolving. Greco himself had recently expanded his trio of bandoneón, violin, and guitar into a sextet including piano and flute. And while tango's precise origins remain the subject of debate, it was undoubtedly a hybrid form that drew on the music and dance traditions of Afro-Argentines, those of the interior provinces, as well as various international influences, including the Cuban habanera and the musical traditions brought by Italian immigrants.[24] Moreover, Greco's own instrument, the bandoneón, whose distinctive tones were just then emerging as the defining sonority within any orquesta típica, was a German concertina only recently introduced in Argentina.[25] Nevertheless, in their efforts to position tango in a competitive marketplace, the record companies constructed tango as *típico*, or traditionally Argentine. Columbia's catalogues reinforced this construction by listing tango records in a section labeled *criollo*, or "native," alongside other sections dedicated to jazz and classical music.

Despite tango's hybridity, its links to rural, folk culture made the criollo label plausible. We have already seen that Carlos Gardel began his career as part of a duo of folk singers before deciding to specialize in tango after 1917. The Gardel-Razzano duo performed both traditional pieces and contemporary songs composed in traditional styles.[26] During the 1910s and 1920s, this sort of folk music, inspired by various musical forms with roots in the Argentine interior, enjoyed great popularity among urban audiences. Ignacio Corsini, later celebrated by many as the second greatest male tango singer, also began his career as a singer of rural folk songs as did Agustín Magaldi, who, before becoming a major tango star, performed as one half of a duo modeled on Gardel-Razzano.[27] Gardel, Corsini, and Magaldi were, in effect, professionalizing folk traditions. In particular, they drew on the rich tradition of the payadores, traveling, guitar-playing singers who specialized in competitive, lyrical improvisation. Their commercial success was part of a broader vogue for rural, popular culture in Buenos Aires. During this era of rapid modernization and massive immigration, porteños of various social classes embraced everything criollo, applying the label to rural cultural practices that contrasted with the culture of Europeanized aristocrats or working-class immigrants. The 1890s witnessed an explosion of criollista literature, popular pulp fiction that narrated in verse the heroics of renegade gauchos. At the same time, both working- and middle-class porteños flocked to the city's criollo circuses, where they watched equestrian acrobatics, clowning, and theatrical melodramas based on criollista stories.[28] In so doing, they were celebrating Argentina's pre-modern, rural roots.

As a commercial trend, *criollismo* had impressive staying power. A revival in 1915 of the most famous of the criollo melodramas, Eduardo Gutiérrez's *Juan Moreira*, provided Gardel with an important early break, when several songs by the Gardel-Razzano duo were included in scene 6 as part of a "grand country fiesta."[29] Tango's links to criollismo, though, go well beyond Gardel, Corsini, and Magaldi. An early staging of *Juan Moreira*, by the Podestá brothers in 1889, had included a *milonga*, a dance form that was a precursor to tango. In addition, early tango lyrics often had a decidedly criollista feel.[30] As late as 1924, Glücksmann's first tango contest was won by Francisco Canaro's "Sentimiento gaucho." Even though the song was performed without lyrics, the title alone was enough to evoke criollismo. As a child, Canaro was a devoted fan of the criollo circuses and the gaucho dramas they featured.[31] In short, countrified popular culture formed a significant part of the urban milieu in which the tango was born. It was, in this sense, hardly a stretch for tango bands to be considered orquestas típicas playing criollo music. Tango performers could enhance their claims of national authenticity by emphasizing their connection to rural culture.

By the 1920s, tango was easily eclipsing folk music. Gardel's transformation was part of a larger trend, visible in the record catalogues of the day. Glücksmann, for example, recorded a diverse mixture of Argentine folk music, tango, and jazz, but over time, tango became the centerpiece of Nacional's offerings. Of the 500,000 phonograph records sold in Argentina in 1925, some 90 percent were tangos.[32] In hindsight, tango's commercial victory over folk might seem surprising. Despite its connections to criollista culture, tango was rooted in the cosmopolitan world of Buenos Aires. Not only did the genre originate in the capital, but tango lyrics also obsessively explored the music's roots in the *arrabales*, or slums of the big city. By contrast, the appeal of criollismo, whether in the circus, in pamphlets, or on records, lay precisely in its opposition to urban cosmopolitanism, its embrace of the national culture that preceded immigration. Surely the folk music played by the Gardel-Razzano duo and countless others would seem to have been a better candidate for the role of national symbol. But as the Brasso advertisement reveals, tango could be paired with the sophisticated, refined jazz of the 1920s, while the rustic folk music of the criollo circuses could not. Tango's combination of the traditional and the modern—what Florencia Garramuño has recently described as its "primitive modernity"[33]—explains why this genre emerged as the most popular Argentine musical form and the one most capable of representing the nation. In a sense, tango occupied the space between cosmopolitan jazz and traditional folk; it represented a modernized national identity.

An important element in tango's rise to national prominence, and one that has been emphasized in nearly all accounts of the genre's history, occurred outside of Argentina. The tango craze that first erupted in Paris and New York in 1913 and 1914 undoubtedly helped solidify the tango's status at home.[34] In particular, the stamp of approval that tango received in Europe and North America helped overcome the lingering resistance of Argentine elites who had been scandalized by the dance's immorality, its associations with prostitutes and with the urban rabble more generally. Tango's passage through transnational cultural circuits transformed it, for it was embraced by Europeans and North Americans under the sign of exoticism. For Parisian sophisticates, its appeal, like that of the American turkey trot and the Brazilian *maxixe*, lay in its titillating associations with primitive sensuality. Yet as Marta Savigliano has pointed out, tango was a different kind of exotic. Partly because the dance was less obviously associated with blacks (despite its significant roots in Afro-Argentine culture), tango enjoyed a certain distinction among the various exotic cultural practices available for European consumption. As Savigliano puts it, "Tango could be clothed in tails and satins. But it could also be put in its place. . . . Tango was a versatile, hybrid, new kind of exotic that could adopt the manners of the colonizer while retaining the passion of the colonized."[35] Here, again, is tango's capacity to straddle the traditional and the modern, or from the perspective of Paris, the savage and the civilized.

The exoticizing gaze of Europeans and North Americans led inevitably to a process of stereotyping. Argentine tango artists performing abroad were obliged to appear in traditional gaucho attire, linking the tango directly to rural Argentine culture in a way that would have made little sense in Buenos Aires.[36] Occasionally, these stereotypes reached the level of caricature. Rudolph Valentino's famous tango performance in the 1921 film *The Four Horsemen of the Apocalypse*, the first of many Hollywood tangos, featured Valentino in a strange gaucho costume that included an Andalusian hat and a Mexican poncho. Valentino used this stereotyped tango to establish his image as the prototypical "Latin lover" and to launch his career as an international star.

The tremendous success of Valentino's film and of the tango more broadly meant that foreign stereotypes were now transmitted back to Argentine audiences.[37] At the same time, artists like Carlos Gardel were packaged in order to appeal to audiences beyond Argentine borders. In both of these ways, the international cultural marketplace exerted a powerful influence on the tango. Gardel's first feature-length film, *Las luces de Buenos Aires* (Millar, 1931), reveals this process. Gardel's films were not Argentine productions; they were made by Paramount and filmed in France and the United States. Spoken in Spanish and featuring numerous singing performances, the films proved enormously successful in making Gardel a star throughout Latin America, yet they were also hugely popular at home. *Las luces de Buenos Aires* had a Chilean director, but its script was written by two Argentines, Manuel Romero and Luis Bayón Herrera, who were well versed in the lyrical conventions of the tango. The film tells what by 1931 was a very well-worn story—the prototypical tango story, in fact—that of the innocent girl seduced by the bright lights of the city. In the film, the girl (Sofía Bozán) leaves her rural home in the Pampas to sing tango in Buenos Aires. She abandons her boyfriend, a ranch owner played by Gardel, in pursuit of fame and fortune. Inevitably, her success in the big city is accompanied by a descent into immorality and vice, until she is rescued by the boyfriend. The film's very explicit opposition between the purity of the country and the sinfulness of the city is signified musically. While Gardel, the morally upright representative of the country, sings folk songs, tango is the music of Buenos Aires. Yet, as Garramuño has shown, Gardel also plays a mediating role in the film. While in Buenos

Aires, he sings the tango "Tomo y obligo," in order to denounce his girlfriend's betrayal.[38] The film thus enables Gardel to personify both the rural folk and urban tango traditions.

The international association between gauchos and tango made it possible for Gardel to represent both the country and the city simultaneously, and in so doing to serve more convincingly as a national symbol. Tango's fiercest critics, including right-wing intellectuals like Leopoldo Lugones, emphasized the urban, cosmopolitan, and immoral roots of the genre in order to contrast it with Argentina's allegedly more noble, rural traditions.[39] Ironically, the exoticizing stereotypes that attached to the tango as it was consumed in Europe and North America established the genre as an internationally legible symbol of Argentine national identity by linking the tango directly to the countryside and thereby reconciling Argentine tradition with cosmopolitan modernity. These stereotypes were not adopted wholesale in Argentina, but as *Las luces de Buenos Aires* suggests, they did influence mass cultural products consumed in Argentina. It is not incidental that in the voluminous press coverage that ensued after Gardel died in a plane crash on June 24, 1935, images of Gardel in gaucho attire were numerous. He clearly donned this clothing to satisfy foreign expectations. Yet the ability of Gardel, and by extension of the tango itself, to mediate between country and city, tradition and modernity, made the genre into a powerful symbol of national identity within Argentina (see figures 3 and 4). Accounts of the reaction to Gardel's death described the intense sorrow of both "el arrabal porteño" and "el rancho criollo."[40] Similarly, long after Ignacio Corsini made his own transition from folk singer to tango star, he continued to speak to interviewers about his boyhood in the Pampas and the "country flavor" that experience lent to his interpretation of tango.[41]

Both the effort to market tango as a national alternative to jazz modernity and the international adoption of the genre as a civilizable exotic encouraged a deepening association between tango and Argentine national identity. Not only was tango típico, but tango stars were seen as the reflection of certain essential qualities of local identity. Azucena Maizani was not just a talented singer; she was "the greatest, most exact and most popular expression of the porteño feeling that condenses the psychology of our race, more sentimental, emotive, and melancholy than any other on earth."[42] If tango was here described as a symbol of Buenos Aires, other descriptions extended its representative power to Argentina as a

3 & 4 Carlos Gardel in rural and urban attire. Courtesy of Archivo General de la Nación.

whole. *Sintonía*, for example, found national identity in the voice of another tango singer: "Mercedes Simone is very Argentine. Her songs are a piece of the guts of the people from every place in the country (la entraña popular de todos los ámbitos del pais)."[43] These recurring depictions in music magazines may simply have reflected the marketing strategies of the local culture industries. Yet evidence suggests that the power of tango as a symbol of the nation was real enough. When Boca Juniors, a soccer team from Buenos Aires, traveled to Europe in 1925 to play a series of matches against European teams, local newspapers reported their exploits as a gauge of the nation's prowess in the sport. Describing the transatlantic journey, the reporter for the porteño daily *Crítica* noted that the players brought tango records to remind them of home, and he pointed out how wonderful this "música criolla" sounded on the sea.[44] Likewise, the paper's coverage of the Argentine Olympic soccer team in 1928 included photographs of the players dancing tango with each other in order to entertain themselves "far from the fatherland."[45] Regardless of whether these tango moments were staged by the press, they reveal that tango, more than any other Argentine musical genre, could be used to depict these athletes as representatives of the national community.

Tango's status as an alternative, authentically Argentine modernism translated into both commercial success and national symbolic status. Nevertheless, the genre's reconciliation of tradition and modernity was never definitive. The pressures unleashed by competition with jazz pushed in opposing directions—toward emphasizing tango's modernity and toward stressing its traditional Argentineness—and the tension between these two efforts would emerge repeatedly in the 1930s. Fan magazines celebrated tango musicians as national symbols, but they also denounced stagnation and the recycling of stale formulas in popular music. A typical issue of *La Canción Moderna* from 1933 invoked the need for change in three separate articles. The first piece decried the lack of "renovation" and congratulated one radio station for holding a contest in order to discover new talent. A second article complained about the "monotonous" state of popular music in Argentina and called on the famous tango composer Enrique Santos Discépolo to come up with something original. Finally, a reviewer complimented Francisco Pracánico's orchestra for its radio performance of the tango "Pampa": "It was not just another tango offered by a new orchestra similar to all the others." The reviewer concluded that Pracánico was sure to be successful since his band was offering "new modalities in the interpretation of tango."[46] And many fans seemed to agree with these critics on the need for progress and innovation in popular music. The letters to the editor published in *Sintonía*, for example, frequently featured complaints that Argentine music was stagnating because artists were content to copy proven formulas. One sarcastically suggested that Carlos Gardel and Azucena Maizani ought to retire and simply collect a tax from their many imitators.[47]

But what form should progress take? Given its popularity and modernist prestige, jazz was the most obvious source of inspiration and, as we have seen, tango's New Guard was open to its influence. Yet many tango fans rejected efforts to jazz up Argentina's music. Calling himself "a defender of tango," one letter writer denounced the rumba version of the classic tango "La cumparsita" played by Harry Roy's jazz band on a radio station in Buenos Aires: "No foreign bandleader, no matter how good he thinks he is, has the right to adulterate that expression of the Argentine soul which is the tango."[48] And if a Cuban-jazz tango played by an American wounded Argentine national identity, then the incorporation of jazz by Argentine tango musicians posed an even greater threat. As another letter writer put it: "There are many orquestas típicas, or bands that were orquestas típicas, but unfortunately the crazed rhythm of jazz has transformed them. And that hurts those of us who truly, sincerely feel Argentine." Tango bands that incorporate saxophones or lengthy piano solos "have fallen in the error of imitating the North Americans"; they are "stealing something that is ours, that musical fortune that Argentines carry in their soul."[49]

Tango's capacity to offer an alternative modernism thus remained problematic. The effort to modernize the music and the struggle to preserve its authenticity—both rational responses to the marketplace—often clashed with each other. Moreover, this tension was often figured in terms of class. Whereas emulating jazz modernity involved social climbing, putting on "tails and satins," embodying national identity often required an affiliation with the humble masses, both rural and urban, or what *Sintonía* referred to as "the guts of the people." As Argentina's mass cultural entrepreneurs embraced the tango and made it central not only to record catalogues but also to radio programming and to domestic movies, they were endorsing popular culture. And despite many efforts to modernize, civilize, and improve it, the tango would never lose its popular associations.

RADIO AND THE HOMOGENIZATION OF MASS CULTURE

Companies like Victor, Columbia, and Nacional sold many records in Argentina, and particularly in Buenos Aires, but the market they served was limited. Records remained a luxury item throughout the 1920s, accessible only to a fraction of the population. A single disc, with one song on each side, cost between 2.50 and 3 pesos. And if that was expensive, the price of the phonograph itself was prohibitive. Record players dropped from about 75 pesos in 1920 to 30 pesos in 1929, but that still put them out of reach for most people in a city where even a skilled worker might only bring home between 160 and 200 pesos per month. Not surprisingly, only an estimated 4.5 percent of the Argentine population purchased records in 1925, and record sales plunged after 1930 as a result of the Depression.[50] But if the impact of the phonograph was limited, another new mass cultural technology would exert much greater influence. During the 1930s, the radio emerged as a more important medium, capable of reaching Argentines of virtually all classes in most of the country.

Radio technology was adopted in Argentina within a few years of its appearance in the United States and before most of Europe had discovered it. The creation of the Radio Club Argentino in 1921 revealed the existence of a large and growing movement of amateur radiophiles who built sets, developed their own technical improvements, and began broadcasting.[51] But radio as hobby soon gave way to radio as business; by 1930 there were eighteen commercial radio stations broadcasting in Buenos Aires.[52] These stations reached a much broader audience than the one to which the record companies catered. Although estimates of the number of radio receivers in Argentina vary widely, several sources suggest that there were well over one million by the middle of the 1930s, or roughly one radio for every ten people, a proportion that must have been significantly higher in urban areas.[53] These sets were not cheap, but in sharp contrast to a record player, once a consumer purchased a radio receiver, the music was free, as was a range of other entertainments, including sports, news, comedy, and radio theater. As a result of its far greater reach, it was the radio, more than the phonograph, that forged a national public, made stars out of artists like Gardel, and effectively disseminated new versions of national identity.

Although it did not face significant foreign competition, Argentine radio was nonetheless shaped by the transnational mass cultural marketplace. Station owners and program directors built an audience by catering to demands for both modern and authentically Argentine programs. During the early 1930s, they crafted a formula that managed to satisfy these competing demands. This menu of offerings, which featured both jazz and tango, but also radio theater, folk music, and comedy programs, constituted an alternative modernism with enormous commercial appeal. It was so successful, in fact, that it became ubiquitous. Despite the large number of stations, the Argentine radio grew increasingly homogenous over time. By the late 1930s, radio audiences throughout the country were largely listening to the same things.

In contrast to the local record business, the Argentine radio industry was never dominated by North American and European business interests. The early popularity of radio in Argentina did create an opportunity for foreign manufacturers of radio equipment, but they were slow to capitalize, allowing local suppliers to step in. While American sets were the most popular in 1932, by 1940 the U.S. Commerce Department reported that "virtually all of the receiving sets are now produced within the country."[54] By 1935 some 115 Argentine factories employing fifteen hundred workers supplied most of the parts and accessories to the local market.[55] In an early attempt to dominate the Argentine market, a consortium of wireless companies from the United States, England, France, and Germany founded the broadcast station Radio Sudamérica in 1922, in order to increase the sale of radio equipment manufactured by member companies. But the consortium's high prices as well as its inability to enforce its patents in Argentina limited its success. Officials at Radio Sudamérica complained that the quality of the station's programming actually expanded demand for cheap, domestically produced radio equipment.[56] In late 1922, a new radio station received a commercial license from the municipal government of Buenos Aires and immediately began jamming Radio Sudamérica's signal. The Argentine owners of Radio Cultura, as the new station was called, agreed to stop the interference in exchange for a payment from their foreign competitor.[57]

The key turning point for Argentina's nascent radio industry came in 1923, when Luis Firpo challenged Jack Dempsey for the heavyweight championship. The North American company RCA, a member of the multinational consortium that owned Radio Sudamérica, transmitted the fight to Argentina using Morse code. The consortium now partnered with its former nemesis, Radio Cultura, which broadcast an instant translation of the round-by-round description. The fight was a major event in Argentina, as Firpo's attempt to unseat the American champion became a matter of national pride. Thousands of fans congregated outside newspaper offices, in theaters, social clubs, and even political party offices to hear the broadcast.[58] Although Dempsey's controversial victory was disappointing, the fight demonstrated the exciting potential of radio technology. Local manufacturers and dealers took advantage of the fight to run advertisements and offer discounts on radio equipment.[59] With popular interest in the radio exploding, a host of new stations quickly joined Radio Cultura on the dial.

In this rapidly expanding market, foreign capital played only a marginal role. Unable to compete with the domestic companies as well as the many individuals who dedicated themselves to assembling radio sets, the consortium disbanded in 1924. In November 1925, the prominent porteño newspaper *La Nación* took over the station that had once broadcast as Radio Sudamérica. As we have seen, local tastes were influenced in important ways by American and European culture, but this influence was transmitted on radio stations that were owned and operated by Argentines. Even if RCA and its European partners had enjoyed better luck with Radio Sudamérica, it is doubtful that they would have had a decisive influence on the content of radio programming in Argentina. In its effort to sell radio equipment, the consortium had largely deferred to local tastes. Radio Sudamérica's program for September 13, 1923, for example, included several "English, American, and Scotch songs," but these were far outnumbered by opera and by dozens of tangos performed by a local orquesta típica.[60] With the rise of commercial broadcasting, the pursuit of advertisers shaped the programming of all successful Argentine radio stations, and it is unlikely that foreign capital would have behaved differently.

Not only was the Argentine radio industry free of foreign ownership, it also faced only limited interference from the state. After an early period in which jurisdiction over the granting of broadcast licenses in Buenos Aires belonged to the navy, the Yrigoyen administration transferred regulatory authority to the Postal and Telegraphic Service of the Ministry of the Interior in 1928. The following year saw the imposition of a series of new regulations, including bans on tasteless advertising and limits on the use of recorded music. More important, the Postal and Telegraphic Service required that all radio towers be relocated outside the city of Buenos

Aires, a measure favoring well-established stations that could afford to move their antennas. A law enacted in 1933 established intellectual property rights and the remuneration of copyright holders. Finally, in 1934 an executive decree imposed a series of rules about radio content: advertising between "numbers" had to be limited to one hundred words, singing in ads was banned, as were deliberate mispronunciations of Spanish, off-color jokes, immoral songs, and offensive dramas.[61] While these regulations were certainly intrusive, they did not differ significantly from the sort of government oversight that functioned in the United States, where despite rules against censorship, licenses were revoked for programs deemed contrary to the public interest.[62] There is little evidence that Argentine radio operators found these regulations problematic, as they did not provoke substantial complaint.

By regulating advertising and programming content, the government implicitly accepted the commercial and competitive character of Argentine radio. Although non-commercial radio stations run by provincial and municipal governments and by universities were more numerous in Argentina than in the United States, they never posed a significant challenge to the for-profit stations. Moreover, as Robert Claxton has argued, "stations survived as noncommercial entities to the extent that they behaved like their commercial counterparts."[63] While these stations did broadcast educational programs, they held onto their audiences with healthy doses of popular music and other light entertainments. In contrast to the publicly financed, state-run broadcasting systems created in Europe, Argentina thus followed the United States in creating a system in which the airwaves were publicly owned but licensed primarily to private individuals or entities aiming to make a profit. With the rise of anti-liberal, statist ideologies in the 1930s, there were significant campaigns to place the radio industry under government control. The daily newspaper *La Prensa* saw the new medium as a threat to its own circulation and argued that the poor quality of radio programming required the nationalization of the broadcasting system.[64] By the late 1930s, the government seemed to agree. In 1938 President Roberto Ortiz appointed a Commission for the Study and Reorganization of the Radio System. Released the following year, the commission's report found grave defects in Argentine radio, arguing that the competitive system had produced "bad programs" and turned the radio into "a true enemy of public culture."[65] The report recommended the termination of all existing licenses and the expansion of state oversight. The proposal included a 50 percent reduction in advertising and the formation of a governing board to include license owners as well as government appointees. Nevertheless, the commission's recommendations met with widespread resistance and were not implemented. Argentine radio would remain in private hands until the media takeovers of the Perón regime.

In the absence of a powerful foreign presence and an interventionist state, radio emerged as a lucrative arena for small entrepreneurs. The founders of early stations tended to be immigrants or the sons of immigrants of modest backgrounds. Lacking any advanced education, these self-taught businessmen typically invested in a radio station after having achieved success in some other sector, often radio equipment sales.[66] The recording industry pioneer Max Glücksmann partnered with the radio equipment dealer Benjamín Gache and the engineer Antonio Devoto to found Radio Grand Splendid in 1924.[67] But the most influential radio entrepreneur was Jaime Yankelevich. Like Glücksmann, Yankelevich was a Jewish immigrant whose family had come to Argentina when Jaime was a small boy. By the early 1920s, he had trained as an electrician and owned a small shop in Buenos Aires, specializing in radio equipment. In 1926, having made a substantial profit from the excitement generated by the Firpo-Dempsey fight, Yankelevich purchased Radio Nacional, one of the stations on which he had advertised his store.[68] By 1934, when Radio Nacional changed its name to Radio Belgrano, the station dominated the market, charging the highest advertising rates and signing the biggest stars.

Yankelevich and Glücksmann bear comparison to the Jewish immigrants who founded the major Hollywood film studios in the late 1910s. As the film historian Lary May has argued, producers like Adolph Zukor, Samuel Goldwyn, and Louis B. Mayer exemplified Max Weber's concept of the "pariah capitalist" who seizes opportunities scorned by established elites. Their outsider status and experience in marginal trades gave them the ability to tap into consumer preferences that challenged Victorian values as well as to imagine a more open and inclusive nation.[69] Similarly, neither Glücksmann nor Yankelevich had any previous experience in music or entertainment, but their retail background made them experts in catering to popular tastes. Glücksmann gravitated to tango because he recognized that genre's commercial potential, and he developed the tango contests to help him respond more efficiently to his audience. Similarly,

Yankelevich, as an early radio advertiser, saw the medium as a commercial opportunity, not an artistic one, and he embraced tango and other popular genres because of their widespread appeal. As entrepreneurial outsiders, Glücksmann and Yankelevich were unlikely to feel any of the ambivalence that more elite Argentines often felt toward popular cultural practices. Yankelevich in particular amazed both his detractors and his admirers with his gift for appealing to popular tastes. Pedro de Paoli, a severe critic of the lowbrow tendencies of Argentine radio, accused Radio Belgrano of favoring "vulgar programs (programas populacheros)," while another commentator denounced Yankelevich for offering a "course in bad taste."[70] Describing the same tendency more positively, the magazine *Radiolandia* celebrated Radio Belgrano's "popular orientation" and congratulated the station for embracing "the aesthetic orientations of the *pueblo*."[71]

As these comments suggest, Yankelevich took a "give-the-people-what-they-want" approach to radio programming; shying away from anything too erudite, Radio Belgrano offered popular music, radio theater, comic sketches, news, and sporting events. Within a month after purchasing the station, Yankelevich had ended the practice of playing records over the air, relying instead on live performances in order to distinguish his station from the competition. This strategy was quickly imitated, establishing live music as the centerpiece of most broadcast schedules and initiating a fierce, ongoing competition to sign the most popular artists. Among Belgrano's musical offerings, tango singers were most heavily represented. The station's listings in 1938, for example, read like a tango who's who: Mercedes Simone, Libertad Lamarque, Ignacio Corsini, Agustín Magaldi, Charlo, and Alberto Gómez. Folk singers like Martha de los Ríos were also featured, although much less prominently. That same year, Radio Belgrano's program listed ten tango bands and four jazz bands under the heading of dance music as well as a handful of bands that specialized in other foreign genres.[72] In addition to the station's musical offerings, Yankelevich achieved enormous popularity with other types of programming. The comic Tomás Simari created "the italo-criollo detective Nick Vermicelli" by fusing the long-standing criollista tradition of poking fun at Italian "Cocoliches," as well as his own experience growing up with an Italian immigrant father, with the conventions of Hollywood gangster films. Simari's sketches were so popular that thousands turned out at the Boca Juniors soccer stadium to see Vermicelli marry his love interest, Anyulina.⁷³ But the most popular show on Yankelevich's station was *Chispazos de Tradición*, a criollista soap opera that aired daily at 6:45 in the evening. Written in discrete chapters by the Spanish playwright and poet José Andrés González Pulido and featuring folk music composed and collected by the Italian-born Félix Scolatti Almeyda, *Chispazos* was often attacked for its lack of authenticity. Nevertheless, González Pulido's melodramatic stories of gauchos and their women, or *chinas*, attracted a huge following. According to the program's weekly magazine, 114,687 fans voted in a poll to determine whom the character Juan Manuel should marry.⁷⁴

Like Glücksmann, Yankelevich developed various methods for connecting to his audience. Vermicelli's wedding and the poll to pick Juan Manuel's bride were typical of a station that encouraged the active participation of its listeners. In 1937 *Sintonía* reported on a poll organized by Yankelevich, an "expert in popular psychology." Adapting Glücksmann's contests to the radio, Radio Belgrano asked listeners to select the best new tango song played on its airwaves and allegedly received 1,835,235 votes through the mail.⁷⁵ Regardless of the veracity of this claim, the contest promoted the station's commitment to tango as a sign of its adherence to popular tastes. The station even used this sort of contest to pick the name "Belgrano." When the Argentine government declared that the word "national" could no longer be used as part of a private business name, the station polled its listeners to select a replacement.⁷⁶ In addition to write-in contests, Radio Belgrano used theatrical performances to give its audience greater access to its performers. The *Chispazos de Tradición* cast performed regularly—often immediately after its radio show—in movie theaters throughout the barrios of Buenos Aires and even on tour in the interior of the country. The show was such a phenomenon that the radio fan magazine *Antena* dedicated a special letters-to-the-editor section to it, and schools throughout Argentina included *Chispazos* scripts in their theater festivals.⁷⁷

Radio Belgrano's enormous success made it a trendsetter. *Chispazos de Tradición*, for example, inspired a seemingly unending list of imitators. Shows like *Junto al Fogón, Tradición Nacional, En el rancho 'e Don Montiel, Cenizas del Fogón, Juramento Gaucho*, and others all borrowed the *Chispazos* formula: episodic melodramas set in the Pampas among stereotypical gauchos and accompanied by folk songs.⁷⁸ Radio Belgrano's next hit was a historical romance set in the Argentine countryside during the reign of Juan Manuel de Rosas. Written by Héctor Pedro Blomberg and Carlos Viale Paz, *Bajo la Santa Federación* shared its rural setting and its liberal use of folk music with *Chispazos*; the two shows even shared the same composer: Scolatti Almeyda. Nevertheless, *Bajo la Santa Federación* set itself apart by claiming to offer greater literary merit and historical accuracy, and it too inspired copycats on other stations, including subsequent works by Blomberg and Viale Paz, who stuck with their winning formula. Radio Belgrano's musical contests were also imitated by other stations, as was the station's mix of tango, folk, and jazz.[79]

By the mid-1930s, the fierce competition on Argentine radio had produced homogeneity, with virtually all stations seeking to reproduce Belgrano's success. The lack of variety and innovation on the radio was a frequent topic of editorials in entertainment magazines. One typical column blamed the "tendency toward imitation" on the single-minded pursuit of profit, which led stations to copy any popular program, an assessment shared by the official commission appointed by President Ortiz.[80] Similarly, Guillermo Del Ponte, the director of Radio Fénix, complained that most stations competed to sign acts that had already proven popular, ignoring their obligation to "educate the tastes of the public."[81] While listeners who sought out diversity could find it, a random spin of the dial would support this conventional wisdom. The radio listings for September 1933, for example, featured sports and news programs, as well as weekly programs aimed at many of Argentina's immigrant groups. There were programs for children, Hawaiian music shows, two opera performances per week, as well as seven classical orchestras performing regularly. These shows did represent diversity, but they were far outnumbered by the many daily programs that featured tango, jazz, comedy sketches, and radio plays. There were thirteen jazz bands and fourteen tango bands performing on a regular basis. In addition, some forty-one singers and duos who specialized in either tango or Argentine folk music enjoyed regular airplay, often performing as many as four or five times per week.[82]

Statistics compiled by Andrea Matallana reveal the ubiquity of the Yankelevich formula. In 1936 70 percent of all radio programming was dedicated to music and radio theater. Five years later, other types of programs—chiefly news—had gained some modest ground, but music and radio theater continued to account for 61 percent of the total.[83] And within these categories, most stations hewed close to Radio Belgrano's aesthetic preferences. In 1938 tango represented 54 percent of the music played on porteño radio stations, while jazz was second with 19 percent. By comparison, only 6 percent of music programming was dedicated to classical music.[84] Stations like Radio Splendid and Radio Excelsior did attempt to distinguish themselves as highbrow alternatives to Radio Belgrano by playing a greater percentage of classical music. But advertising rates suggest that these stations had a significantly smaller audience; Belgrano's rates were twice as high as Excelsior's and up to 33 percent higher than Splendid's.[85] Moreover, even these stations offered a great many programs that would have fit right in on Radio Belgrano. In March 1935, Radio Splendid's Saturday schedule included several classical performances, but its nighttime lineup featured the jazz band Blue American Jazz alternating with the orquesta típica of Edgardo Donato. For its part, Radio Excelsior offered opera on Sundays, but its Saturday program featured jazz by the Santa Paula Serenaders and tango by Juan de Dios Filiberto's orquesta típica.[86] Tango, jazz, and radio theater were programming staples all across the dial.

Yankelevich's approach was so successful that it proved difficult to resist. In fact, the one station that emerged in the 1930s with sufficient economic backing to challenge Radio Belgrano's dominance saw no alternative but to adopt a very similar program. In 1935 Editorial Haynes, the company that owned *El Mundo*, one of the top-selling daily newspapers in Buenos Aires, launched Radio El Mundo with the intention of creating "the leading station in South America." In particular, the station bragged of its intent to improve the content of Argentine radio. Toward that end, it named as its artistic director Enrique del Ponte, one of the founders of Radio Cultura, a station long praised by critics of Radio Belgrano's vulgar populism.[87] In the weeks preceding the station's inauguration, *El Mundo* celebrated its artistic director as a man committed to the "constant improvement of the cultural and artistic level of the radio," a "solid guarantee of quality for the station . . . because of the vast culture and exquisite sensibility that characterizes him."[88] Del Ponte's inaugural transmission included a performance by the tango star Azucena Maizani, but also symphonic music by Weber and de Falla, as well as several songs by Juan Arvizú, the Mexican bolero singer. The prominence of both classical music and international artists was, in fact, intended to be a hallmark of Radio El Mundo's style.[89] In order to make the new station into a model of high cultural standards, del Ponte announced his plan to assemble a house orchestra as skilled in symphonic music as those that played in the prestigious Colón Theater in Buenos Aires.[90] Nevertheless, within a few weeks, the station had reversed course, firing del Ponte and replacing him with the former artistic director of Radio Belgrano, Pablo Osvaldo Valle. From that moment on, Radio El Mundo employed a distinctly Yankelevich-inspired approach. Valle attempted to re-create the lineup he had assembled for Radio Belgrano, luring away popular artists whenever he could.[91] By emphasizing programs with mass appeal, Radio Belgrano and Radio El Mundo dominated the radio market, absorbing some 60 percent of all the advertising revenue on Argentine radio by 1939 and alarming observers who worried that without state intervention the radio would become a de facto monopoly.[92] Radio El Mundo's hiring of Valle and its embrace of Belgrano's programming style suggest that the critics were right: competition in the radio market did produce a trend toward uniformity.

The enormous success of Yankelevich's formula and the tendency of all local radio stations to adopt it reflected the position of Argentina in global mass cultural circuits. Just as the commercial success of the tango reflected its capacity to mediate between cosmopolitan modernity and Argentine tradition, successful radio stations struck a similar balance. Since its inception as a hobby for amateur enthusiasts, the radio apparatus itself had epitomized technological modernity.[93] In the 1930s, stations like Belgrano and El Mundo boasted of their technical achievements and their use of the most up-to-date equipment as much as of the excellence of their programs. Toward this end, advertisements for radio stations often featured photographs of radio towers in order to buttress their claims of technological sophistication (see figure 5). On the occasion of Radio El Mundo's inauguration, *La Canción Moderna* ran an extensive pictorial of the station's multiple studios, characterizing them as examples of "modern and comfortable elegance" and noting their use of the latest noise-reduction technology. The grand dimensions of Studio A, the magazine declared, "place it among the largest in the world."[94] Yet alongside these claims, radio stations also needed to deliver local authenticity. Efforts to elevate the foreign at the expense of the national were, like Enrique del Ponte's attempt at Radio El Mundo, doomed to fail. Argentine listeners appreciated the tango's ability to deliver modernity on Argentine terms; they expected the same from their radio stations.

The programming mix that dominated Argentine radio reflected these competing pressures. Radio stations prided themselves on contracting both the biggest international stars and the most popular Argentine

5   Radio advertisement, *Radiolandia*, June 18, 1938.

artists. By programming jazz as well as Brazilian, Cuban, Central American, and even Gypsy music, Radio Belgrano achieved "the modern miracle" of bringing together "all the rhythms of the world," thereby realizing the "ideal of the twentieth century."[95] The station's inclusion of musical variety reinforced the amazing power of radio technology to bring the whole world into porteño homes. Yet amid this variety, Yankelevich was careful to give special prominence to tango. By highlighting tango alongside jazz as well as a dizzying array of other international genres, Radio Belgrano reconciled local tradition with cosmopolitan modernity. Similarly, among the soap operas listeners could find on Argentine radio in the 1930s were gaucho stories modeled on *Chispazos de Tradición*, detective stories modeled on Hollywood films, and "universal" literary works from the European canon. By imitating foreign models and placing Argentine programs among a variety of North American–style options, radio offered Argentine listeners access to modernity on local terms. The success of Jaime Yankelevich's radio station, no less than that of Glücksmann's record label, rested on its capacity to construct an alternative modernism.

If competition yielded imitation in the radio market of Buenos Aires, the development of national networks broadcast this increasingly homogenous porteño mass culture to the rest of the country. Radio networks emerged in Argentina just a few years after the appearance of the networks CBS and NBC in the United States in 1927. In 1930 Yankelevich founded the first and most important Argentine network, linking the five stations he owned in Buenos Aires with stations in Rosario, Bahía Blanca, Córdoba, and Mendoza. Over the next several years, he added five other stations across the Argentine interior. By the middle of the decade, the Yankelevich network had been joined by two others: RADES, launched by the group who owned Radio Splendid, and the Blue and White Network, whose flagship was Radio El Mundo.[96] Affiliated stations benefited from higher advertising rates as well as access to the latest technology and the most popular artists and programs. Clearly, independent stations in the interior were at a major disadvantage, and the result was to reinforce the mass cultural dominance of Buenos Aires. Scholars have argued that the emergence of networks in the United States helped produce a trend toward standardized programming; as the number of independent stations declined, so did the incentives to specialize in programs that would appeal to niche audiences.[97] In Argentina, this effect was even greater. Buenos Aires had long exerted a powerful leadership role in the nation's cultural life, one that reflected the capital's overwhelming economic domination. Long before the invention of the modern mass media, singers and theater companies from Buenos Aires toured the interior, spreading porteño popular culture. Record players and radios only deepened this cultural transfer. Already in the 1920s, peasants from the remote Calchaquí valley who migrated to the Tucumán lowlands to work in the sugar harvest returned home with records, gramophones, and a taste for tango.[98] In the 1930s, more and more Argentines in the nation's interior were able to listen to radio, and increasingly, the radio stations they heard were affiliates of national networks based in Buenos Aires and broadcasting a predictable mix of tango, jazz, and radio theater. By the 1930s, the radio had unified the national mass cultural marketplace.

THE CINEMA AND AUDIENCE SEGMENTATION

Like the radio, cinema technology came early to Argentina. Little more than a year after the Lumière brothers held their first motion picture exhibition in Paris in 1895, several of their films were screened at the Odeon Theater in Buenos Aires. By 1897 Max Glücksmann and his collaborator, Eugenio Py, were producing their own short films for the Casa Lepage.[99] Over the next decade, the Argentine cinema would remain primarily an object of curiosity for porteños anxious to sample the most impressive of modern technology. Unlike the radio, the high cost of film equipment meant that the cinema never produced an extensive community of amateur producers.[100] Instead, the well-to-do could watch imported and locally produced newsreels and other short films at downtown theaters. Beginning in 1909, with the release of *La Revolución de Mayo*, Mario Gallo's fictional recreation of Argentina's independence movement of 1810, Argentine cinema began to emerge as a popular form of commercial entertainment. Argentine silent film boomed in the years between 1915 and 1921, when about one hundred feature films were produced. With the European film industry shuttered by the First World War, Argentine filmmakers were even able to sell their products abroad. The most successful Argentine film of the silent era, *Nobleza gaucha* (Cairo, 1915), was a hit not only in Buenos Aires but also throughout Latin America and Spain.[101]

Although the profitability of *Nobleza gaucha* was hardly typical of Argentine cinema in these years, its thematic content was. With intertitles drawn from José Hernández's epic poem *Martín Fierro*, the film tells the story of a brave gaucho whose girlfriend is abducted by an evil ranch owner and taken to his mansion in the city. *Nobleza gaucha* thus introduces the city versus country opposition that would appear sixteen years later in the Gardel film *Las luces de Buenos Aires* and in so many subsequent Argentine movies. This theme allows the film to revel in Argentine modernity—for example, via shots of automobile traffic on the luxurious Avenida de Mayo in Buenos Aires—even as it celebrates rural traditions as the essence of Argentine nationhood.[102] Just as tango's broad appeal relied on its capacity to reconcile jazz with Argentine popular culture, films like *Nobleza gaucha* offered domestic audiences an alternative modernism, a way of inserting a mythical national past into a rapidly modernizing present.[103] And as in the case of tango, the cinema's thematic concerns reflected the dynamics of the transnational marketplace. Unlike Argentine radio programmers, who after the decline of Radio Sudamérica faced no foreign competition, Argentine filmmakers needed to distinguish their products from the imported films available to local moviegoers, and they did so by emphasizing the national. Many followed the example of *Nobleza gaucha* by repackaging stories drawn from criollista literature and the enormously popular criollo circus, while others narrated famous episodes from Argentine history.

Argentine silent film entered a crisis in the early 1920s. The end of the war facilitated the recovery of the European film industry, increasing the competition that Argentine movies faced abroad. More important, however, was the rise of Hollywood cinema to a position of unrivalled international dominance. Beginning in 1916, American studios adopted new strategies, opening their own offices around the world so as to avoid having to negotiate with local distribution firms. After the war, the active support of the United States government helped Hollywood studios prize open foreign markets. But more than distribution strategies or government backing, the international success of the North American film industry during the 1920s reflected the sheer size of its domestic market. With huge movie audiences at home, Hollywood films paid for themselves before they were exported. Film companies based in the United States entered foreign markets needing only to recover distribution costs, while their local competitors had to recover the costs of production as well. Moreover, huge domestic receipts meant that Hollywood studios could afford to produce longer films with more lavish production values than those produced in other countries, and these movies attracted audiences throughout the world.[104] As theater owners in Argentina became aware of the appeal of expensive feature films, they were increasingly willing to deal directly with North American companies, and local distribution companies began to lose control of the market.[105] Unlike the recording industry, in which local producers were also the exclusive agents of foreign music companies, the Argentine film industry confronted foreign producers who enjoyed direct access to the local market. By 1931 seven large North American companies directly distributed 62 percent of all films screened in Argentina. These companies used the same distribution techniques in Argentina as they did at home: they rented films to theater owners demanding a percentage of box-office receipts, and they insisted that theater owners seeking to book a popular film also accept several less profitable movies.[106]

Faced with Hollywood's technical and artistic competence as well as its economic power and aggressive marketing strategies, local filmmakers could not compete. As early as 1916, the United States consul found American films on the program in almost every theater in Buenos Aires.[107] By the early 1920s, Argentine film production had dwindled. Over the next decade, locally produced films would account for only 10 percent of box-office receipts.[108] Argentine filmgoers avidly followed the exploits of Douglas Fairbanks, Rudolph Valentino, and Greta Garbo, but they were only rarely able to see an Argentine production. In 1931 in the midst of economic crisis, only four Argentine films were released; the following year, the number had dropped to two.[109]

The introduction of sound in movies brought with it the resurrection of Argentina's film industry. The "talkie" emerged in the United States with the release of *The Jazz Singer* (Crosland) in 1927. By 1930 Argentine filmmakers were experimenting with records as a way of producing synchronized sound in feature films. In 1933 the country's first two modern studios—Argentina Sono Film and Lumiton—were created in order to make films using optical sound technology for the domestic market. The industry took off almost immediately, growing steadily over the next decade. Local filmmakers released thirteen films in 1935, twenty-eight in 1937, forty-one in 1938, and an average of fifty films per year over the following four years. By 1937 there were nine film studios and thirty production companies in Buenos Aires.[110] This rapid growth came despite the fact that Hollywood continued to enjoy a significant competitive advantage over domestic producers. By 1935 Paramount, Metro, Warner, Fox, Columbia, Universal, and United Artists all had branch offices not only in Buenos Aires, but in the important provincial cities as well. In contrast to these powerful companies, Argentine film studios were tiny operations. Lacking the bargaining power of their foreign rivals, Argentine producers were unable to secure a distribution system that guaranteed them a percentage of the gross receipts. Forced to sell films to distributors on a flat fee basis and lacking any protectionist assistance from the government, they remained severely undercapitalized.[111] The steady growth of the domestic film industry in such adverse conditions reveals that filmmakers had tapped a powerful demand for Argentine sound films.

As in the recording and radio industries, the growth of Argentine cinema resulted from the efforts of small entrepreneurs who proved adept at catering to local tastes. Typical of these was Angel Mentasti, who founded Argentina Sono Film, perhaps the most successful of the country's film companies. An Italian immigrant who arrived in Argentina at the end of the nineteenth century, Mentasti worked as a wine distributor. At the behest of one of his clients, the director of a company that distributed foreign films, Mentasti began to carry a movie catalogue on his sales trips through the provinces. Soon thereafter, he quit the wine business and went to work full-time in film distribution. Like Max Glücksmann and Jaime Yankelevich, Mentasti was an immigrant entrepreneur of modest means, whose expertise lay not in cultural production but in sales and marketing. Just as Glücksmann had relied on men like José González Castillo, the tango lyricist who encouraged him to record Carlos Gardel, Mentasti's partner in Argentina Sono Film was Luis Moglia Barth, an Argentine-born son of a shopkeeper. Like González Castillo, Moglia Barth had extensive experience in adapting European films for the Argentine market, a process that in his case involved extensive editing and even occasionally refilming a scene, in addition to writing subtitles. With the knowledge he gained from these adaptations, Moglia Barth began to direct his own silent films. After the introduction of optical sound and the impressive commercial success of *Las luces de Buenos Aires*, Mentasti and Moglia Barth became convinced of the potential profit to be made by following the formula developed in Gardel's film: a series of tango songs performed by well-known stars, tied together by a simple narrative drawn from the recurring tropes of tango lyrics. Well versed in the challenges of film distribution, the partners approached two investors separately with the idea for the movie that would be called, simply, *¡Tango!* (Moglia Barth, 1933) and thereby raised more capital than they needed. With its next two films already financed, Argentina Sono Film entered the marketplace in a relatively strong position.[112]

The filmmaking style inaugurated by *¡Tango!* was heavily influenced by Hollywood. It was, after all, a Paramount film that had suggested the basic formula. And just as tango musicians adopted a 4/4 beat and occasionally imitated jazz instrumentation, Argentine filmmakers copied North American cinematic techniques. Manuel Romero, who would become the nation's most prolific director in the 1930s, was clearly influenced by his experience working on *Las luces de Buenos Aires*. Enrique T. Susini, one of the founders of Lumiton, was also present for the filming of Gardel's first full-length talkie at Paramount's studio in Joinville, outside Paris. There, he befriended John Alton, a Hungarian American cinematographer who had moved from Los Angeles to France to work with the Hollywood director Ernst Lubitsch and who now headed the camera department at Joinville. Susini, who was in the process of building the Lumiton studio, convinced the cinematographer to return with him to

Buenos Aires. There, Alton helped design the studio and served as cinematographer for *Los tres berretines*. Between 1932 and 1940, Alton remained in Argentina, where he directed the camera work and lighting on more than twenty films, chiefly for Lumiton's rival, Argentina Sono Film. The Argentine cinema's technical and artistic debt to North American film was more than simply a result of imitation; in the figure of John Alton and others, the Argentine film industry imported Hollywood expertise directly.[113]

Nevertheless, if Mentasti and other Argentine film producers were to wrest some share of the domestic market away from the powerful Hollywood studios, they needed to do more than replicate North American style. Although financially weak, local studios did have certain competitive advantages. Domestic filmmakers benefited from the long tradition of popular theater in Argentina, particularly the short comic plays known as sainetes; by providing comparable entertainment at a lower admission price, they could capture an already existing audience. Moreover, an important segment of this audience was either unable or reluctant to read the subtitles that accompanied films in English, and demands for films in Spanish were common in the entertainment press.[114] In the early 1930s, Hollywood companies tried to satisfy this demand by producing films spoken in Spanish, but with the important exception of Gardel's films for Paramount, they met with only limited success. With Gardel's death in 1935, Hollywood lost its one bankable Spanish-language star, and Argentine productions quickly eclipsed Spanish language films made in the United States.[115] Ironically, Paramount's success with Gardel showed Argentine filmmakers that they could compete with Hollywood by emphasizing their own authenticity. Argentine movies could speak to local audiences in a way that Hollywood films could not. They were set in familiar locales, and they starred actors who spoke Spanish in the local dialect and who were often recognizable to filmgoers from their previous careers in theater and radio. Moreover, these films drew their material from Argentina's popular cultural traditions. While Argentina Sono Film turned to the tango, Lumiton's *Los tres berretines* was based on the biggest hit of the previous theatrical season. The movie's use of the immigrant stereotypes that were the sainete's comic trademark, as well as its celebration of soccer and tango, rooted it firmly in Argentine popular culture. Of course, both the tango and the sainete were from Buenos Aires. Since the vast majority of Argentine films were produced in Buenos Aires and since the barrios of the capital city constituted the biggest local market for these movies, the cinema, like the radio, reinforced the hegemony of porteño culture throughout the nation.

The tendency of these early sound movies to emphasize and celebrate the cultural practices of ordinary Argentines repeated a process that had occurred much earlier in the United States, where the emergence of nickelodeons at the turn of the century had produced a cinema that catered to a heavily working-class audience.[116] In order to appeal to these viewers, filmmakers in the United States appropriated and repackaged pre-existing popular entertainments, such as melodrama and burlesque, and offered movies that featured explicitly working-class characters and concerns. Moreover, in the early years of North American cinema, movie-going was an experience that reinforced social divisions. In big cities, workers went to movie theaters in their own neighborhoods and with their own ethnic and class-based communities.[117]

However, in the United States, the cinema soon lost its working-class character. Various campaigns emerged to clean up and moralize the movies, to purge them of scandalous elements. And from the 1920s on, Hollywood studios embarked on a new strategy, achieving enormous profits by manufacturing films that appealed to a multiclass audience. As downtown movie palaces began to replace the old neighborhood theaters, filmmakers rejected the spectacular melodrama that had been so popular among working-class audiences in the earlier period. They stopped making films about and for the working class and instead embraced more conservative "cross-class fantasies."[118] More fundamentally, "classical" Hollywood cinema created a new mode of spectatorship that blurred the class and ethnic divisions of movie audiences. Beginning in the late teens, North American filmmakers used set design, composition, continuity editing, deep focus, and other techniques in order to produce seamless narratives in which the spectator was granted an omniscience denied to the film's characters. By actively positioning spectators, these new strategies of narration encouraged viewers' absorption and identification with the film, and, in so doing, they tended to standardize reception. While viewers still brought their own perspectives to bear on films, this new cinematic style facilitated Hollywood's efforts to pitch its products at a homogenous mass audience.[119]

Many of the same ideological and commercial forces that worked to dissolve the cinema's working-class commitments in the United States were present in Argentina as well. Alarmed by the power of movies to shape the "culture" of the masses as well as the image of Argentina abroad, many intellectuals and politicians urged the cinema to raise its standards. These critics echoed those who attacked radio stations for pandering to the lowbrow tastes of the masses, and they proposed the same solution: state intervention. Particularly vocal in their demands for official regulation of the film industry were Carlos Alberto Pessano, the Catholic intellectual and editor of the film magazine *Cinegraf*, and Matías Sánchez Sorondo, the conservative senator. These cultural critics linked their campaign to the demands of filmmakers who wanted the government to protect the local film industry against foreign competition. In 1936 President Agustín P. Justo created the Argentine Cinematic Institute and appointed Pessano and Sánchez Sorondo as its directors. Nevertheless, under Ortiz's administration, the institute's functions were severely limited, and although some instances of censorship did occur during the 1930s, these were relatively minor.[120] But while official censorship remained limited in these years, criticism of the supposed bad taste displayed in national films was nearly omnipresent in the print media. In *Crítica*, Ulyses Petit de Murat denounced "certain dishes seasoned with coarse sauces, certain situations that affect good taste, the stylistic rudeness of many films."[121] Likewise, in *El Mundo*, the film reviewer Calki (Raimundo Calcagno) insisted, "our cinema needs quality!"[122] while his colleague Néstor (Miguel Paulino Tato) irritated movie fans by fulminating against the "vulgarity and bad taste" displayed in local films.[123]

For these critics, what threatened the quality of Argentine cinema was precisely its tendency to borrow from lowbrow popular cultural forms such as the tango and the sainete. In its review of *Los tres berretines*, *Cinegraf* put it succinctly: "We have repudiated a cinema based on specimens from the *suburbios*, on carnival parade peasants. It seems to us equally absurd that films are falsified based on *sainete* immigrants in order to lapse into situations that can never adequately reflect national life and that films resort to humor through the language of the *arrabales*, which is inherently in bad taste."[124] "Bad taste," according to this reviewer, was epitomized by the tango and the sainete, cultural forms that sprang from the suburbios and arrabales that were home to the urban poor. While *Cinegraf*'s conservative politics and glossy covers stood out among Argentine film magazines, its elitist hostility toward popular culture did not. Most film reviewers were ambivalent at best about the local cinema's appropriation of lowbrow cultural forms.[125] They wanted Argentine films to emphasize the national without at the same time catering to the uncultured tastes of the popular sectors. In its positive review of *La vida de Carlos Gardel* (de Zavalía, 1939), a biography filmed four years after Gardel's death, *La Razón* lauded the film for having avoided "the sin of reproducing the hackneyed and unedifying world of the tango (*ambiente tanguero*). In effect, Carlos Gardel rose in the suburban barrios, singing in the markets, as the film says. But the film has not gone poking around in that dirty atmosphere of the bar counter and the suburban tough (*compadrito suburbano*)."[126] Even though this reviewer acknowledged the rags-to-riches story that helped make Gardel a national icon, he complimented the film for avoiding any depiction of the gritty urban milieu from which Gardel emerged. What the reviewer appreciated was the movie's sanitized version of a popular national legend. Critics like this one hoped that film, if it could avoid pandering to popular tastes, might serve as a vehicle for educating and improving the masses. They saw the cinema as an opportunity to redefine the nation by aligning it with progress and modernity while preserving its distinctive essence.

High-minded critics were hardly the only influence encouraging filmmakers to raise their standards. Competition with Hollywood gave Argentine filmmakers a chronic case of nationalist insecurity. Before the boom in domestic film production, the cinema was often figured as a dangerously seductive threat to the nation; foreign movie stars threatened to woo local girls away from Argentine men. In a column in 1931, Roberto Arlt worried that women who watched movies would become disillusioned with their own lives. He reports the words of a female informant, referring to a Hollywood film star popular in the Spanish-speaking world: "I have known many happily married women who after going to the movies for one year, look at their husbands as if to say: 'Ramón Novarro smokes more elegantly than you.' "[127] Likewise, in *Los tres berretines*, the patriarch of the family complains that when women return from the movies, their lives seem "miserable" by contrast. Once Argentina began producing its own sound films, the competition with Hollywood was often depicted as a matter of national importance. The fan magazine *Sintonía* regularly ran ads calling on patriotic readers to attend Argentine films: "Watch Argentine movies in your barrio theater: It is patriotic (*Es hacer patria*)."[128] Eventually, the success of the local film industry gave Argentine men the chance to undo their emasculation. In

1939 the film and radio magazine *Radiolandia* actually celebrated the suicide of a girl from the province of Misiones, whose desperation was caused by the recent death of the local film star José Gola. The fact that Argentine girls were killing themselves for national idols as they had once done for Rudolph Valentino represented a major victory: "Native competition (*la competencia criolla*) has become great and strong."[129] In this atmosphere of national anxiety, movie critics used each review of an Argentine film as an occasion to measure the progress of the nation's film industry against the Hollywood standard. As one positive review put it, "The eyes of the spectator, accustomed to the brilliance, elegance and movement of foreign cinematic productions, will not much miss those virtues watching this film from local studios. And these days, any Argentine production that places itself on that level of spectacle, which has cost the foreigner so many years of work and so many millions, deserves frank applause."[130] The transnational marketplace itself gave the domestic studios an incentive to refine and elevate their films.

Just as competition with jazz led musicians and radio programmers to stress tango's modernity, filmmakers facing competition from Hollywood responded by embracing the modern. In the silent era, *Nobleza gaucha* had demonstrated that Argentine movies could succeed by offering viewers both modern Buenos Aires and the rural traditions of the gauchos. The sound films of the 1930s deployed similar strategies to construct an alternative modernism. If films like *¡Tango!* and *Los tres berretines* celebrated Argentine popular culture, they also reveled in porteño modernity. The opening montage of *Los tres berretines*, in which images of congested city streets are accompanied by jazz music, is a case in point. Likewise, as Florencia Garramuño has pointed out, among the first images of *¡Tango!* is the bridge over the Riachuelo River in the busy port of Buenos Aires, an image that signifies both the industrial modernity of the port and the picturesque flavor of La Boca, the working-class portside neighborhood. The poster for Argentina Sono Film's third feature, *Riachuelo* (Moglia Barth, 1934), used the same bridge as a backdrop, along with bustling ship traffic in the port to represent the city's thriving commerce.[131] These images served much the same purpose as radio station advertisements featuring photographs of giant antennas: they associated local mass cultural productions with the latest achievements in modern technology.

The Argentine studios had good reasons to abandon their commitment to lowbrow popular culture, just as Hollywood had done in the

1920s. Not only did critics demand moral and artistic improvement, but also local audiences accustomed to North American cinematic virtuosity expected a more modern cinema. By 1933, when the local film industry finally took off, Hollywood had long since rejected its own working-class origins in favor of a more cross-class mode of address. By continuing to produce cinema rooted in popular culture, Argentine filmmakers risked seeming antiquated to audiences who were used to the Hollywood style. Yet at the same time, other forces discouraged the local studios from following Hollywood's lead. Most important, the Argentine movie audience was segmented in ways that made it difficult to embrace Hollywood's pursuit of a homogenous, multiclass audience. Unlike the radio, movies were consumed in public places and therefore lent themselves more readily to attempts at distinction. In Buenos Aires, a preference for foreign films became a marker of upper-class status. The resulting audience segmentation reinforced domestic filmmakers' embrace of plebeian cultural practices.

From the beginning of the sound era, the movies were a popular source of entertainment in Argentine cities. As early as 1929, there were 972 theaters showing movies in the country as a whole, 152 of them in the city of Buenos Aires.[132] Seven years later, Argentina ranked first in Latin America with 1,425 movie theaters.[133] On the basis of film receipts for 1942, the U.S. Commerce Department calculated that the average Argentine went to the movies seven or eight times per year.[134] Many of these moviegoers belonged to the ranks of the working poor. Of the 147 theaters listed on one porteño newspaper's movie page in 1939, 101 were located in the barrios outside the city center,[135] and as early as 1930, even predominately working-class areas like Nueva Pompeya and La Boca had their own movie theaters.[136] Admission prices were high at the downtown, first-run theaters: 1.50 pesos for the balcony and 2.50 for orchestra seats. But barrio movie houses were much more accessible to popular audiences. There, tickets went for as little as 20 centavos, or the equivalent of U.S. $0.05, at a time when the average daily wage for an unskilled worker was between U.S. $1.00 and U.S. $2.00. And for that relatively low price, patrons at barrio theaters were entitled to a program that consisted of at least three and as many as five feature films.[137] The lack of ethnic segregation in Buenos Aires meant that moviegoing never reinforced immigrant identities the way the nickelodeons did in North American cities. On the other hand, Argentine movie audiences continued to be at least partly segregated by class throughout the 1930s, long after the neighborhood theaters of the United States had given way to the downtown movie palaces. In the barrios of Buenos Aires, the movies were a cheap night out, affordable even for manual laborers. The weekly magazine of Argentina's principal union confederation, the CGT, probably only exaggerated slightly when it declared that "90% of the clientele for the production of films comes from among our readers."[138]

No doubt the working-class members of the CGT enjoyed all sorts of movies, but they made up a particularly large segment of the audience for domestic films. Throughout the period, the Argentine movie audience was divided roughly along class lines: while Argentines of all social classes saw Hollywood films, the audience for domestic movies was composed primarily of the lower and middle classes. As the U.S. Commerce Department put it, "The so-called better class Argentine ... has a predilection for American films."[139] In fact, for much of the 1930s, many downtown, first-run theaters refused to show Argentine films at all, and the film industry trade paper, *El Heraldo del Cinematografista*, labeled most domestic productions "suitable, especially, for popular theaters."[140] According to the movie page from 1939 cited above, only 30 percent of the downtown theaters were showing any Argentine films. But in the barrio theaters, the figure rose to 53 percent, and most of those theaters offered several domestic productions.[141] If we were to exclude such well-to-do districts as Norte, where only one of seven theaters was showing a domestic film, the proportion would be substantially higher. The movies constituted a cultural field marked by a hierarchy of taste. At the top of this hierarchy were the major new Hollywood films, shown for a high price at fancy downtown theaters. At the other end of the spectrum were Argentine films, shown at barrio theaters at prices accessible to nearly all. As we have seen, the barrios of Buenos Aires housed a heterogeneous population of diverse class commitments. Yet within the market for cinema, the barrios represented the "popular" in contrast to the elite world downtown.

Argentina Sono Film and Lumiton initially acquiesced to this audience segmentation because they lacked the big budgets that would have enabled them to challenge Hollywood's control of the high-end market. Eventually, as we shall see in subsequent chapters, the studios did pursue wealthier consumers, appropriating storylines from North American films in order to attract these audiences. But at the same time, local filmmakers needed to hold on to their base audience in the barrios. Even at low-cost barrio theaters, moviegoers had a choice between films from the United States and local productions, and Argentine movies that simply copied North American models risked appearing second best by comparison. Just as the innovations of tango modernizer Julio de Caro were measured against the achievements of Paul Whiteman, Argentina's cinematic efforts would always be judged by Hollywood standards. Given the enormous disparity in budgets, the playing field was anything but level. In response, local studios continued to play to their comparative advantage, producing films rooted in Argentine popular culture in order to appeal to the humble viewers who made up the bulk of their audience.

Moreover, popular culture, and particularly tango, helped domestic filmmakers expand their audience beyond the country's borders. Thanks in large part to the international star power of Gardel, itself a product of the North American film industry, tango had major commercial appeal throughout Latin America. After Gardel, the biggest beneficiary of this demand was Libertad Lamarque, whose tango films became major hits both inside and outside of Argentina, making her the nation's biggest and highest-paid box-office attraction. Lamarque, already a star on the radio, had a singing role in ¡Tango! and went on to star in a series of film melodramas that allowed her to show off both her singing voice and her screen appeal. Her films were international hits and paved the way for other Argentine productions, allowing Argentina's studios to dominate the Latin American market until they were overtaken by the Mexican film industry in the mid-1940s.[142] Foreign demand for Argentine tango thus reinforced the young film industry's embrace of popular culture and its commitment to the aesthetic preferences of a popular audience.

The transnational marketplace pushed the Argentine cinema in two directions at once. Effective competition required filmmakers to emulate Hollywood as well as to distinguish their products by delivering the Argentine particularities that audiences could not get in Hollywood movies. The resulting cinema, built out of a combination of elements drawn from Hollywood and from Argentine popular culture, offered an alternative modernism that reconciled Argentine tradition with cosmopolitan modernity. But as in the recording and radio industries, this reconciliation was always unstable. The Argentine cinema's subordinate relationship to the North American film industry prevented it from fully embracing Hollywood's strategy of building a homogenous mass audience. Argentine producers found it extremely difficult to make films that could satisfy both the elite customers who preferred foreign films and the barrio crowds that made up the bulk of their audience. Just as tango music maintained its identification with the humble masses and Radio Belgrano boasted of its fealty to the tastes of the pueblo, the Argentine cinema retained a commitment to plebeian popular culture that limited its efforts to emulate Hollywood modernity. As the chapters that follow will make clear, the persistent tensions between modernity and tradition, between the cosmopolitan and the authentic, and between efforts at cultural elevation and the embrace of the popular shaped virtually all Argentine mass culture in this period.

For Argentina's heterogeneous audiences, mass culture had brought the whole world closer, but it put them into particularly close contact with the output of the powerful culture industries in the United States. Jazz and Hollywood were "global vernaculars," in Hansen's phrase, discourses that facilitated an everyday engagement with modernity. When Argentines consumed locally produced music and film, they did so as part of a mass cultural diet that contained hefty servings of these hegemonic modernisms. Jazz always accompanied the tango on porteño radio stations, and North American films always outnumbered Argentine movies in local theaters.[143] But unlike imported cultural products, tango music and domestic movies purported to tell these audiences something about themselves. The pressures of the transnational marketplace helped produce a deeply contradictory discourse about Argentine national identity, as cultural producers reshaped pre-existing popular cultural traditions in order to compete against foreign imports. No tradition was more important in this process than popular melodrama.

3 REPACKAGING POPULAR MELODRAMA

Melodrama, more than any other cultural mode, shaped the form and content of Argentine mass culture in the 1920s and 1930s. Producers working in the new media repackaged local traditions in order to offer consumers the Argentine authenticity they could not get from Hollywood or jazz. And when these producers looked to popular culture, what they found was deeply melodramatic. From the late nineteenth century on, the stylistic, formal, and thematic conventions of melodrama were visible on the porteño stage, in popular poetry, in the criollo circuses, and in pulp fiction. As a result, melodrama was omnipresent in the mass culture of this period. Both its aesthetic of emotional excess and its Manichean vision of a society divided between rich and poor were visible in every medium and in almost every genre. Melodramatic mass culture disseminated an image of a rigidly stratified Argentina that contrasted sharply with the complex and fluid class structure of the porteño barrios.

Of course, the influence and popularity of melodrama in Argentina is but one instance of a much larger, in fact global, phenomenon. As Peter Brooks revealed more than thirty years ago, melodrama first emerged in Europe in the wake of the French Revolution. According to Brooks, this new mode became a "central fact of the modern sensibility" because it posited a system of meaning—a vision of good and evil—at a time when religion had begun to lose its power and "the traditional imperatives of truth and ethics [had] been violently thrown into question."[1] Expanding on this analysis, scholars have examined the particular appeal of melodrama for working-class audiences in nineteenth-century Europe and North America. In the context of modernization, industrialization, and the rise of market culture, melodrama neatly expressed the anxieties and fears of poor people confronting a brutal and often unpredictable capitalist system, even as it offered these audiences the promise that moral order could be restored. In melodramas, good people endured tragedy, but in the end the villain usually paid a price. Crucially, this retribution was the result of fate, rather than of any action taken by the suffering protagonist. In this way, melodrama dramatized workers' feelings of radical disempowerment even as it reassured them that in a harsh modern world, some form of cosmic justice still functioned.[2] Seen in this light, the dominant message of melodrama was conservative; its reassurances and its moralism praised conventional virtue and self-abnegation, not assertiveness and political action.

Within Latin America, where melodrama has retained its cultural centrality from the theater and serialized fiction of the nineteenth century to the era of radio plays and early cinema right through the advent of the telenovela, most scholars have emphasized this conservatism. They have stressed melodrama's tendency to divert attention away from exploitation and oppression based on class, race, or gender. As Jesús Martín-Barbero describes early Latin American cinema, "The melodrama made it possible for film to . . . dissolve tragedy in a pool of tears, depoliticizing the social contradictions of daily life."[3] Likewise, scholars have drawn attention to melodrama's power to reconcile subordinate groups to a profoundly unequal society. According to Carlos Monsiváis, Mexican melodrama offered its audiences an "aesthetic of consolation," in which suffering is rewarded with a sense of belonging and with a certain dignity and beauty. Melodramatic stories taught lessons in how to survive by adapting to conventional morality.[4] In Latin America as elsewhere, these lessons were particularly confining for women, who were typically relegated to the role of victim.

This conservatism was undeniably present in Argentina's melodramatic mass culture. Tango lyrics, radio plays, and movies were often imbued with a spirit of fatalistic resignation; these texts gave their protagonists little hope of challenging their victimization. Yet Argentine melodrama disseminated subversive messages as well. As in the United States, the melodramatic mode was stigmatized by elites and intellectuals as a lowbrow form designed to appeal to the base instincts of the masses. This condescension toward plebeian tastes produced distinction and legitimized social hierarchy,[5] but it also provoked, on the part of melodrama's fans, a critique of snobbery and a tendency to wear an affiliation with popular culture as a badge of honor. And this effect was heightened in Argentina, where the only alternative to locally produced, melodramatic mass culture was often a foreign import. Moreover, even if melodrama's fatalistic ethos encouraged audiences to accept the status quo, that same conformism contradicted one of the dominant discourses of Argentine society: namely, the pursuit of upward mobility. While barrio associations, magazines, and advertisements counseled self-improvement as a realistic path to a higher standard of living, melodramatic stories premised on the eternal, unbridgeable chasm between rich and poor suggested the futility of such endeavors. In their work on Hollywood melodramas, feminist film theorists have emphasized the "radical ambiguity" at the heart of these movies. While the rules of the genre require moral resolution in the form of the ultimate punishment of transgression, the aesthetic excess of melodramatic films and their success at eliciting identification with female victims enable and encourage alternative, and even subversive, readings. As Linda Williams puts it, "The female hero often accepts a fate that the audience at least partially questions."[6] In Argentina, the counterhegemonic potential of melodrama was heightened by its insistently classist orientation. The visceral anti-elitism of Argentine melodrama often spoke much louder than any lessons about the need to submit to conventional morality and social hierarchy.

THE VARIETIES OF POPULAR MELODRAMA:
THEATER, MUSIC, LITERATURE

Long before the advent of the radio and the cinema, melodrama was a staple of Argentina's popular theater. Although the nation's theater history stretches back to the colonial period, 1884 often appears as a foundational moment. That year, the Podestá brothers included in their criollo circus a pantomime version of Eduardo Gutiérrez's gaucho tale *Juan Moreira*. Quickly given a script, the play evolved in order to please its growing audience. In keeping with the carnivalesque atmosphere of the circus, the Podestás included musical and dance performances and frequently incorporated the audience into the action. Perhaps most famously, an improvised exchange with an Italian-born member of the circus crew led to the creation of Cocoliche, an Italian whose comic efforts to act and speak like a gaucho made him a stock character in popular theater. But alongside these innovations, the stage version of *Juan Moreira* also incorporated a melodramatic subplot; in addition to Moreira's violent rebellion, viewers were now treated to a sentimental dramatization of his separation from wife and child.[7]

Criollista dramas like *Juan Moreira* were one of two main antecedents for the new brand of popular theater that emerged in turn-of-the-century Buenos Aires; the other was the popular theater of Spain. During the 1890s, porteño theaters were dominated by Spanish troupes performing various genres, but especially the zarzuela, a sort of light opera in which musical and spoken scenes alternated.[8] Spanish popular theater had its own melodramatic tradition; both the zarzuela and the one-act play known as the sainete typically told stories of impossible love featuring evil villains and resolutions in which destiny rewarded the good and punished the bad. In addition to this melodramatic orientation, Spanish zarzuelas and sainetes adapted the nineteenth-century literary tradition of *costumbrismo*, which sought to depict the everyday customs and mannerisms of local people. The result was what Osvaldo Pellettieri describes as a parody or "carnivalization" of the form as playwrights livened up their works with formulaic, stereotyped caricatures of well-known social types. After 1910, when Argentine authors secured the rights to a percentage of the gross receipts generated by each performance, domestic theater production increased rapidly. The resulting genres, of which the sainete criollo was perhaps the most popular, represented reworkings of Spanish forms. The sainete criollo injected the carnivalesque atmosphere of the circus into the theater—many circus troupes, including the Podestá brothers, had begun performing plays in theaters in the 1890s—and it deepened the parody of costumbrismo already visible in Spanish plays. Argentine sainetes featured not just Italian Cocoliches, but many other stereotyped representations mocking both immigrants and criollos. The domestic sainete combined this satiric style of comedy with more somber moments focused increasingly on the personal struggle of the protagonist, a feature that distanced it from its Spanish antecedent while deepening its reliance on melodrama.[9] The resulting form—a tragicomic hybrid—was extremely popular. By 1928 Buenos Aires had some forty-three theaters with an average of seven hundred seats each; in 1925 some 6.9 million theater tickets were sold in the city.[10] And while a more serious theatrical tradition existed as well, it was the sainetes and similar "light" fare that drew the biggest crowds.

Both the criollo circus and the Spanish popular theater had included musical performances, and as plays written and performed by Argentines came to predominate in porteño theaters, Argentine music and dance genres necessarily replaced Spanish forms. The Podestás' *Juan Moreira* had featured a milonga, the antecedent to the tango, among other rural dances, but sainetes were set in Buenos Aires and required an urban music. During the 1910s, just as foreign recording companies were bringing the orquestas típicas into the studio, the tango quickly gained a starring role in the sainete criollo. The partnership between tango and sainete, as well as the eventual appropriation of both forms by the new mass media, enshrined one particular melodramatic narrative as the paradigmatic Argentine story. Nearly omnipresent by the 1920s, this was the story of the innocent, young girl who leaves her simple, safe life in the barrios for the temptations of downtown, where she is inevitably ruined.

This particular take on the fallen-woman theme emerged first in popular poetry, another arena of cultural production that drew heavily on melodrama. In the late nineteenth century, Argentina's anarchist and socialist circles produced poetry that described the horrors of class exploitation with intense imagery. Perhaps most widely read among the working class was the poet Pedro Palacios, who published under the pseudonym Almafuerte. Almafuerte denounced the immorality of the new industrial order, referring in one poem to working women "straining their lungs like a bloody blasphemy that explodes" and to "the open, insolent, triumphant chuckle" of the rich laughing at the poor.[11] Among Almafuerte's disciples was Evaristo Carriego, who would become the great poet of the porteño barrios. Carriego's poems described the city's outlying neighborhoods as a picturesque refuge peopled by familiar figures—the organ grinder, the blind man, the godmother, the drunk husband—and associated with the security of home. While he retained Almafuerte's sympathies for the poor, Carriego's tone was less angry, and his emphasis was not on exploitation, so much as on the sadness and humility of barrio residents. In 1910 Carriego published "La costurerita que dió aquel mal paso" (The little seamstress who stumbled). In this, his most famous and influential poem, and in several others, Carriego explored the story of a humble, naïve girl from the barrios who is tempted by the bright lights of the city and ends up destroyed by prostitution and tuberculosis. Carriego's tale, with its implicit critique of a woman's striving for upward mobility as well as its opposition between the innocence and goodness of the barrio and the morally dangerous world of downtown, provided a whole generation of tango lyricists and playwrights with their most familiar material. The melodramatic tale of the *costurerita*, typically referred to in tango songs as a *milonguita*, or cabaret girl, would recur in hundreds of songs and plays.[12]

In the first two decades of the twentieth century, tango was still primarily an instrumental dance music, although the so-called Old Guard did produce some songs with lyrics. These typically featured a male narrator who boasted of his bravery, his quickness to violence, his skill at dancing, and his ability to attract women. The aggressive male bravado of songs like "El porteñito" (Villoldo, 1903) reflect the tango's debt to criollista tales of violent rebels like Juan Moreira as well as to the tradition of the payadores. But the boom in tango song, whose beginning is often dated to Gardel's recording of Pascual Contursi's "Mi noche triste" in 1917, ushered in a major transformation in the poetry and thematic content of tango lyrics. The advent of the phonograph and the radio helped turn the tango into a music for listening, thereby accentuating the importance of the lyrics. At the same time, the new form of tango song was also a product of the alliance forged between tango and sainete. "Mi noche triste" was included in the 1918 production of *Los dientes del perro*, a sainete written by Alberto Weisbach and José González Castillo, the lyricist and playwright who had encouraged Max Glücksmann to record Gardel the previous year. In the play, which told the story of a transgressive love affair between a cabaret singer and a young man from a wealthy family, the actress Manolita Poli sang "Mi noche triste" as part of a cabaret scene. The performance helped make the play a huge hit: it ran for more than five hundred nights and inspired a sequel, which itself became one of the most popular plays of the season in 1919.[13]

Success bred imitation, and the sainete and tango lyric continued to develop symbiotically. Tangos that proved themselves before a theatrical audience were recorded by Gardel and other singers. They then inspired new sainetes. Samuel Linnig's tango, "Milonguita," written for his sainete *Delikatessen Haus* (1920), revisited the melodrama of the barrio girl attracted to the cabarets of downtown. Two years later, he turned the lyric of "Milonguita" into a new sainete with the same name, for which he wrote another tango, "Melenita de Oro," covering very similar terrain.[14] Contursi's follow-up to "Mi noche triste" was "Flor de fango," another tango on the milonguita theme, which in 1919 became the second tango Gardel recorded. That same year, the song was included in Alberto Novión's *El cabaret de Montmartre*, the most performed play of 1919, and its fourth line, "Tu cuna fue un conventillo" (Your cradle was a tenement) became the title of Alberto Vaccarezza's hit sainete of 1920.[15] That play's winning formula—its combination of melodrama and the humor of stereotypes, its heavy use of lunfardo, its focus on the romantic lives of the urban poor, and its inclusion of tango songs—inspired dozens of copies; Vaccarezza himself wrote some 120 plays that made it to the porteño stage.[16] By this point, the cabaret was, by far, the most common setting for sainetes and other plays, and the tango was never absent. Linnig, Vaccarezza, González Castillo, and others wrote both plays and tango lyrics, many revisiting the story of the milonguita.

The transformation of tango lyrics from bravado to melodrama, which accompanied the music's new prominence in porteño popular theater, has inspired a great deal of commentary. Most famously, Jorge Luis Borges denounced the lyricists of the 1920s for having abandoned the early tango's virility, its cult of courage, and its expression of "the belief that a fight may be a celebration." In his reading of Evaristo Carriego's poetry, Borges preferred the violent tough guys of the barrio to the seamstress who stumbles, and he extended this preference to the tango. For Borges, the brave *compadritos* (urban toughs) of early tango songs were the descendants of the gaucho rebels of criollista literature, models of masculine honor and bravery, if not necessarily intelligence. By contrast, "the later tango is like a resentful person who indulges in loud self-pity while shamelessly rejoicing at the misfortunes of others." Purging the tango of violence made it respectable, he argued, but at the cost of incorporating "a streak of vulgarity, an unwholesomeness of which the tango of the knife and the brothel never even dreamed."[17] If, for Borges, the later tango's unwholesomeness has to do with the emasculation of its protagonists, its vulgarity was at least partly the result of its commercialization on a mass scale. Many scholars have followed Borges's lead, linking the rise of tango's new protagonist, who, in Eduardo Romano's words, "exchanges the provocative snub for a sentimental lament," to the music's new audience in the barrios. As Romano argues, the consumers of mass culture listened to music not in brothels and seedy dance halls, but in respectable homes. These listeners required a more decent music.[18]

The rise of the new tango lyrics clearly exemplifies the familiar process whereby commercial culture depoliticizes the popular traditions that provide its raw material.[19] Just as the Podestás' melodramatic-comic *Juan Moreira* was better suited to drawing a cross-class audience to the criollo circus than Gutiérrez's more anti-authoritarian original, Carriego's nostalgic, picturesque depictions of the porteño poor offered a more viable model for tango lyricists than the harsh class discourse of Almafuerte. Seeking to attract the broadest audience possible, recording companies and theater troupes were understandably more enthusiastic about love stories than they were about celebrations of violent rebellion or denunciations of exploitation on the factory floor. Yet the tango's marriage to melodrama was not merely a turn to respectability. If melodrama is a particularly compelling genre for workers experiencing the dislocations of modernization, then the tango lyric's transformation must have been crucial to the genre's success as an alternative modernism. The tango's urbanity as well as its openness to new instrumentation allowed it to compete effectively with jazz by embodying an authentic, yet modernizing national identity. The melodramatic bent of the new lyrics fit this purpose as well, by neatly expressing many of the anxieties of the working poor, especially men. Barrio associations and advertisers promised upward mobility for those willing to pursue education and self-improvement, but for men who often experienced competitive capitalism as unfair and arbitrary, these promises could seem empty. Melodramatic tango lyrics offered a clear contrast: they described a world in which the rich had all sorts of advantages and the poor suffered the consequences. Tango lyrics expressed a working-class male perspective while providing the compensatory comfort of simple moral judgment.

In the most typical tango lyrics written after 1917, a compadrito, or "whiny ruffian," to borrow Marta Savigliano's apt phrase, complains about being abandoned by a girl from his neighborhood.[20] It is from his vantage point that tangos describe the perilous journey of innocent girls from the barrio to the immoral cabarets of downtown. As Contursi puts it in "Flor de Fango" ("Gutter Flower," 1917):

> Mina que te manyo de hace rato,
> perdoname si te bato
> de que yo te vi nacer.
> Tu cuna fue un conventillo
> alumbrao a querosén.
> Justo a los catorce abriles
> te entregaste a la farra,
> las delicias del gotán.
> Te gustaban las alhajas,
> los vestidos a la moda
> y las farras de champán.

> *Woman whom I've understood for a long time*
> *forgive me if I tell you*
> *that I saw you born.*
> *Your cradle was a tenement*
> *lit by a kerosene lamp.*
> *At fourteen*
> *you gave yourself to partying,*
> *the indulgences of tango.*
> *You liked jewelry,*
> *fashionable clothing*
> *and champagne parties.*[21]

In tangos like this one, the male singer blames the woman for allowing herself to be seduced. In "Margot" (Flores, 1919), the accusation is even more explicit:

> . . . no fue un guapo haragán ni prepotente,
> ni un cafishio de averías el que al vicio te largó;
> vos rodaste por tu culpa, y no fue inocentemente:
> ¡berretines de bacana que tenías en la mente
> desde el día en que un magnate cajetilla te afiló!
> . . .
> Si hasta el nombre te has cambiado como ha cambiado tu suerte:
> ya no sos mi Margarita ¡ahora te llaman Margot!

> . . . *it was not a handsome or arrogant layabout,*
> *nor an immoral pimp who delivered you to vice;*
> *it was your fault you rolled over, and not innocently:*
> *the impulses of a rich girl you had in mind*
> *since the day a millionaire dandy courted you!*
> . . .
> *You have even changed your name, just as your luck has changed:*
> *you're no longer my Margarita, now they call you Margot!*

In "Pompas de jabón" ("Soap Bubbles," Cadícamo, 1925), the singer sees a girl from his barrio riding in the car of a *bacán*, or big shot, and warns her that her luxurious lifestyle will not last long; when her beauty fades, she'll be abandoned and forced to beg in order to survive. Here is the schadenfreude that so offended Borges; the singer may have lost his woman, but he gets the last laugh when she ends up old and alone.

Not all tango lyrics were so nasty. Samuel Linnig's "Milonguita," which provided the tango's fallen woman with her most familiar name, treats her as a victim: "Men have treated you badly / and today you would give your soul / to dress in percale." The reference to the cheap fabric of a humble woman's dress alludes ironically to the milonguita's material aspirations, but the singer remains sympathetic. In "Mano Cruel" ("Cruel Hand," Tagini, 1929), blame falls squarely on the male seducer: "That man who offered you riches lied / with a cruel hand he abused your grace and your virtue." Still, the current of misogyny that runs through these lyrics is unmistakable. As the historian Donna Guy argues, these songs "berated women for the desire for conspicuous consumption that allowed men to lead them into lives of degradation."[22] For having dreamed of escaping the drab world of the barrio and enjoying the excitement and luxury of the cabaret, the milonguita pays a high price: prostitution, tuberculosis, abandonment. This misogyny expresses the anxieties of men facing a modern world that threatened their patriarchal privileges. The milonguita melodrama was invariably set in a cabaret, but metaphorically, it likely spoke to other concerns as well. In Buenos Aires of the 1920s, it was not just the sinful cabaret that lured women away from the home; the presence of women in the workforce also threatened to undermine traditional gender roles. Unsurprisingly, then, the new tango lyrics express a "doubting masculinity"; no longer so quick to violence, the compadrito is now at least as likely to cry over his lost love as he is to challenge the man who stole her away.[23] But even if revenge fantasies were less common, melodrama offered other compensations: by dispensing moral judgment and poetic justice, tango helped assuage masculine anxieties.

As melodramatic texts, tango lyrics were essentially fatalistic. They counseled resignation, implying that any effort to challenge one's fate was futile. As Diego Armus observes of Carriego's little seamstress, her story "lacks suspense: her descent is predetermined."[24] And this applies as well to the milonguita, who is doomed from the moment she aspires to a different life. In "No salgas de tu barrio" ("Don't Leave Your Barrio," Rodríguez Bustamante, 1928), a female singer cautions a young girl to accept her station in life:

> Como vos, yo, muchachita
> era linda y era buena,
> era humilde y trabajaba
> como vos en un taller;
> dejé al novio que me amaba
> con respeto y con ternura,
> por un niño engominado
> que me trajo al cabaret.
>
> *Like you, little girl, I*
> *was beautiful and good*
> *I was humble and worked*
> *like you in a workshop;*
> *I left the boyfriend who loved me*
> *with respect and with tenderness*
> *for a hair-creamed boy*
> *who brought me to the cabaret.*[25]

This fatalistic message was not aimed exclusively at women. Tango lyricists often ridiculed men as well for the crime of social striving. "Niño bien" ("Rich Kid," Fontaina and Soliño, 1927) scolds a boy from the barrios for smoking English tobacco and claiming to be from a good family, when he was really born in a poor barrio with "a pretty cloudy pedigree." Likewise, "Mala entraña" ("Bad Guts," Flores, 1928) expresses disdain for a man who puts on airs:

> Mezcla rara de magnate
> nacido en el sabalaje,
> . . .

> ¡Compadrito de mi esquina,
> que sólo cambió de traje!
>
> Strange mix of millionaire
> Born in the mob
> ...
> ...
> Ruffian of my corner
> Who only changed suits!

Tango's critique of social climbing was not applied equally across gender lines; male strivers were criticized, but unlike the milonguitas abandoned in old age, men typically got away with it. Nevertheless, within the world constructed by tango lyrics, social striving amounted to fakery and inauthenticity, pretending to be something one was not.

By replacing the rebellious, violent heroes of criollista tales and early tango lyrics with whiny compadritos more likely to cry than to fight, tango lyrics certainly offered a safer product, more appropriate for a mass cultural industry intent on attracting a cross-class audience. But the fatalism of tango was not necessarily conservative. The tango's insistence on the immorality and dangerousness of social mobility offered a powerful critique of one of the most prominent discourses in Argentine society, the notion that through hard work, one might improve oneself and attain a better life. According to the tango, not only is the milonguita doomed, but the entire notion of self-improvement is morally suspect. Lyricists could be quite blunt in debunking the promises of upward mobility. "Mentiras criollas" (Arona, 1929) provides a long list of "lies" that Argentines are asked to believe: that girls kiss you out of love, but also that your boss will give you a raise if you work hard and that you can learn to be a musician or a doctor through a correspondence course.[26] One of the greatest tango lyricists, and undoubtedly the most cynical, was Enrique Santos Discépolo. His tango "Cambalache" (1935) compares the modern world to a pawnshop in which the beautiful and valuable share equal billing with the ugly and worthless:

> Es lo mismo el que labura
> noche y día, como un buey
> que el que vive de los otros,
> que el que mata, que el que cura,
> o está fuera de la ley.

He who works
day and night like an ox
is the same as he who lives off of others
or kills, or cures the sick
or is an outlaw.

Discépolo's outlook may be bleaker than that of most tango lyricists, but his diagnosis of society fits comfortably within tango's fatalistic tradition. Rather than a world in which anyone who works hard can get ahead, this is one that rewards thievery and punishes the good. Moreover, even if Discépolo unsettles the melodramatic notion of poetic justice, he certainly does uphold the idea that our lives are governed more by fate than by our own actions.

Despite this insistent fatalism, the marketing of tango singers often did appeal to the fantasy of striking it rich. The public image of Carlos Gardel is perhaps the best example of this phenomenon. Although Gardel sometimes appeared in gaucho attire, his most typical costume was an elegant smoking jacket. The image of tango singers in black tie was, in fact, part of the effort to market the music as an alternative modernism. In 1920s Buenos Aires, jazz was associated with elegance, sophistication, and the high life; in order to compete, tango needed to be dressed up. But more than an assertion of pedigree, the smoking jacket was a symbol of upward mobility. Gardel's lower-class origins were a major component of his image, reinforced by his nickname, "el morocho del Abasto," which referred to his dark hair and eyes as well as to his roots in a humble neighborhood of Buenos Aires. Gardel in black tie was then the quintessential poor kid made good. As Marta Savigliano has argued, this rags-to-riches story was a crucial element of his appeal. In the film *El día que me quieras* (1935), Gardel plays a wealthy young man in love with a lower-class dancer. The plot gave him ample opportunity to dress in black tie, giving Gardel's fans the vicarious thrill of seeing a humble kid like them play the role of an aristocrat.[27] Tango lyricists undercut this message at every turn, even using the symbols of tango's social ascent in order to express the genre's essential fatalism. Thus in Celedonio Flores's "Viejo Smocking [sic]" (1930), a lonely, impoverished old man sings to the tuxedo he wore when he was a young gigolo: "You'll see that one of these days, I'll use you as a pillow, and thrown down on the bed, I'll let myself die." Still, even if the tango's cynicism spoke louder than its promise of upward mobility, Gardel's omnipresent smoking jacket allowed the music's fans to indulge their dreams of acquiring wealth and status.

Gardel was hardly the only poor boy made good in tango.[28] Humble origins were a key component of the tango image. A report on the composer and bandleader Francisco Canaro in the fan magazine *Sintonía* exemplifies the strategy. The article describes Canaro's childhood in the working-class dockside neighborhood of La Boca and rehearses the familiar story of tango's rise to social acceptance. After achieving popularity in La Boca and in other humble Buenos Aires neighborhoods, Canaro got his big break when his orchestra was invited to play at the home of the aristocratic Señora de Gainza Paz. But according to the reporter, Canaro's legitimacy comes not from his acceptance by the elite but from his lower-class origins: "He represents the emotional superstructure of that human, grey, humble and combative belt that encircles our capital city. . . . Francisco Canaro is the product of a blind determinism, the one chosen by destiny to act as an authentic representative of the social environment where he spent his youth."[29] *Sintonía* struck a similar chord in a report on the tango composer and band leader Juan de Dios Filiberto.[30] Visiting Filiberto in La Boca, the reporter depicts the musician as both a product and a symbol of his working-class milieu. As reporter and subject enjoy an evening stroll along the port, they see "tired workers" returning from the factories and, as if to establish Filiberto's popularity among this crowd, they encounter a child singing "Caminito" and a man whistling "Malevaje," two of his most famous compositions.

As these reports suggest, tango's proponents emphasized the music's connection to poor Argentines even as they celebrated its acceptance by the national and international elite. Wishing Carlos Gardel well on the eve of one of his many European tours, the magazine *La Canción Moderna* reminded the star not only of his own plebeian origins but of the tango's roots in working-class neighborhoods: "Tango, tell the traveler who now carries you on the wings of his triumphs . . . tell him that the suburbio gave to you as well a big bunch of love and sadness. Tell him not to abandon you because you never abandoned him. . . . Tell him that there in the sad shadow of a proletarian tenement, one night the little seamstress who vomited blood gave you your first note in the rattle of a tragic cough; that you found in the sobbing complaint of the poor woman battered by her drunk husband another motive for your harmony."[31] Invoking Carriego's tubercular seamstress, the magazine located tango's birth in a scene of proletarian suffering, offering this creation myth as proof not only of the purity and nobility of the music, but also of its authentic Argentinidad.[32] This article reveals the melodramatic logic of the tango. Tango lyrics, after all, were premised on a Manichean vision of society, in which the innocent, humble barrios stood in opposition to the morally debased downtown world of fancy cabarets. The milonguita was often blamed for her own downfall, but her journey downtown was usually inspired by the seductive promises of some wealthy villain. Tango stars tantalized their fans with stories of rapid social ascent, but a close connection to the noble world of working-class tenements and suffering seamstresses was crucial to their image. By stressing proletarian origins even as it encouraged strike-it-rich fantasies, this marketing strategy expressed an ambivalence about the working-class desire for upward mobility.

Alberto de Zavalía's film *La vida de Carlos Gardel* (1939) builds its fictionalized account of the singer's life around precisely this ambivalence. As I described, critics lauded the film for avoiding the world of compadritos and milonguitas in favor of a wholesome vision of the working-class barrio. Yet this sanitized story still foregrounds the divide between rich and poor. In fact, the movie reimagines Gardel's life as a struggle between the pursuit of upward mobility and the moral imperative of loyalty to one's social class. Early in the film, Gardel, played by Hugo del Carril, a tango singer then emerging as Argentina's most popular leading man, asserts his class pride: "We may be poor, but we have dignity." Later, though, with his judgment clouded by ambition, he falls for a wealthy socialite who can advance his career, and he rejects the true love of his life, a poor but virtuous girl from his barrio. Although he soon comes to his senses, his fame and a series of melodramatic accidents conspire to keep the lovers apart, until both die and are finally united in the afterlife. *La vida de Carlos Gardel*, like the marketing of tango more generally, offers Gardel's lower-class fans the fantasy of wealth, but it suggests that achieving that dream constitutes a betrayal of one's social class and results inevitably in suffering.

This cautionary tale about the dangers of upward mobility reflects the deep classism of tango melodrama. Tango lyrics offered a fundamental critique of the rich and an endorsement of values associated with the working class. In their rejection of social striving, lyricists foresaw a distinctly moral peril. Celedonio Flores concludes "Mala entraña," for example, by passing harsh judgment on the would-be millionaire:

> Se murió tu pobre madre,
> y en el mármol de tu frente
> ni una sombra, ni una arruga
> que deschavara, elocuente,
> que tu vieja no fue un perro,
> y que vos sabés sentir.
>
> *Your poor mother died*
> *and on the marble of your forehead*
> *not a shadow, not a wrinkle*
> *that might eloquently reveal*
> *that your mother was not a dog*
> *and that you know how to feel.*

Here, upward mobility is a perversion that destroys basic human values. Beyond the love of one's mother, the moral values that tango lyricists held in highest esteem were solidarity and generosity. In "Yira . . . yira" (1930), Discépolo described his bleak vision of the modern world by insisting on the absence of these sentiments: "never expect any help, nor a hand, nor a favor." "Mano a mano" (Flores, 1920) revisits the perennial theme of the milonguita, but instead of taking pleasure in the suffering of the woman who left him for the bright lights of downtown, the singer concludes by offering her solace:

> si precisás una ayuda, si te hace falta un consejo,
> acordáte de este amigo que ha de jugarse el pellejo
> p'ayudarte en lo que pueda cuando llegue la ocasión.
>
> *if you require some help or need some advice,*
> *remember me as a friend who will risk his skin*
> *to help you anyway he can, when the time comes.*

The singer's claim to the moral high ground results from his unselfishness, which sets him apart from the world of rich kids and aristocratic playboys, who care only about their own pleasure.

Tango's class consciousness varied with the lyricist. Celedonio Flores, for example, was far more likely than Discépolo to exalt the poor at the expense of the rich. Similarly, not all tango singers presented themselves as the defenders of the poor. The prominence of socially conscious lyrics in the repertoire of Agustín Magaldi was unusual enough to earn him the nickname "the singer of the destitute" (*el cantor de los desamparados*).³³ Even the most explicitly classist of tangos remained skeptical of any effort to challenge the status quo. The tango scholar Blas Matamoro recognizes that the lyrics of the Golden Age describe a rigid social structure in which upward mobility is impossible, and he acknowledges the genre's anti-elitism. Nevertheless, he argues that tango's fundamentally passive response to the fact of inequality, its deep fatalism, facilitated the hegemony of the Argentine oligarchy, who ceded cultural recognition to the poor but monopolized political and economic power for themselves.³⁴ Yet tango songs, like other melodramatic texts, were ideologically multivalent. While they modeled a cynical, embittered sense of resignation, they also accepted as a given the moral superiority and national authenticity of the poor. They offered the poor more than just cultural recognition; they encouraged listeners to identify themselves in opposition to the rich.

The tango envisioned class conflict primarily as a competition over women. The lyrics expressed a poor man's anxiety about his ability to keep the woman he loves away from a rich suitor. In this way, tango offered male listeners an emotional outlet as well as the pleasures of melodrama's moral judgments. Similarly, it expressed the audience's skepticism about the possibility of upward mobility, even as it indulged fantasies of overnight wealth. But what did tango offer women? The vast majority of tango lyrics were written by men, a fact that helps explain the genre's tendency toward misogyny. Within tango lyrics, women played only a small number of roles. Most often, they were humble girls from the barrios whose moral virtue was threatened by the seductions of the cabaret. Nevertheless, if women were not prominent among tango lyricists, they gained a great deal of visibility as singers. Manolita Poli, the actress who debuted Contursi's "Mi noche triste" on stage in 1918, was one of many female performers who sang tango in the porteño theater. By 1923 Victor had recorded Rosita Quiroga, a major star for the label throughout the rest of the decade. Azucena Maizani, discovered by Francisco Canaro in 1920, debuted on stage in 1923 and made her first recordings for Odeon the following year. Her frequent appearances on the radio, on stage, and on tours throughout the country and beyond helped make her the female counterpart of Carlos Gardel. The success of Quiroga and Maizani paved the way for Mercedes Simone, Ada Falcón, Sofía Bozán, and Libertad

Lamarque, among others. By the end of the 1920s, female tango singers were a major part of the entertainment landscape.[35]

The emergence of these stars gave rise to what Anahí Viladrich has called "female transvestism," the phenomenon of women singing lyrics written to be sung by a man.[36] Typically, female singers did not alter the gender of the lyrics; they simply ignored the dissonance between lyrics and performance. Maizani literalized this transvestism by frequently performing in men's clothing (see figure 6). Still, even this practice cannot be considered an attempt at passing, since Maizani's soprano was unmistakably feminine. The film ¡Tango! (1933) ends with the singer, dressed as a prototypical, male compadrito, singing "Milonga del 900" (Manzi, 1933). Maizani was not a character in the film; she appears in this scene as a symbol of the tango itself, using hypermasculine imagery to tell the story of a man who cannot forget the woman who has left him: "The guitars playing their song say her name to me, as do the streets of my barrio and the blade of my knife." According to the film and theater director Luis César Amadori, Maizani enjoyed dressing as a man so much that she came up with the idea of performing a tango dressed as a soccer player. He was only able to dissuade her by encouraging her to debut Discépolo's "Esta noche me emborracho" ("Tonight I get drunk," 1928) instead. With Maizani on more familiar masculine turf, her performance of Discépolo's tale of a man driven to ruin by a woman helped launch the composer's career.[37] Maizani's enthusiasm for transvestism reveals how confining tango's gender code was: in order to represent the tango and to avoid the role of passive victim, female singers needed to sing as men.

If "Milonga del 900" and "Esta noche me emborracho" gave Maizani the chance to speak as a man, her performance of gauchesque tangos like "Amigazo" allowed her to go one step further by performing masculine violence. More typically, though, Maizani's repertoire emphasized male vulnerability. In "Llevátelo todo" (Sciammarella, 1928), a man begs his friend not to steal his lover, while in "Malevaje" (Discépolo, 1928) a tough guy bemoans how his love for a woman has made him timid and fearful: "Tell me, for God's sake, what you have given me that I am so changed, I don't know who I am any more." Applying a woman's voice to tangos like these underscored the feminization already implicit in the lyrics. In her own most famous composition, "Pero yo sé" (1928), Maizani avoids revealing the gender of the singer, while focusing instead on the emotional life of the male object of the singer's attention. Addressing a wealthy

6 Azucena Maizani in masculine attire. Courtesy of Archivo General de la Nación.

playboy who appears to enjoy a carefree lifestyle, the singer reveals his secret: "But I know that inside you pine for a love, that you are trying to forget by going through so many women." It was the prominence of this sort of lyric in the tango repertoire, lyrics that either exemplified or described male vulnerability and emotionalism, that created space for female singing stars.

Tango's validation of male emotion was directly linked to its class message. Celedonio Flores's attack on the upwardly mobile subject of "Mala Entraña" for failing to feel emotion at the death of his own mother reflected a sentiment typical of many tangos sung by women. "Muchacho" (1924), a tango Flores wrote especially for Rosita Quiroga, denounces a rich man for his lack of true emotion, implying that this failing makes him unworthy of the tango: "Your soul does not cry when you hear a bandoneón."[38] Within the melodramatic world constructed by tango lyrics and particularly those sung by women singers, the capacity to feel and express sadness was a key component of working-class masculinity, part of what made them morally superior to the rich.

If tango's female stars helped disseminate this particular notion of masculine, working-class emotionalism, they also expressed the genre's contradictory combination of the fantasy of easy wealth and the denunciation of social striving. Like their male counterparts, female singers were celebrated in the press for having risen from humble origins. One magazine story showed Maizani wearing a luxurious fur coat as she walked through the working-class neighborhood of La Boca, but it insisted that she was one of the people. Shaking the singer's hand at the end of the interview, the reporter comments: "A small hand without jewelry. Prettier for that. The hand of a *muchacha criolla* (native girl)."[39] Maizani's female fans were excited to see their favorite singer wearing such a lovely coat, but they also needed to be reassured that she had not abandoned them in her quest for material success. Just as tango lyrics punished women more harshly for the sin of social striving than they did men, tango fans seem to have held female stars to a higher standard of class solidarity. In a letter to *Sintonía*, a "woman worker" denounces the arrogance of an unnamed female "star" who refused to sign a photograph the writer had sent her. The writer claims to have known the star when they worked side by side in a bag factory, but now that good fortune has lifted her out of the working class, the star has turned her back on her community: "Who do you think has elevated you to the place you occupy? We have, Madam, the members of that anonymous mass, the humble people of this nation, to which you also once belonged when you were not yet the shining 'star' you are today.... Your impoverished co-workers are too far beneath you for you to descend to them."[40] Female tango singers embodied the fantasy of an escape from drudgery, but the melodramatic logic of tango required that they retain their allegiance to the poor.

Tango was not the only melodramatic form available to female audiences in this period. Even as Gardel and Maizani were dominating the radio, the so-called weekly novels disseminated in newspapers and aimed explicitly at women readers enjoyed immense popularity. Although equally melodramatic, this serial romance literature envisioned a different social world. Like the milonguitas of the tango, the heroines of the weekly novels were *bellas pobres*, beautiful girls from poor families in the barrios. But instead of pursuing upward mobility in the exciting, immoral world of the downtown cabaret, these girls hoped only to marry the men of their dreams, often men of higher social status. Whereas tango's love affairs were invariably illegitimate and fleeting, the weekly novels endorsed the bourgeois ideal of marriage and the constitution of a family as the route to happiness.[41] Moreover, if the tango envisioned loving, generous, and emotionally vulnerable men abandoned by women who crave upward mobility, the weekly novels featured women who pursue true love in the face of social obstacles and men who are unwilling to make that sacrifice.[42] Yet if the genres' gender judgments were mirror images, they shared a common vision of social class. As melodramatic narratives, both the tango and the weekly romance novel unfolded in a world in which the poor were generous and good, while the rich were selfish and frivolous.[43] Similarly, the weekly novels shared the tango's conformism. Although both happy and tragic endings were possible, the weekly novels as a whole observed the rule that, as Beatriz Sarlo has put it, "love is *not* stronger than social barriers."[44] Like other forms of melodrama, both genres discouraged any attempt to transform the social order. They portrayed the division between rich and poor not so much as a class conflict, but as an immutable, inevitable backdrop for tales of romance, transgression, punishment, and, occasionally, redemption. Together, these genres constituted a rich tradition of popular melodrama with an established audience among both men and women. It is hardly surprising, then, that when Argentina's sound film revolution began in 1933, its producers drew their subject matter overwhelmingly from this tradition.

FILM MELODRAMA: JOSÉ AGUSTÍN FERREYRA AND LIBERTAD LAMARQUE

The centrality of melodrama in the Argentine cinema of the 1930s was overdetermined. Not only were Argentine popular music, theater, and literature saturated with melodrama, but also Hollywood cinema itself was born with "melodramatic predispositions."[45] Given Hollywood's status as a model for imitation and competition, this orientation inevitably influenced Argentine filmmakers. Yet competition with Hollywood had an ambivalent effect on them. Hollywood influence reinforced the Argentine cinema's melodramatic impulses, but it also reshaped them. Seeking to modernize their offerings in order to compete with the sophisticated imports from the North, Argentine filmmakers developed a melodramatic language that combined the tropes of tango songs and weekly novels and pushed them in new directions. The alternative modernism they produced positioned the local cinema to compete with Hollywood, even as it reinforced the subversive messages of Argentina's popular melodramatic tradition.

The transformation of popular melodrama is particularly visible in the work of José Agustín Ferreyra, a director whose career spanned the silent and sound eras. Born in the Buenos Aires barrio of Constitución to a white father and an Afro-Argentine mother, "El Negro" Ferreyra, as he was known, grew up in a family of modest means. Largely self-taught, he worked as a theatrical set designer before producing his first film in 1917. He was an avid fan of Buenos Aires's bohemian nightlife and of the tango in particular, and his films betrayed that influence. As Ferreyra explained in an article published in 1921, he saw the cinema as "the art that is most accessible to easy and quick comprehension," a democratic vision that inspired a straightforward, "urban realist" style.[46] His silent movies as well as his first few sound films depicted the lives of working-class Argentines with extraordinary detail and sympathy. In his article, Ferreyra complained that the Argentine cinema was being unjustly ignored in favor of films from the United States. This analysis proved overly pessimistic, since the introduction of sound film in the early 1930s would spark a revival of the domestic cinema. Still, the massive appeal of Hollywood film created a marketplace that favored some styles of filmmaking over others. As local studios began to produce films on an industrial scale, Ferreyra found himself increasingly out of step and unable to pursue his distinctive style of filmmaking.

The titles of many of Ferreyra's silent films, including *La melenita de oro* (1923), *La muchacha del arrabal* (1922), *Mi último tango* (1925), *El organito de la tarde* (1925), and *La costurerita que dió aquel mal paso* (1926), reveal their reliance on melodramatic narratives taken directly from tango lyrics or from Carriego's poetry. Some of these films were based on specific tangos; others inspired the composition of new tangos, occasionally with lyrics by Ferreyra himself, to be played alongside the film. Ferreyra drew on other elements of popular culture as well. He adopted the sainete's comic use of ethnic stereotypes in several films, and he also appropriated the thematic content of the weekly novels. In *Perdón, viejita* (1927), he told the story of a bella pobre who is in love with a noble, hardworking man. Their marital union is threatened, however, when the man's mother becomes convinced that the girl has stolen her jewelry. His film *Muñequitos porteños* (1931) was Argentina's first sound film, although its use of recorded discs was quickly surpassed by the optical sound technology introduced two years later in *¡Tango!* and *Los tres berretines*. The film's story about an Italian immigrant woman and her alcoholic father gave Ferreyra ample room to display his trademark sympathy for the poor.

Ferreyra immediately realized that the new technology would enable Argentine cinema to compete for the domestic market, but he did not see the need to adapt either his business practices or his cinematic style to the new context. Uninterested in affiliating with either Sono Film or Lumiton, he continued to raise funds on an ad hoc basis in order to finance his films independently. This financial independence went along with a resistance to industrial work discipline. According to Floren Delbene, the male lead in several of Ferreyra's films, the director avoided following a screenplay, preferring to improvise instead.[47] Between 1933 and 1935, Ferreyra made three films which largely reproduced the thematic and stylistic approaches he had pursued in the silent era. *Calles de Buenos Aires* (1934), for example, includes the now stereotypical poor young woman seduced by the temptations of downtown. She loses her love interest, an honest and noble tango singer, to a hardworking woman who resists temptation, accepts her poverty, and remains in the barrio. The story thus combines the weekly romance novel's conformist emphasis on marriage with tango's misogynistic depiction of the milonguita. It takes tango's vision of working-class masculine goodness and emotional sincerity and embodies it in the person of a tango singer. The film also featured Ferreyra's loving depictions of daily life in the humble barrios of Buenos Aires: children playing soccer, men and women engaged in mundane chores.

In *Puente Alsina* (1935), Ferreyra pursues similar themes without the tango setting. The film opens with a vivid depiction of workers building a new bridge over the Riachuelo River in Buenos Aires. In addition to long shots of the work site as a whole, there are close-ups of calloused hands, of men wiping the sweat from their brows, of workers pulling, digging, and hammering. Into this visceral scene of labor, Ferreyra inserts a conventional melodramatic plot: Lidia, the privileged daughter of the chief engineer on the project, rejects the wealthy fiancé chosen for her by her father and falls in love with Edmundo, one of the workers. As Lidia walks across the work site in the opening scene, Ferreyra announces the film's melodramatic theme by contrasting her fancy dress, white gloves, and elegant gait with the stooped shoulders and drab clothing of the workers. Later, once Edmundo and Lidia are romantically involved, several comic scenes emphasize the social gulf that separates them. When she is shocked by his rustic bathroom, he rigs up a makeshift shower for her. With a quizzical look, she responds "very interesting." Lidia's fiancé has Edmundo falsely arrested, but in the end the truth comes out. The couple's reconciliation is made possible when Lidia's father realizes that the "real gentleman" is Edmundo, "the honest worker." Despite its overt sympathy for the working class, *Puente Alsina* is hardly a subversive film. Edmundo proves his virtue in part by talking his fellow workers out of an illicit strike. Moreover, by vesting the ultimate power of judgment in the person of Lidia's father, the film stops well short of subverting hierarchy. Nevertheless, what *Puente Alsina* does do is argue for the dignity and goodness of working-class men. Edmundo's virtues—his honesty and diligence—raise him above the moral level of Lidia's rich fiancé. In this way, Ferreyra's early sound films reproduced the essential class message of popular melodrama; like tango lyrics and romance novels, these movies relied on a stark opposition between the noble poor and the immoral rich.

Puente Alsina represents a brief moment at the beginning of the sound era when the cinematic representation of manual laborers was possible; by 1936 the rise of a more profitable film industry had made those sorts of representations increasingly rare. That year, Ferreyra's career took a sharp turn when he began a series of three films for the SIDE company. Founded by a young inventor named Alfredo Murúa, SIDE had rented its services as a studio and laboratory to Sono Film and to independent producers like Ferreyra. In 1936 Murúa decided that SIDE would make its own films and seek a place in the domestic market alongside Lumiton and Sono Film.[48] Among the company's first projects was a tango film modeled on Gardel's movies and starring Libertad Lamarque. By this time, Lamarque was easily tango's biggest female star. She had debuted on the Buenos Aires stage and on the radio in 1926, and had been under contract with RCA Victor ever since. In 1931, after a successful run in Alberto Vaccarezza's sainete *El conventillo de la Paloma*, she won a contest organized by the municipal government of Buenos Aires and was declared the

"Queen of Tango."[49] Over the next few years, frequent tours and recordings, as well as regular performances on Radio Splendid and Radio Belgrano, made her a household name. Lamarque had a singing part in ¡Tango!, and she starred in *Alma de bandoneón* (Soffici, 1935), a mediocre Sono Film product in which she played an aspiring tango singer. Nevertheless, she had yet to translate her success on the radio into movie stardom. Murúa's idea was to replicate Carlos Gardel's winning formula. Gardel had followed *Las luces de Buenos Aires* with a string of hits for Paramount—*Melodía del arrabal* (Gasnier, 1933), *Cuesta abajo* (Gasnier, 1934), *El tango en Broadway* (Gasnier, 1934), *El dia que me quieras* (Reinhardt, 1935)—until a plane crash ended his life in June 1935. These movies gave Gardel ample opportunity to show off both his singing voice and his winning personality. Lamarque's films for SIDE would enable her to step into the void left by Gardel's death.

Murúa's idea originally involved a screenplay written by the playwright and tango lyricist José González Castillo, but Lamarque rejected it because she thought the character she was to play, a woman who goes to jail for murdering a man, "did not suit" her personality. She then wrote a new script herself, taking the opportunity to craft her own image. Uninterested in reproducing either the transvestism of Azucena Maizani or the role of a tough-talking milonguita, Lamarque self-consciously aimed to construct a more conventionally feminine role for herself. She recognized that she could probably not attain international stardom playing the sort of "coarse, common (*arrabalera*)" character she had been embarrassed to play in *El conventillo de la Paloma*.[50] The film, called *Ayúdame a vivir* (1936), borrowed heavily from the conventional melodrama of the weekly romance novel. Lamarque plays a middle-class woman doubly victimized, first by her husband's infidelity and second, when she is wrongly accused of killing her husband's mistress. In order to take full advantage of Lamarque's star power, the film included several scenes in which she suddenly interrupts the action by singing a tango, communicating with the other characters through the lyrics. This formula, labeled a "tango opera" by the film historian Domingo Di Núbila, would be employed again in the next two films Lamarque made with Ferreyra for SIDE: *Besos brujos* (1937) and *La ley que olvidaron* (1938).[51] These movies were perfect vehicles for Lamarque because they enabled her to free herself from tango stereotypes, in much the same way as Gardel had done. She could be a tango-singing melodramatic heroine without locking herself into the role of the milonguita. In a tango opera, Lamarque's character sang tangos not because she lived in a gritty arrabal or prostituted herself at a cabaret, but simply because Lamarque herself was a tango star. Playing on this movie-star logic, Lamarque's character announces one of her songs in *Ayúdame a vivir* by bragging "Libertad Lamarque . . . bah! I sing better than her."

For Ferreyra, who agreed to direct *Ayúdame a vivir* after Mario Soffici had rejected the tango opera conceit, the Lamarque trilogy represented the abandonment of his realist depiction of lower-class, urban life in favor of stories set among the bourgeoisie. Modern art deco living rooms and rural exteriors replaced the conventillo patios and barrio street scenes of his early films. What remained, though, was popular melodrama's class message. Muted in *Ayúdame a vivir*, this message was explicit in *La ley que olvidaron*, for which Lamarque accepted González Castillo's polemical screenplay. Lamarque plays María, a humble servant of a wealthy family who agrees to raise the love child of the family's spoiled daughter, so that the daughter's "honor" might remain intact. Central to the film is the familiar melodramatic opposition between the moral poor and the immoral rich: whereas María loves the child as if she were her own, her employers think only of appearances, ruthlessly separating the two as soon as the child's mother is respectably married. Ferreyra underscores the class divide in the opening scene, which juxtaposes images of the humble women of María's barrio with the wealthy women at her workplace. Later, he accomplishes the same juxtaposition by dissolving from a champagne bucket to a wash bucket. Lamarque's positioning on the lower, and therefore morally superior, side of this simple class divide makes her an object of audience identification. Like the other tango operas, this film is a long way from stories of violent compadritos or milonguitas condemned to prostitution, but it retained popular melodrama's affiliation with the poor and condemnation of the rich.

The SIDE trilogy was enormously popular throughout Latin America and turned Lamarque into Argentina's biggest box-office attraction. She now commanded a salary that the upstart company could not afford, and she signed with Sono Film. Although SIDE had played a key role in opening foreign markets for Argentine cinema, the company was unable to capitalize on its own success. The popularity of these movies outside of Argentina was largely due to the transformation of Ferreyra's filmmaking. By abandoning urban realism, he was able to fashion a more universally accessible brand of melodrama that did not rely on viewers' familiarity with the world of porteño barrios. Moreover, by imitating the stylistic and technical attributes of Gardel's films, Ferreyra attracted viewers who were accustomed to Hollywood movies. Yet SIDE was forced to achieve modern results with backward technology. The Hollywood style relied on extensive cutting in order to deliver a seamless narrative, but SIDE could not afford a Moviola, the modern machine that enabled an editor to view the film while editing. The result was a tremendous waste of time and money. Unable to produce films rapidly, SIDE remained financially fragile, vulnerable to any box-office setbacks.[52] And once Lamarque had left, Murúa's company was unable to reproduce its earlier success. Ferreyra continued to make films for SIDE, but without Lamarque's star power he did not produce another hit. By 1941, the year of his final film, he had been eclipsed by directors whose style better suited a young film industry locked in competition with Hollywood.

After leaving SIDE, Lamarque increased her box-office appeal by continuing to trade on her tango stardom. In *Madreselva* (Amadori, 1938), her first movie for Sono Film, she plays Blanca, a young woman who sings in her father's humble puppet show. She meets and falls in love with a movie star named Mario, played by Hugo del Carril. A series of misunderstandings drives Mario into the arms of Blanca's sister, while Blanca leaves Argentina for Europe and a career as an international opera star. When the misunderstandings are sorted out, the path is clear for Mario and Blanca to marry, but having promised her father that she would look after her sister's happiness, Blanca does the honorable thing and accepts a life of lonely stardom. *Madreselva* enacts one of the central themes of tango lyrics: the warning against upward mobility. Although she pursues wealth and fame, Blanca avoids the fate of a milonguita by retaining the moral fiber that results from her humble upbringing. However, she does so at the cost of her happiness. The film's title comes from a tango whose lyrics were written seven years earlier by Luis César Amadori, the director of the film. The song, which Lamarque sings twice in the movie, offers a classic bit of tango cynicism that neatly encapsulates Blanca's predicament: "I've learned that one must fake it in order to live decently." Amadori reiterates the idea of fakery throughout: in Blanca's marionettes, in

Blanca's first meeting with Mario, when he arrives in her father's bar still dressed in the tough-guy costume he was wearing in his current film. Blanca's acceptance of her fate is the exception that proves the rule: upward mobility entails pretending to be something one is not and, at least for women, leads inevitably to moral disaster.

The opera storyline represented something of a departure for Lamarque, who was more often cast as a tango singer. She had played this role in both *Alma de bandoneón* and *Besos brujos*, and she would return to it in *Puerta cerrada* (Saslavsky, 1939) and *Yo conocí a esa mujer* (Borcosque, 1942). In all of these films, tango functioned as the prime mover of melodramatic narrative: Lamarque's character falls in love with a wealthy suitor, but his elitist family blocks the romance because they consider tango singers disreputable. In a sense, casting Lamarque as a tango singer achieved the same purpose as the tango opera format: it gave her a reason to sing tangos without requiring that the film be set in a seedy arrabal. More important, though, was the class message of these films. By the 1930s, tango had long since achieved broad cross-class acceptance. No longer relegated to the slums, tango was danced in fancy cabarets and savored by elites, including President Marcelo T. de Alvear (1922–28) himself.[53] Moreover, the transformation of tango lyrics had made the music suitable for domestic consumption by decent families. Nevertheless, as Diana Paladino points out, the domestic cinema continued to depict tango as a popular genre rejected by snobbish elites.[54] In Lamarque's movies, tango served to locate the protagonist on the noble and popular side of the class divide and to facilitate audience identification. Melodramatic logic dictated that Lamarque be punished for the transgressive act of singing tango, but surely that judgment was not shared by audience members, who were drawn to Lamarque's early movies precisely by the star power she had earned as a tango singer. Tango was not merely a popular musical genre; it was a powerful symbol of Argentina. Playing the part of a tango singer, Lamarque represented her popular audience in terms of both class and national identity. For that audience, her victimization at the hands of condescending rich people could not be experienced as a legitimate punishment for some real transgression, but only as classist persecution.

In *Puerta cerrada*, Lamarque plays Nina Miranda, a tango singer who sacrifices her career in order to marry a rich man whose family disapproves of her occupation (see figure 7). When her self-serving brother tricks her into believing that her husband has abandoned her, she decides to return to the stage in order to support her child. Briefly unsure about whether to challenge propriety by singing a tango, she turns to her brother who reassures her: "Decency does not reside in singing a waltz instead of a tango." Thus heartened, she performs a stirring rendition of the classic early tango, "La morocha," whose lyrics by Angel Villoldo emphasize the national authenticity of the performance:

> Soy la morocha argentina
> la que no siente pesares
> y alegre pasa la vida
> con sus cantares.
> Soy la gentil compañera
> del noble gaucho porteño,
> la que conserva el cariño
> para su dueño.
> Yo soy la morocha
> de mirar ardiente,
> la que en su alma siente
> el fuego de amor.
> Soy la que al criollito
> más noble y valiente
> ama con ardor.
>
> *I am the Argentine brunette*
> *the one who feels no sorrow*
> *and happily passes through life*
> *with her songs.*
> *I am the gentle companion*
> *of the noble porteño gaucho,*
> *the one who saves her affection*
> *for her master.*
> *I am the brunette*
> *of the burning gaze,*
> *the one who feels in her soul*
> *the fire of love.*
> *I am the one who loves the*
> *most noble and valiant criollito*
> *with ardor.*

7 Libertad Lamarque as the tango star Nina Miranda with her lover (Agustín Irusta) and his disapproving aunt (Angelina Pagano) in *Puerta cerrada*. Courtesy of Archivo General de la Nación.

Although Villoldo underscores both the singer's submissiveness and her passionate sensuality, Nina's performance highlights the latter. The gaucho of the lyrics is not present on stage, and when she stops singing to execute a few tango steps, she treats her male partner as a prop. As she sings the final verse, the camera zooms into a tight close-up. She smiles, seductively stretching out the first syllables—"Yo soy . . ."—and as the orchestra waits for her to continue, she inserts a spoken word that does not figure in the original lyric: *pimpollo*, meaning "flower bud" or, in lunfardo, the popular slang of Buenos Aires, "beautiful, young woman."[55] This scene, whose lighthearted sexiness contrasts markedly with the somber, melodramatic tone that characterizes the bulk of the film, harnesses Lamarque's star power, enabling the audience to identify with Nina not simply as a passive melodramatic victim, but as the proud bearer of an authentic and exciting popular culture. Nina's association with this particular version of tango heightens the film's critique of the hypocritical and moralistic elite whose disdain for the genre (along with her brother's selfishness) causes her downfall.

Since Lamarque's films displace class conflict from collective struggles over exploitation to individual battles over marriage choice, they can be considered conservative. In Silvia Oroz's words, these films, like film melodramas throughout Latin America, "point out social inequality, not to modify it, but to *humanize* it."[56] But melodrama's truly subversive potential is realized when the pleasure and power of the transgression outweigh the ultimate moral resolution that upholds the dominant ideology. In *Puerta cerrada*, elite prejudice against the tango leads to a misunderstanding that results in the accidental death of Nina's husband and the wrongful incarceration of Nina herself. Given the strength of the audience's identification with Nina on the level of both class and national identity, her punishment reads not only as personally unjust, but also as an elitist attack on the Argentine people. Even in gender terms, this punishment is suspect. The ending of the film, in which Nina sacrifices herself in order to save her son, seems to uphold her husband's insistence that she give up her career in order to be a wife and mother. But for an audience that has delighted in Libertad Lamarque's performance of "La morocha," this patriarchal lesson is, to say the least, difficult to accept. Although *Puerta cerrada* was likely influenced by the Hollywood melodrama *Stella Dallas* (Vidor, 1937),[57] the contrast between the films is instructive. In both, the protagonist's frustrated dreams of upward mobility are eventually realized by the child that had been taken from her. But Stella Dallas spends much of the film striving ridiculously for upper-class status, and her downfall reads as punishment for this transgression. By contrast, Nina Miranda is never an object of ridicule for the audience; she is punished merely for being a tango singer, for representing, in other words, Argentine popular culture.

Striving to compete with Hollywood, Argentine filmmakers reshaped popular melodrama. Tango's extreme cynicism as well as its celebration of illegitimate romance were jettisoned in favor of the more conventional, marriage-focused narratives of weekly novels and radio plays. Likewise, the urban poor became less visible on Argentine movie screens. "El Negro" Ferreyra, whose sympathetic depictions of barrio life went hand in hand with his passion for the tango, abandoned this trademark style in favor of tango operas set in bourgeois homes. Reshaping melodrama along these lines facilitated the local movie industry's efforts to compete with Hollywood by harmonizing cinematic modernism with local authenticity: art deco interiors could coexist with the tango. Yet tango provided these films with more than just local color. Film melodrama, including Lamarque's output for SIDE and Sono Film, retained the essential premise of the popular traditions it inherited: a strict opposition between the noble poor and the hateful rich. Lamarque's glamorous star power, as well as the fancy interiors that served as backdrop, likely appealed to audiences' fantasies of upward mobility. Yet at the same time, her association with the tango served a classically populist function: by presenting popular culture as oppositional to the dominant class, these films enabled a critique of patriarchal and antinationalist elitism.[58] Pushed and pulled by the conflicting pressures of the transnational marketplace, Argentina's cinematic melodramas were fundamentally ambivalent, offering viewers both conformism and populism.

THE POPULIST-MELODRAMATIC COMEDY:
LUIS SANDRINI AND NINÍ MARSHALL

The populist undercurrent in Lamarque's film melodramas reverberated with more explicitly subversive expressions that coursed through Argentine mass culture in this period. Soccer, for example, carried a powerful, populist charge. The sport's tendency to disrupt propriety and respectability was captured in one of the urban chronicles, or *aguafuertes porteños*, that Roberto Arlt wrote for the newspaper *El Mundo*. In this column, published in 1929, Arlt describes a game between Argentina and Uruguay. While he notes the Argentine victory, Arlt is more impressed with the unrestrained enthusiasm of the fans: they cheer and applaud thunderously; they climb onto the roof of a nearby building to get a view; they throw rotten oranges at their rivals' supporters; and they even urinate from the top of the stadium.[59] If Arlt presents soccer as a site of carnivalesque transgression, other accounts stress the sport's anti-elitist meanings. For José Gabriel, a sports columnist for the popular paper *Crítica*, soccer could help forge a national community that excludes the rich. One of his columns addresses an imaginary "señor muy aseñorado," whose chauffeured car passes by the stadium just as a match between Argentina and a visiting team from Scotland is ending. The rich man is bewildered as a crowd of thirty thousand fans pour into the street, blocking his passage. He is entirely unaware of even the presence of a soccer field there, let alone of its significance. The columnist fills him in and goes on to explain just how important soccer and other mass cultural events can be: "Soccer and cinema are the great spectacles of our days. If you do not want to recognize it, so much the worse for you." More than just the setting for a game, the stadium contains "the agglomeration of the happiness of a people."[60] Even though by the late 1920s, soccer already had a cross-class audience, José Gabriel identifies the sport's fans in opposition to a scornful and condescending elite. This populist image of soccer, and of mass culture in general, found expression in *Los tres berretines*, in which the sons' mass cultural pursuits triumph over their father's commitment to education and respectability. The film comedies of the 1930s would mine this populist vein extensively, combining it with the Manichean social vision of melodrama to produce a hybrid that challenged dominant values even more directly than Lamarque's films.

The film scholar Pascual Quinziano has argued that the hybrid character of Argentine comedies makes these movies more conservative than their Hollywood counterparts. For Quinziano, Argentine film comedy represents an "impure genre" in which melodrama's inevitable restoration of the moral order limits the potential for comic subversion.[61] But while Quinziano is correct to emphasize the presence of melodramatic elements in the comedies of the 1930s, this "impurity" does not necessarily prevent the films from challenging the status quo. By appropriating a melodramatic vision of society, these comedies, like Lamarque's films, compel identification with the poor, while condemning the hypocrisy and mean-spiritedness of the rich. Equally important, the comic elements in these movies often undermine the neat, moral resolutions offered by melodrama. This tension is particularly apparent in the films of Luis Sandrini and Niní Marshall, the two biggest comic stars to emerge in this period. Cast in the role of providing comic relief to melodramatic love stories involving other characters, both Sandrini and Marshall subverted this hierarchy by stealing the spotlight with comic personas modeled on typical characters they observed on the streets of Buenos Aires. These characters stand outside the moral universe of melodrama and import a current of more transgressive populism into their films.

Luis Sandrini was an accomplished circus performer and stage actor who in 1932 was performing in the hit play *Los tres berretines*. Sandrini's performance as Eusebio, the brother who dreams of hitting it big as a tango composer, was so popular that the Lumiton producers adapted the script to afford him a bigger role in the film version. Sandrini modeled his performance on a neighborhood personality from La Paternal, the barrio where he lived. The barrio was (and still is) home to the soccer team Argentinos Juniors, and a group of fans would gather on the sidewalk near Sandrini's house to discuss the games. One member of this group drew Sandrini's attention because of his persistent stutter. In *Los tres berretines*, Sandrini imitated and embellished this form of speech to great comic effect, and he went on to play the same character in dozens of subsequent films.[62] To the stuttering, he added a series of character traits, including an amiable laziness, a rejection of respectability, and a tendency toward altruism, creating a somewhat Chaplinesque everyman at once ridiculous and heroic. Although tango would not play a central role in Sandrini's oeuvre, his character's association with the genre in *Los tres berretines* helped establish his connection to popular culture, in much the same way as it did for Lamarque. Similarly, Sandrini's character, presumably like his model in La Paternal, used an extremely colloquial and local vocabulary that identified him instantly with the popular classes of Buenos Aires.

Sandrini's next film, the box-office hit *Riachuelo* (Moglia Barth, 1934), was set in La Boca and belongs, with Ferreyra's *Puente Alsina*, to the small group of early sound films whose main characters were urban proletarians. Sandrini plays a happy-go-lucky pickpocket named Berretín (presumably to remind audiences of his earlier role) who meets Remanso, a recently released convict intent on living an honest life. Berretín offers Remanso the "thieving umbrella" that he uses to hide the watches and wallets he steals, but Remanso refuses, explaining that he wants to work "honorably." Remanso convinces Berretín to return the money he has stolen from a poor man, and when this act of conscience is rewarded with a kiss from a pretty girl, Berretín decides to give up his life of crime and become an honest worker. The film's climax comes when Berretín catches the neighborhood gangster in the act of robbing the shipyard where he works and delivers him to the police. In the end, Remanso and Berretín both get the girl; a double wedding ends the film. On its surface, *Riachuelo* offers a heavy-handed moral lesson about the virtues of hard work and honesty. By taking a job, Berretín enters a respectable, decent working-class community: the manager of the conventillo where he and Remanso rent rooms insists that the property is a *casa de familia*. Moreover, Berretín's honesty pays dividends. The factory manager rewards him with enough money to get married and to fix the boat on which he had been living. Nevertheless, Sandrini's comic presence in the film subverts this message. Berretín's "thieving umbrella" is part of his comic persona; it hardly disqualifies him from gaining the audience's sympathy.[63] Even after his conversion, Berretín remains a far less compelling model of diligence and honesty. In fact, he explicitly resists the discipline of the workplace: in a recurring gag he drops his tools and walks away the instant he hears the bell signaling the end of the shift. As in virtually every other movie Sandrini would make, his character undermines the moral lesson of the melodramatic plot. The character of Remanso is a familiar type: an honest, diligent worker, nearly identical to the character of Edmundo in *Puente Alsina*. And *Riachuelo* shares with *Puente Alsina* its defense of working-class virtue. Yet in a comic twist on the embittered cynicism of tango lyrics, Sandrini's performance encourages the audience to laugh at the notion that hard work and honesty can lead to upward mobility.

Following *Riachuelo*, Sandrini made a series of films that repackaged this simple comic formula. Since the local film industry had abandoned its focus on urban manual laborers, Sandrini would not reprise his role as a dockworker. Nevertheless, his comedies continued to play out against the backdrop of a society divided between the noble poor and the hateful rich. In these films, Sandrini's characters were always situated clearly on the lower end of this melodramatic class divide. In *El cañonero de Giles* (Romero, 1937), he is a small-town rube with an unlikely talent: every time he hears a dog bark, he unleashes a powerful kick capable of rocketing a soccer ball past any goalkeeper. Recruited to play for a major team in the capital, he resists the discipline of athletic training: "I'm a football player, not a showgirl," he says, when the coach asks him to do leg lifts. Manipulated by the hypocritical and greedy team owners, he is initially seduced by the party life of the big city, until he recovers his values and wins back his small-town girlfriend. In *Don Quijote del Altillo* (Romero, 1936), Sandrini plays an unemployed layabout in love with Urbana, a girl who is seduced by her boss in the office where she works. Here again, Sandrini's character resists the idea of hard work and happily resorts to theft in order to acquire the ingredients for a birthday party he wants to throw for Urbana. Meanwhile, desperate to escape her poverty, Urbana convinces herself that her boss means well and enters a relationship with him. When she discovers that her boss is married, Urbana finally realizes that it is Sandrini's character who actually deserves her love.

These films revisit the central theme of tango melodrama: the young man or woman seduced by the promise of wealth into abandoning the simple but moral life of the barrio. They mine the melodramatic opposition between rich and poor for its comic potential. Thus, every movie has its fish-out-of-water scenes, in which Sandrini's character is thrust into the company of the wealthy and fails to fit in. In *El canillita y la dama* (Amadori, 1938), Sandrini plays Cachuso, a poor newspaper vendor who pretends to be the long-lost son of a wealthy industrialist. After falling for Martha, the industrialist's daughter, he helps her run away to avoid being forced to marry the unscrupulous man her father has selected for her. The comic culture clash between rich and poor plays out largely on the level of language. Cachuso's colloquial vocabulary, his use of the term *viejo* (old man), for example, instead of *papá* (father) clashes with the formal language of the wealthy characters. At one point, he struggles to find the proper form of the second person singular pronoun, starting with the colloquial Argentine *vos*, then trying the more universal *tú*, before opting for the formal *usted*.

The subversive potential of Sandrini's lazy but good-hearted simpleton is most fully realized in *Chingolo* (Demare, 1940). Sandrini plays the title character, a hobo who makes a comic philosophy out of his refusal to work (see figure 8). Preferring to steal chickens, he and his two friends take offense when a rich man offers to pay them to change his car's flat tire. When he rescues the son of a wealthy family who had fallen into the river, Chingolo gets his chance to try life on the other side of the class divide. Chingolo proves his essential moral rectitude by refusing a monetary reward from the boy's family: "One does not charge for such things." Impressed, the boy's mother awards Chingolo the annual prize of the women's charity association she heads. Intent on transforming him into a "respectable man (hombre de bien)," she has him cleaned and dressed up, and she gets him a non-taxing managerial job in her husband's canned peach factory. At first Chingolo resists these changes because they offend both his anarchic spirit and his sense of morality. Speaking into the boss's dictation machine he orders that the excess fruit be given to the poor, rather than thrown out—an act of goodwill rejected by his employer on the grounds that keeping people hungry is part of business.

Eventually, Chingolo is corrupted by his new surroundings. He has his

8 Luis Sandrini as the hobo Chingolo in the film of the same name. Courtesy of Museo del Cine Pablo Ducrós Hicken.

friends pretend to get sick from a competitor's peaches, thereby boosting his sponsor's business and successfully currying favor. He then conceives of a machine that will allow the boss to increase profits by firing many of his workers. In the end, though, Chingolo repudiates the immorality of the rich, rejects his new life, and returns to his hobo ways. The catalyst of this moral reawakening comes from a subplot lifted directly from Argentine melodrama. Chingolo is enamored of Elvira, the nanny for the boy who nearly drowns at the beginning of the film. Unfortunately, she is in love with Eduardo, the family's eldest son, a typical *niño bien*, or spoiled, lazy rich kid. Elvira, despite her poor romantic judgment, is the film's most consistent moral voice. Impressed with Chingolo's virtue at first, she scolds him for helping enrich the factory owner at the expense of poor workers. When Elvira gets pregnant, and Eduardo and his parents refuse to recognize the child, Chingolo recovers his sense of morality. He offers to give the child his own last name in return for a small fortune, which he then gives to Elvira so that she can pay for the child's education. This act returns Chingolo to the virtuous side of the class divide, but it does not get him the girl. Eduardo, inspired by Chingolo's example, comes

REPACKAGING POPULAR MELODRAMA | 121

to his senses, asks for Elvira's forgiveness, and promises to marry her and recognize the child. In the last scene, Chingolo and his friends hop a train; he misses Elvira, but he is happy to have returned to the life of a hobo.

Chingolo's ending dilutes the movie's subversive message. Not only is Chingolo content with life on the bottom of the socioeconomic ladder, but the interclass marriage of Eduardo and Elvira presents a hopeful model of class reconciliation, implying that the fundamental class divide depicted throughout the film can in fact be bridged. In this sense, *Chingolo* seems to substantiate Quinziano's argument that melodramatic elements work to contain the subversive potential of comedy. Yet the film's ending feels false. Eduardo is a one-dimensional character whose last-minute conversion is implausible to say the least. Moreover, class reconciliation and the restoration of moral order is only possible at the level of subplot. Chingolo cannot be incorporated into the dominant Argentine society, and his critique of hypocrisy, capitalist exploitation, and inequality remains uncontested. While Sandrini's films adopt melodrama's vision of society as hopelessly divided between good and evil, poor and rich, they do not embrace melodrama's moralism. On the contrary, Sandrini's character represents an alternative morality, within which the solidarity between poor people, their essential generosity, is a much more important value than either hard work or obeying the law. Chingolo's essential moral goodness derives from his rejection of capitalist greed and is not threatened by his tendency to steal wallets from rich people, to dine on stolen chickens, or to refuse work. In the end, he confirms his morality through an act of selfless generosity toward a fellow poor person.[64]

The film reviewer for the conservative newspaper *La Nación* expressed concern about the message of Sandrini's films: "With that character of contradictory moral profile, [Sandrini] exploits with ease his particular brand of popular humor."[65] As the reviewer implied, these films pose a critique of the dominant moral code by compelling audience identification with Sandrini's character. Yet at the same time, the movies seek to impose conformist, melodramatic resolutions. This ambiguity reflects the conflicting commercial pressures faced by an Argentine film industry locked into competition with Hollywood. Like Lamarque's films, Sandrini's fish-out-of-water comedies gave audiences the visual pleasures of lavish interiors and luxurious lifestyles. Nevertheless, the ability of audiences to identify with the characters depicted by both Lamarque and Sandrini depended upon their being firmly situated on the economically inferior but morally superior side of the class divide. In other words, Argentine melodrama demanded a certain class consciousness on the part of viewers. The transgressive populism of Sandrini's comic persona pushed these films even further, undermining the conventional moralism of their melodramatic endings. In this alternative moral universe, theft is excusable if its victims are wealthy; idleness is liberating; exploitation and greed are the worst sins; and selfless sacrifice for a fellow poor person is the noblest calling.

Sandrini's ability to step outside of melodrama's strict moral code owed something to his gender. Unlike so many melodramatic heroines, his characters are not inevitably punished for their sins. Chingolo might not get the girl, but he proves clever enough to outmaneuver the rich and powerful. By contrast, Lamarque's characters do not typically achieve this level of agency; they either give up their dreams of upward mobility or reconcile themselves to a life of unhappiness. Nevertheless, at least one female actress did manage to circumvent melodrama's harsh gender codes. During the 1930s, Niní Marshall emerged as a radio and film performer with a comedic style that proved enormously popular: by the end of the decade, she was as big a star as Sandrini or Lamarque. Marshall's performances were open to a range of different readings. Her comic personae could be enjoyed as snobbish caricatures of the uncultured masses, yet they also offered a populist anti-elitism every bit as powerful as Sandrini's.

Born Marina Esther Traverso, Marshall was the daughter of Spanish immigrants and grew up in relative comfort in the Buenos Aires neighborhood of San Telmo. Marshall emerged first on the radio, where she created a series of memorable characters that she later brought to the screen. She got her first break when she was cast as Cándida, a Spanish maid, on a Radio Municipal program. In 1937 Pablo Osvaldo Valle, the program director of Radio El Mundo, gave Marshall her own program, allowing her to write the script herself.[66] Although Marshall claimed to have modeled Cándida on the maid who worked in her own childhood home, the Spanish domestic had long been a stock character on the porteño stage. In sainetes, Spanish maids were ridiculed for their uneducated form of speech, their smelly food, their stupidity, and often their promiscuity, but they were typically portrayed as loyal servants, a reassuring depiction for well-to-do theatergoers.[67] In Marshall's version, the Spanish maid remained an object of ridicule, but one who often got the last laugh. In one script, she argues with the program host, insisting that Christopher Columbus was Spanish and that it was the Spanish who civilized the Argentines: "If it weren't for the *Gallegos* [Galicians, but in Argentina, a name for all Spaniards] you would be walking around naked . . . you indecent, shameless person!" When the host angrily responds that he is no Indian, Cándida teasingly imagines him wearing ostrich feathers, except that she mispronounces *avestruz*, the Spanish word for ostrich, as *vistruz*. Her host corrects her, but she insists, "I know very well what *vistruz* is and what *avestruz* is."

HOST: *Vistruz* isn't anything!!!
CÁNDIDA: I know that too! Hah! A coat with four feathers from a *vistruz*, which were the only birds that existed here, since we imported all the others.
HOST: *(angry)* The birds that you imported, were *pájaros de cuenta* (criminals)!!!
CÁNDIDA: The *pájaros de cuenta* were products of cross-breeding, my lord!!![68]

Here, Cándida's dimwittedness and lack of education serve as effective weapons against her condescending interlocutor. She subverts hierarchy by identifying herself with the civilizer and him with the savage, while her persistent misunderstandings and her attitude of superiority drive him to exasperation.

Marshall's version of the Spanish maid had much in common with another one from the same period: Ramona, the character created by the cartoonist Lino Palacio. In this comic strip, which first appeared in 1930 but achieved enduring success in the 1940s, the maid's obtuseness tends to enact revenge on her social superiors. When Ramona's employers leave for the evening, they tell her not to open the door because there are thieves in the neighborhood. Following this instruction literally, she refuses to let them in when they return later that night. In another strip, Ramona mails a letter for her boss even though it has yet to be addressed. When confronted, she explains that she figured her employer had left the envelope blank because she didn't want her maid to know who the recipient was. Ramona may be dumb, but it is generally her employers who suffer the consequences of her mistakes. Much of the pleasure of the strip comes from this revenge of the weak against the strong.[69] Marshall's Cándida had a similar, anti-elitist appeal; her ignorance provoked laughter, but her ability to frustrate and ridicule those who considered themselves superior to her was just as enjoyable.

When Cándida was first brought to the screen in Luis Bayón Herrera's *Cándida* (1939), she had to be inserted into a more developed plot. Alongside the comic mispronunciations and confusions of the radio program, Cándida now played a role in a conventional story involving a widower who marries a materialistic, pretentious, and self-centered woman. Outraged by the maid's tendency to speak her mind, the new wife fires Cándida and then proceeds to drive her husband into bankruptcy. In the end, the selfless Cándida secretly uses the money she has been saving for her own wedding in order to rescue her former employer. The cinematic version of Cándida retains the ignorance and stubbornness of the radio character but now also exhibits the essential goodness and generosity that Argentine movies tended to attribute to the poor. The result is a revival of the old prototype of the loyal servant and, in general, a far less subversive performance. In the end, the new wife is rehabilitated and rejects her earlier selfishness, while Cándida's generosity is rewarded. She and her boyfriend are able to marry and start a life together. But despite this moralistic and conformist resolution, what makes the character compelling is her deep sense of pride. Reprising her old joke from the radio, she teaches her employer's son that before "we Gallegos" came, "you" were all Indians, running around naked. Likewise, her dismissal results from her insistence on standing up to her employer's wife; she has her own ideas about how to serve food and how to dress, and she refuses to submit to the rich woman's authority.

Cándida's pride is analogous to a Libertad Lamarque character's insistence on singing tango despite the disapproval of her social superiors or to the refusal of Luis Sandrini's Chingolo to trade in his hobo lifestyle for the trappings of wealth. This same attitude—what critic Abel Posadas calls "class pride"—is also characteristic of Catita, the most popular of Marshall's radio and film characters.[70] Marshall modeled Catita on the young women who used to wait outside the radio station hoping to get an autograph from Juan Carlos Thorry, a movie actor who played the role of the host on the Cándida program. As Marshall recalled years later, these women were "gossips, busybodies, and meddlers [who] dressed with bad taste, almost extravagantly. They represented a social stratum, the product of the tenements (*conventillos e inquilinatos*) that existed in that period."[71] In addition to their pushiness, what drew Marshall's attention was their form of speech, which included idiosyncratic pronunciations as well as a host of distinctive phrases, many of Italian origin. Marshall's condescension toward the "Catitas" is not surprising. Before beginning her own radio career, she had written a column in the fan magazine *Sintonía* in which she had criticized the incorrect pronunciations of a soccer player interviewed on the radio and frequently mocked the bad taste on display in programs like *Chispazos de Tradición*.[72] In the character of Catita, she had simply picked a new target for this sort of ridicule. Like Cándida, Catita was a caricature that poked fun at a recognizable social type. Emilio Córdoba, the owner of La Piedad department store and the program's sponsor, initially balked at the idea of associating his store with Marshall's new character, arguing that his customers were just like Catita and would take offense. Since the show was an overnight sensation and La Piedad's sales immediately increased, Marshall concluded that the store's customers must not have seen themselves in the character, "a very logical reaction of 'the Catitas.'"[73] While there may be some truth to Marshall's assessment, many of Catita's fans likely responded to the character's intense self-esteem and the implicit populism it entailed. In other words, Catita's unapologetic class pride and her rejection of elite preferences and judgments may well have had an impact that Marshall herself did not intend.

After her triumphant appearance on the radio in 1937, Catita made her cinematic debut the following year in Manuel Romero's film for Lumiton, *Mujeres que trabajan* (*Women Who Work*). The film tells the story of Ana María, a wealthy, young woman who loses her fortune and her social standing when her father is unable to pay his debts and commits suicide. Rejected by her hypocritical friends and by her fiancé's aristocratic family, Ana María is rescued by her loyal chauffeur, who invites her to take a room where he lives, a boarding house that is also home to a group of female department store clerks, including Catita. Over the course of the film, Ana María is transformed by her contact with these "women who work." She takes a job at the store, develops good work habits and even a sense of solidarity, coming to the aid of one of her co-workers, who has been seduced and abandoned by the store's wealthy owner. Though the focus on women in the workplace represented an important challenge to the dominant cinematic practice of the day, the film's melodramatic structure and romantic plot are thoroughly conventional. In heavy-handed fashion, Romero juxtaposes the hypocritical superficiality of the rich with the generous nobility of the poor. Ana María overcomes her earlier arrogance and is welcomed into the community of working women. In the end, she is reunited with her fiancé, and they decide to marry over the objections of his family. As he puts it, they will now live together as "a woman who works and a man who works."

While Catita plays a marginal role in the melodrama, she is the central engine of comedy in the film. Marshall steals every scene she is in, deploying all of the comic devices she developed for the radio: rapid-fire speech, a squeaky, high-pitched voice, a tendency to run words together, and a grab bag of uncultured catch phrases. Catita is unabashedly envious of the rich and longs to find a husband who can support her materialistic aspirations. Wearing an ostentatious fur stole, she is the embodiment of the *guaranga*, the pretentious, inelegant social striver who preoccupied intellectuals of the period. In fact, when Lorenzo, the chauffeur, declares his love for Catita, the landlady asks, "Isn't she a bit *guaranga* for you?" His response—that he is attracted to the "contrast" she presents with the "high society" people he drives around all day—reveals the secret of Catita's comic appeal. As Posadas points out, most characters in the Argentine cinema of the 1930s speak in an exceptionally mannered style, using a formal vocabulary rarely heard in everyday speech. In this context, Catita's use of language had an explosive impact.[74] Catita explicitly rejects the standards of her social superiors; her distinctive speech patterns reflect not just ignorance, as in the case of Cándida, but a self-conscious rejection of elite aesthetic standards. When Lorenzo insists that she return the Venus de Milo replica she has stolen from the home of the wealthy villain, she responds that she doesn't want it anyway, since "this piece of junk is broken." Among the group of women employees in the film is a tie-wearing Communist, whom the film ridicules as sexually frustrated. In contrast to that character's Marxist pronouncements, Catita's aspirations—marriage, luxury, comfort—are entirely conventional. Nevertheless, her style, coupled with her complete lack of embarrassment, represents a powerful subversion of hierarchy.

Following the success of *Mujeres que trabajan*, Lumiton made a series of Catita vehicles. While these films continued the formula of combining a melodramatic love story with Marshall's special brand of humor, they moved Catita to center stage. In *Divorcio en Montevideo* (Romero, 1939), Catita and her friend, Adriana, are manicurists who listen to radio soap operas and fantasize about marrying millionaires (see figure 9). A rich

9   Niní Marshall as Catita in *Divorcio en Montevideo*. Courtesy of Museo del Cine Pablo Ducrós Hicken.

man named Claudio offers to pay Adriana to marry and then quickly divorce him so that he can collect an inheritance. She accepts in order to pay for an operation for her sick father. After an improvised trip to Paris, Claudio falls in love with Adriana, and his friend falls for Catita. As in *Mujeres que trabajan*, Catita's inelegant, materialistic pushiness plays out against the backdrop of a melodramatic culture clash between rich and poor. She gets drunk in public, wears gaudy dresses, and complains about all the "foreigners" in Paris. Adriana proves her worthiness by refusing the money that Claudio offers her, but Catita subverts this moralistic lesson. Angry at her friend for not taking the money she has earned, Catita steals the wedding ring that Adriana asks her to return to Claudio. Catita is loyal to her friend throughout the film, even giving Adriana the stolen ring as a memento of her love for Claudio. Nevertheless, if Adriana is the prototypical good girl from the barrios, who acts selflessly and morally and is rewarded when Claudio finally comes to his senses, Catita rejects this melodramatic logic. She takes what she can and never doubts that she deserves her share of the good life.

Catita's aggressive materialism was particularly striking coming from a woman. As we have seen, the tango repertoire was filled with stories of young women seeking upward mobility in downtown cabarets. These milonguitas were almost invariably doomed in the long run. Similarly, Libertad Lamarque's characters rarely escaped the punitive logic of melodrama. Of course, Niní Marshall's films typically did include melodramatic victims, women for whom the only hope of upward mobility was to marry a rich man. Marshall's characters, especially Catita, escaped this fate partly because Marshall did not play the romantic lead. Marshall and the directors with whom she worked essentially invented a new genre, in which her comedy stole the spotlight from a conventional melodramatic plot. Catita, in other words, was the friend of the melodramatic heroine and, as such, she was not subject to the same strict gender code.

Evidence suggests that Catita's popularity crossed class lines.[75] The reviewer for the elite newspaper *La Prensa* described the "guffaws" Marshall's performance inspired when *Mujeres que trabajan* opened at the downtown Cine-Teatro Monumental.[76] While the critic praised her "picaresque modalities" and "sparks of playful popular ingenuity," one imagines the well-to-do, opening night audience laughing primarily *at* Catita and her ridiculous attempts at style. But Catita's primary audience was in the barrios. Marshall performed with Thorry on Radio El Mundo four nights a week, twice as Cándida and twice as Catita. Following the program, they performed live shows in movie theaters throughout the city. According to Marshall, they appeared in every barrio in the city, always leading with Catita and almost always filling the house. Later, they toured the interior of the country.[77] The letters section of the fan magazine *Sintonía* provides some insight into the various types of connection Marshall forged with her fans. When Marshall was criticized, it was most often for "deforming" the Spanish language, popularizing and legitimizing mispronunciations and other vulgarities. In response, one reader praised Marshall's intelligence, arguing that she had perfectly captured a "type of woman of whom there are thousands in our metropolis." This reader implicitly emphasized the cultural distance that separated Catita from himself as well as from Marshall. He celebrated the actress as a caricaturist who poked fun at people who deserved to be teased.[78] Similarly, another reader argued that Marshall actually improved people's speech by making thousands of real-life "Catitas" aware that they were speaking incorrectly.[79] But other readers praised Marshall in very different terms. One letter writer from the remote province of Formosa on the Paraguayan border enthusiastically defended her against critics: "Niní Marshall is, currently, the number ONE comic actress (like that, in capital letters) in radio and cinema. For those of us who live in Formosa, as for all the 'normal' inhabitants of the country, it is a delight to hear her." The writer signaled her identification with Catita, in particular, by signing off with one of the character's signature phrases, *as noche*, a truncated version of *buenas noches*.[80] The writer's use of Catita's own words as well as the sense of community affiliation implicit in the letter suggest that many non-elite fans identified directly with Catita's aggressive class pride; they were laughing *with* her, not just *at* her.

Both Luis Sandrini and Niní Marshall combined melodrama with a more transgressive populism in order to fashion a subversive brand of comedy. Both actors created characters of humble origins who lived in a society starkly divided between the rich and the poor. The essential goodness and generosity of these characters contrasted with the pettiness and cruelty of the rich. Like the melodrama of the tango, the weekly novel, the radio soap opera, and the Libertad Lamarque film, these comedies dramatized the anxieties faced by poor people living in a rapidly modernizing capitalist society, even as their happy endings supplied a satisfying poetic justice. Yet Argentina's populist-melodramatic comedies provided other satisfactions as well. Sandrini and Marshall undermined conventional moralism by creating characters that refuse to conform to the strict rules of melodrama. Within the melodramatic universe, goodness involved a fatalistic acceptance of one's lot in life and an avoidance of unseemly social striving, yet both Sandrini's character and Catita are openly envious of the luxuries enjoyed by the wealthy; both even resort to theft. Likewise, Sandrini's trademark aversion to hard work and Catita's pushiness challenged accepted norms of behavior. These characters prove their goodness through acts of solidarity and generosity, even as they refuse to acquiesce to the aesthetic, behavioral, and ethical demands of the wealthy. The barrio residents who made up the bulk of the audience for domestic movies must have enjoyed these characters' explicit affiliation with popular styles and practices.

Throughout the 1930s, commercial and ideological pressures pushed many Argentine filmmakers away from this sort of populism. As we have seen, José Agustín Ferreyra abandoned his sympathetic depictions of the urban working class and began producing tango operas. By the end of the decade, this conservative tendency had deepened. In an effort to attract more elite moviegoers, the studios released a steady stream of so-called white telephone films set in the luxurious homes of the bourgeoisie. These films, clearly influenced by Hollywood and other foreign models, catered to the audience's desire to indulge vicariously in the swank lifestyles of the rich.[81]

Nevertheless, populism persisted. Even the most benign "white telephone" comedies often trafficked in the class messages of melodrama. *Los martes orquídeas* (Múgica, 1941) tells the story of a lonely girl, played by Mirtha Legrand, who is unable to attract boyfriends like her sisters. Her wealthy father seeks to comfort her by inventing a secret admirer and eventually hires an unemployed young man to play the part. In the end, the deception is revealed, but by then the actor has fallen in love with the girl, and the two happily plan to marry. The movie's populist subtext echoes the working-class pride that was so central to the films of Sandrini and Marshall. The wealthy father is certain that his daughter will reject her suitor once she learns that he is unemployed, has an Italian surname, and lives in a humble pension. But the girl, a dreamer who writes love poetry and reads romantic fiction, does not share her father's class prejudice. She immediately accepts the young man, in his words, "as I am." The man's comic attempts to act the part of a wealthy suitor—wearing fancy clothes, riding horses, attending frivolous parties—were unnecessary. *Soñar no cuesta nada* (Amadori, 1941), another of Mirtha Legrand's early films, offers an even more explicit populism. Here, Legrand plays a poor girl who gets to experience how the other half lives when she is mistaken for the daughter of a wealthy family (played by Mirtha's real-life twin, Silvia). Once again, the positioning of Legrand's character as an outsider who does not belong in the world of the rich guarantees her innocence and virtue: among other accomplishments, she teaches the spoiled son of the family to appreciate the opportunities his class position affords him. The director, Luis César Amadori, had perfected the depiction of upper-class luxury in films like *Madreselva* and *El canillita y la dama*. Amadori's frequent set designer, Raúl Soldi, recalled that he used to keep a high-class nightclub and a mansion with a grand staircase ready, since the director's films always required such fancy settings.[82] Yet even as they played to the popular desire to experience the good life, films like *Soñar no cuesta nada* reinforced the idea that we, the poor, are morally superior to them, the rich.[83] They appealed simultaneously to class pride and class envy, encouraging viewers to look down on the rich even as they fantasized about being rich.

The mass cultural melodrama of the 1920s and 1930s represented an alternative modernism, but as the variety of fan responses to Catita suggest, it offered different things to different audiences. For many, including those who may have aspired to a middle-class lifestyle, the new radio programs and sound movies provided a respectable, safe, and sanitized version of authentic Argentine culture. They could enjoy music and cinema that was rooted in the local context but was just as modern, or at least almost as modern, as those imported from the North. And they could indulge their fantasies of striking it rich. For others, though, melodrama offered a way of processing the dislocations of modernity in class terms, constructing a group identity around certain values associated with the poor, including solidarity, loyalty, and the capacity to express true emotion. By expressing suspicions about motivations that conflict with those values, such as the pursuit of upward mobility, melodrama represented a counter-discourse that pushed back against the appeals of advertisers and barrio associations. In its most subversive incarnations, mass cultural melodrama was packaged with a populist condemnation of the Argentine elite.

4 MASS-CULTURAL NATION BUILDING

Argentine mass culture was the object of persistent attacks by those concerned about the spread of bad taste and low morals. Critics bemoaned the popular programming on Radio Belgrano for appealing to the lowest common denominator. They lambasted *Chispazos de Tradición* for its inauthentic gauchos and formulaic romance plots. They accused comedians like Niní Marshall and Luis Sandrini of deforming the Spanish language and denounced tango lyricists for celebrating the immoral behavior and improper slang of criminals and prostitutes. This preoccupation with the content of popular culture was not new. At the turn of the century, the tango's association with illicit sexuality had made it an object of elite scorn and government regulation.[1] But concerns about the allegedly low level of popular culture took on a new urgency with the advent of the radio and the cinema. The new media's unprecedented capacity to cross barriers of distance and class made it a new kind of threat. In Argentina and, in fact, throughout the world, the spread of mass culture provoked anxiety and inspired diverse campaigns to moralize, elevate, or sanitize the material being broadcast to the masses.

Critics of mass culture quickly recognized the new media's tendency to appeal to plebeian tastes by repackaging popular cultural traditions. Tango music dominated record catalogues and radio lineups, and the biggest stars of the genre quickly crossed over to cinema. Gaucho tales from the old criollo circus were adapted to radio theater. In general, the diverse tradition of popular melodrama put its stamp on virtually every piece of domestic mass culture available to Argentine consumers. And as a result of mass culture's reliance on popular traditions, subversive messages coursed through the films and radio programs of the period. Tango's association with the urban poor and its alleged rejection by snobbish elites were central to its appeal. Film melodramas and comedies encouraged viewers to identify with working-class heroes who refused to conform to dominant moral and aesthetic standards. In short, the critics of mass culture had reason to fear: Argentine radio and cinema had an alarmingly populist cast.

In the 1930s, this fear of mass culture intersected with a larger set of concerns about national identity. In the context of economic crisis, corrupt oligarchic governments, and the rising international legitimacy of anti-liberal, statist ideologies, a new nationalist movement gained influence in Argentina. Combining elements of Italian Fascism with a deep commitment to Catholicism, right-wing nationalists elaborated what Federico Finchelstein calls "clericofascism."[2] They criticized Argentina's liberal democracy and its economic dependence, and they contributed to a revisionist interpretation of Argentine history that demonized the nation's liberal forefathers, celebrated the Federalist *caudillos* (strongmen) of its rural past, and blamed the country's economic woes on British imperialist exploitation.[3] This questioning of Argentina's political and economic traditions was accompanied by a renewed quest to identify and consolidate a national identity that many felt had been lost during the era of massive immigration and liberal subservience to Europe. A series of influential essays on national identity were published in the 1930s, including Raúl Scalabrini Ortiz's *El hombre que está solo y espera* (1931), Ezequiel Martínez Estrada's *Radiografía de la pampa* (1933), and Eduardo Mallea's *Historia de una pasión argentina* (1937).[4] These texts offered diverse diagnoses of Argentina's problems, but taken together, they revealed a rising tide of nationalist anxiety.

Inevitably, much of this anxiety came to be directed at mass culture. In Martínez Estrada's view, the failure of the state to actively regulate the culture industries meant that Argentine radio and cinema, for all their flaws, accurately reflected the values and tastes of the people: "Instead of the radio forging the consciousness of popular taste among us, the consciousness of popular taste has forged the radio in its own image."[5] Given their popularity, domestic radio programs and films offered evidence on which to base one's assessment of the nation as well as obvious targets for reformist projects. In this context, then, the frequent campaigns to improve mass culture often formed part of a concerted effort to remake the nation. Cultural critics and producers hoped to use the new media either to help recover and disseminate the national essence or to elevate the nation's cultural level. These efforts took various forms. Some hoped to improve Argentine mass culture by more closely copying North American models, while others saw commercialism itself as debasing and hoped the mass media might preserve and disseminate the uncontaminated culture of the rural "folk." Still others imitated international trends by seeking to elaborate an Argentine high culture that drew on and improved the nation's folk traditions.

These varied attempts at mass-cultural nation building sometimes reinforced the commercial strategies of Argentina's record labels, radio stations, and film studios. The transnational marketplace encouraged local cultural producers to rely on popular culture, but this strategy also potentially limited their reach. Cultural commodities that appealed to popular audiences might alienate wealthier consumers drawn to prestigious foreign imports. Throughout the 1930s, cultural producers actively sought to unify the market, to broaden their audience by competing for these higher-class consumers, even as they held on to their popular base. Some projects aimed at elevating mass culture might also serve this commercial purpose. Nevertheless, both the attempt to consolidate a national identity and the effort to expand the audience for domestic mass culture were undermined by persistent contradictions. In the end, the powerful populist tendencies in Argentine mass culture proved impossible to reconcile with efforts to unify the nation across class lines.

CAN THE TANGO BE IMPROVED?

Record companies, radio programmers, fan magazines, lyricists, and performers all actively positioned the tango as an alternative modernism, just as modern as jazz and yet authentically Argentine. The claim of authenticity, as we have seen, typically invoked the genre's plebeian associations. Stars like Carlos Gardel marketed their rags-to-riches biographies, stressing their working-class origins. The melodramatic stories exhaustively explored in tango lyrics situated the music in the poor arrabales of Buenos Aires. Even more basically, tango lyricists signaled their affiliation with the poor through their extensive use of lunfardo, the popular porteño slang. The immortal opening line of Pascual Contursi's "Mi noche triste"—"Percanta que me amuraste" ("Woman who left me")—inaugurated tango's self-conscious break with proper Spanish and its explicit affiliation with the popular culture of the urban plebe. Taken to its logical extreme, this populism could even imply a certain class consciousness, an implication visible, for example, in the magazine *La Canción Moderna* during its first year of publication in 1928. That year, the magazine was edited by Dante A. Linyera, a lunfardo poet and tango lyricist. In his lyrics, Linyera, like many other tango lyricists, embraced the popular and denigrated the elite.[6] But in *La Canción Moderna*, Linyera went further, printing the lyrics of the latest tango hits and interviews with tango stars alongside denunciations of the bourgeoisie and celebrations of the working class. The magazine defined itself as "the magazine of the people" and included a regular section called "the voice of the suburbio" which denounced injustice and called for class solidarity. *La Canción Moderna* even printed a special issue for May Day, featuring on its cover a drawing of a protest in the name of "peoples oppressed by capitalism," and including columns on the anarchist heroes Errico Malatesta and Simon Radowitsky, as well as poems celebrating the class struggle.[7] Linyera's articulation of tango with the rhetoric of working-class militancy was unusual, but it reveals the potential for class consciousness in tango's discourse of authenticity.

As tango was appropriated by the new mass media, the genre's plebeian affiliations quickly came to seem problematic. If tango was to appeal to a broad, cross-class audience and if it was to compete with ultramodern jazz, it needed to be freed from the arrabales. Musically, the efforts of New Guard bandleaders like Julio de Caro achieved this purpose by associating tango with the spirit of progress and modernization. But tango lyrics also required transformation; specifically, tango needed aesthetic alternatives to the intensely plebeian language of lyricists like Contursi and Celedonio Flores. In fact, other lyricists did write tangos in a more universal idiom, telling stories about love and betrayal that were less rooted in the social world of the poor. This tendency gained prominence with the emergence of Alfredo Le Pera in 1932 as the screenwriter of Carlos Gardel's films for Paramount. When work began on a follow-up to the enormously successful *Las luces de Buenos Aires*, the screenwriters of that film, Manuel Romero and Luis Bayón Herrera, were unavailable. Their replacement was Le Pera, who, as a translator of subtitles for foreign movies and a former drama critic for various Buenos Aires newspapers, was well suited to the task of packaging Argentine popular culture for an international audience.[8] Since Paramount marketed Gardel's movies throughout Latin America, the films needed to avoid references that would only be accessible to porteño viewers. Le Pera responded to the challenge by elaborating less localist and less plebeian tango stories. Since Le Pera also wrote the lyrics to many of the tangos Gardel sang on screen, his more universal aesthetic had a major impact on the tango canon. Le Pera compositions like "Volver" (1935) retained tango's melancholy nostalgia and its focus on romantic abandonment, but they spurned lunfardo in favor of a lyrical, more traditionally poetic language:

> Yo adivino el parpadeo
> de las luces que a lo lejos,
> van marcando mi retorno.
> Son las mismas que alumbraron,
> con sus pálidos reflejos,
> hondas horas de dolor.
>
> *I make out the blinking*
> *of the distant lights that*
> *mark my return.*
> *They are the same ones that illuminated*
> *with their pallid reflections*
> *deep hours of pain.*

Given Gardel's stature, imitation was inevitable, and tango lyricists gradually abandoned lunfardo.[9] Once again, the effort to compete in the transnational marketplace had transformed Argentine popular culture.

The commercial dynamic that encouraged lyricists to abandon lunfardo dovetailed with an ideological campaign aimed at purging tango of its troubling plebeian associations. This campaign was particularly visible in the pages of Argentina's thriving fan magazines. By the mid-1930s, Buenos Aires newsstands featured several magazines that provided coverage of the local radio and cinema as well as of North American music and film. The owner of *La Canción Moderna* was Julio Korn, the son of Jewish Romanian immigrants, who had first distinguished himself as a publisher of sheet music. Following Dante Linyera's brief term as editor, Korn would steer the magazine in a more mainstream direction, renaming it *Radiolandia* in 1934 in order to emphasize its link to the modern mass media. By the 1940s, *Radiolandia* could boast a circulation of 450,000. Nearly as popular was *Sintonía*, owned by Editorial Haynes, the owner of Radio El Mundo, and edited by the journalist Emilio Karstulovic. The radio impresario Jaime Yankelevich was not to be outdone: he founded *Antena* in order to give Radio Belgrano an outlet for free publicity. Closely tied to the radio milieu that they covered, these editors were "outsider" capitalists like those who founded the recording, radio, and film industries. They sought to attract middle-class readers by emulating the high standards of general interest magazines like *Caras y Caretas*, but at the same time, they embraced the aesthetic preferences of the masses and insisted on their popular credentials.[10] The campaign to elevate and improve the tango betrayed these conflicting agendas.

Even after it had moved away from the class consciousness of its early years, *La Canción Moderna* continued to depict itself as an advocate of the popular. For example, it criticized the radio station run by the state oil company, YPF, for playing classical music of interest only to "distinguished girls" while ignoring "the traditionally popular expression of our porteño music."[11] But if *La Canción Moderna* continued to defend the tango, it now did so in very different terms. The editorial criticizing YPF did so in the name of "the people" but defined that group not as the poor inhabitants of the suburbios but as "the middle class." Similarly, another editorial defended tango lyrics against elitist critics but began by accepting much of their critique:

> We duly recognize that mediocrity has established itself among lyricists, but . . . one cannot base a judgment solely on the bad lyricists. . . . The great popularity of our tango has attracted good writers, whose signatures are known and valued in the world of theatre and litera-

ture. . . . Vulgarity and *lunfardismo* are being eliminated, honest and intelligent lyricists have stood out, in a word, even simple but delicate poems have been put to music. . . . It is true that there is a great deal that is bad, that there are lyricists whose knowledge of the world comes through a café table or a crime report, but let us recognize that successes are no longer based on the prison, the *mina* [lunfardo for "woman" or "prostitute"] or other terms of that sort, which are invariably mentioned when one wants to disparage our tango, sterilizing in this way the efforts of honest lyricists who struggle to elevate it and most of all to clean it.[12]

La Canción Moderna now celebrated the attempts of lyricists to clean up the tango, to purge it of its immoral subject matter and its plebeian language. As an example of the sort of lyrics the magazine sought to cultivate, the editorial cited "Silencio," a tango about the horrors of the First World War co-authored by Alfredo Le Pera. Defending "Silencio" against the charge that it represented an attempt to "foreign-ize" the tango, the editorial compared the song to Remarque's *All Quiet on the Western Front*, praising it as a work of art with a universal message. *La Canción Moderna* argued that by eliminating "vulgarity and lunfardismo," lyricists could transform the tango from popular culture into high art. Five years later, the magazine, now named *Radiolandia*, reiterated the point: "The lyricist has a responsibility: to write while trying to improve. Whoever fails to make this effort is acting against popular song."[13]

Many artists embraced the project of improving the tango with the same enthusiasm as the editors of *La Canción Moderna*. The singer Tania, for example, argued that tango was better in both class and cultural terms than its origins suggested: "The tango has an essence that is superior to the image in which it is always depicted. Even though it may come from the humblest, roughest (*más compadritos*) barrios, it has emotion and universality."[14] Tania's comments reveal that for tango, quality and authenticity could often seem mutually exclusive; she argued that the genre had universal cultural value *despite* its roots in the lower-class suburbios, the very roots that gave the music its claim to represent the nation. In this way, the campaign to improve and clean up the tango threatened the authenticity of the music, a contradiction that *Radiolandia* tried hard to resolve. In an editorial entitled "Authenticity and Clarity (Tipicismo y claridad)," the magazine acknowledged that the noble efforts of composers, lyricists, and performers could easily go too far.

There is an obvious desire to elevate the quality of popular music. . . . In the composer who struggles to avoid vulgar modulation and hackneyed forms. In the lyricist who tries to "dignify" himself in the virtuous search for theme and words. And in the performer who in the fulfillment of his difficult task tries new modalities of expression.

All three are efforts worthy of sponsorship within the urban songbook so urgently in need of improvement. But each of the three efforts entails its own danger. The composer on the path to melodic originality can fall—and almost always does—into the well of distortion and falsification (*retorcimiento*). The lyricist choosing words and themes ends up writing pedantic and affected verses. And the performer, exaggerating the originality of his interpretation, helps to strip traditional emotion from popular music.

It is necessary to progress within porteño song. But it is necessary to progress without avoiding the *porteñismo* of song. Progress does not consist in tango lyrics that describe the dramas of princesses, instead of passions illuminated by streetlamps. That is not it. It consists, on the contrary, in finding within those same passions something poetic, or picturesque, or simply moving.[15]

Radiolandia, like many other cultural commentators, called for progress, originality, and an improvement in quality but recognized that achieving those ends might come at the cost of abandoning or destroying the popular essence of the tango.

In celebrating the thirteenth anniversary of Radio Belgrano, *Radiolandia* congratulated the station for maintaining its popular orientation even as it achieved progress: "Radio Belgrano progressed within its own spirit. Deepening its efficiency. Improving its quality. But without turning away from the route laid down."[16] The hope here was that the quality of a cultural product could be clearly distinguished from its content. There were good tangos and bad tangos, just like there were good symphonies and bad symphonies. The trick was to improve the tango without turning it into something else. Similarly, another article argued that singers needed to excel in both their capacity for expression and the quality of their voice. The former was crucial to their *tipicismo*, their ability to achieve tango authenticity, while the latter was more universal. Unfortunately, according to *Radiolandia*, Argentines had tended to overvalue expression, elevating many poor singers to stardom.[17]

The distinction between improvements in the quality of tango and the introduction of inauthenticity was difficult to discern. For example, on the question of lyrics, *Radiolandia* itself wavered between calling for a stop to the use of lunfardo and arguing that the porteño argot constituted a central aspect of tango authenticity and could be reconciled with improvements in quality.[18] Predictably, debates raged in the 1930s over precisely where to draw the line between authenticity and improvement. In a typical letter published in *Sintonía*, one reader criticized Radio Belgrano and its artistic director, Pablo Osvaldo Valle, for emphasizing "quantity and not quality" when selecting performers.[19] But of course, definitions of "quality" varied. While most of *Sintonía*'s letter writers were fans of the tango, some insisted that radio stations like Belgrano could provide "quality" only by incorporating classical music.[20] The intellectual Bernardo Kordon wrote to say that tango was in clear decline: "There has certainly been an overproduction of [tango songs], but quality is absent in the majority, and what is worse, they easily provoke ridicule when they are inspired by exotic themes."[21] Kordon's letter brought an angry response from a group of readers who rose to the defense of contemporary tango composers.[22] While virtually all letter writers agreed on the need to pursue quality, they disagreed on how to define that concept.

The struggle to reconcile authenticity with quality played out in the context of capitalist mass culture, and many Argentines worried that tango was being warped by those who sought to exploit it for profit. A report in *Sintonía* on Juan de Dios Filiberto depicted the tango composer, musician, and band leader as a tragic figure, at war with modern, market culture: "In a hostile and commercialized environment, he dreams of grand and impossible things. . . . Filiberto directs an orquesta típica with which he is determined to triumph against the commercialization of the tango." And Filiberto himself echoed these themes in his own comments to the reporter: he longed for the day, he said, "when our song, which is the song of all the multitudes who suffer, of all the pain of the poor, can arise in its fullness, without the burden of those who commercialize it, of those who exploit it."[23] Tango's working-class authenticity here stands in opposition to the project of elevating the tango in order to market it to a higher class of consumer.

Many of *Sintonía*'s letter writers agreed. According to one, "The tango is in decline because it is no longer Argentine, it is bastardized, bad, immoral. The tango of today is not art, it is commerce, it is not the expression of our feeling, it is 'plagiarism.'"[24] For this writer, the commodification of tango threatened to falsify it, to strip it of its Argentinidad, presumably because foreign elements like saxophones would be included in the pursuit of popularity. But the market cut both ways. Mass cultural capitalism could threaten tango authenticity, but it could also stand in the way of achieving progress and cultural elevation. Arguing that an unfettered market encouraged vulgarity, the magazine *Antena* called on the state to play a more active role in regulating the moral and cultural content of the radio. Specifically, the magazine insisted that the government should establish a set of credentials required of anyone serving as artistic director of a radio station: this position "must not be held by audacious people, semiliterates, and people of strange combinations, as occurs now." Artistic directors, according to *Antena*, needed cultural preparation in order to distinguish between "the bad, the ordinary, and the good."[25]

Likewise, *Sintonía*'s editors also hoped that radio stations would resist the cultural threat posed by commercialism. They denounced advertisers who insisted that "one has to give the public what it asks for," thereby putting commercial interests ahead of the need to elevate the culture: "Above and beyond the supposed demands of the public is the cultural mission that radio has the obligation to fulfill." The article complimented Radio El Mundo for having rejected "routine and mediocrity" in favor of "more dignified and pure expressions of art," and having done so without losing its audience.[26] This version of the anti-commercialism argument did not make distinctions between jazz and tango, since both were aggressively and successfully marketed on the radio. Like the letter writer who demanded that Radio Belgrano include classical music, *Sintonía*'s editors explicitly praised the inclusion of "the most elevated musical genres" on the radio, implying that to give the people what they want would be to give in to the hegemony of tango and jazz. But of course a magazine that was itself committed to celebrating these popular genres could only push this argument so far. Congratulating Radio Splendid and Radio Excelsior for elevating their programming, *Sintonía* was careful not to denigrate popular culture: "Those happy initiatives, which were echoed on other stations, are responsible for the continuous contact of our public with the best performers and the greatest authors. We are not referring to this or that genre, but rather to all that is good, whether popular or classical."[27] Here, *Sintonía* embraced the argument that quality could be distinguished from content and that popular music like tango could be improved without losing its essence. Nevertheless, the idea that radio stations or the state should engage in efforts of cultural improvement suggested that commercial appeal and cultural value tended to move in opposite directions; if left to the market, the radio would be dominated by the mediocre.

Critics seeking to improve the tango found their hero in the modernizing band leader Julio de Caro, and yet his efforts were also controversial. By 1933 de Caro, who had dominated the tango scene in the late 1920s, was intent on enlarging his band in order to create something new: "In the new year, I plan to realize my old dream of a genuinely Argentine symphonic orchestra, which is completely different from the vulgar orquesta típica, since that type of band plays exclusively tangos, while I will interpret a rigorous selection of those, but within a large repertoire of completely symphonic versions of folkloric music, such as vidalitas, estilizadas, cañas, mediacañas, malambos, etc . . . It is necessary to raise the moral and spiritual concept of our music. . . . The tango needs to develop in another way, so that it acquires quality (*para que tome categoría*) and establishes itself as an elevated musical expression and so that it is listened to with pleasure even in the circles that are most resistant to our popular music."[28] De Caro imagined a large orchestra of the best professional musicians capable of elevating the tango or, as he put it elsewhere, dressing it "in the finery (*ropaje*) it has lacked until now."[29] The attempt to create a symphonic tango earned de Caro frequent praise from *Radiolandia*, *Sintonía*, and *Antena*, committed as they were to elevating Argentine popular culture. *Sintonía* labeled him "a tireless tango worker" and congratulated him for refusing to rest on his laurels.

The notion of tango as a folk genre that could form the basis of sophisticated, symphonic music was inspired by international trends. De Caro explicitly compared the project to the work of the Cuban composer Ernesto Lecuona and the Russian bandleader Dajos Bela, both of whom had composed symphonic works on the basis of folk material.[30] Jazz, in particular, seemed to offer a clear example of how primitive music could be used as raw material by serious composers. *Sintonía*'s jazz writer, León Klimovsky, for example, described jazz as a "rich 'stylization' of the best and most primitive folkloric elements."[31] And de Caro was not alone in thinking of tango in precisely these terms. In the late 1930s, *Radiolandia* often described tango as "urban folklore" and argued that "folklore . . . is the basis of all the great musical creations of the world."[32] Similarly,

Osvaldo Fresedo argued that tango "represents the character of the people" but that it needed to progress "like popular music from all over the world."[33] Inevitably, de Caro's pursuit of quality raised the specter of inauthenticity, leading his interviewer to ask whether "modern orchestrations" would rob the tango of its "traditional flavor." In response, de Caro argued that the fox trot and rumba had both been orchestrated without losing their authenticity.

De Caro's symphonic tango project appealed on various grounds. Built on the concept of folklore, it promised an escape from the taint of commercialism. Since it echoed international developments, it seemed modern and up-to-date. Most important, though, it offered a way to improve the tango, to raise it up from its embarrassingly plebeian origins without losing its ability to represent Argentine national identity. De Caro's own background helps explain his interest in this project. Unlike Francisco Canaro and other members of the Old Guard, Julio de Caro could not claim proletarian roots. His father, an Italian immigrant who had been a conservatory professor in Milan and ran his own music school in Buenos Aires, wanted Julio to attend university and become a doctor. When Julio insisted on playing tango professionally, his father threw him out of the house. Perhaps out of a desire to justify his career path, de Caro's tango ambitions always centered on the pursuit of "quality (*categoría*)," the desire to create "something very special, that would ennoble the tango."[34] In any case, given de Caro's middle-class upbringing, it is not surprising that he agreed with the many critics who hoped to elevate the tango so that it might serve as a more appropriate national symbol.

Although popular with many critics, de Caro's efforts at tango renovation provoked bitter opposition as well. This polemic is today typically understood as a debate between traditionalists and evolutionists, and those terms were used at the time.[35] But in the 1930s these different approaches to tango were also commonly understood to be about rhythm and melody. In one typical account, *Radiolandia* sorted Radio Belgrano's extensive lineup of tango bands into two broad categories: "From rhythmic tango to melodic tango, each director imposes a definite personality on his band." Devotees of symphonic tango, like Roberto Zerrillo, along with other innovators of the New Guard, like Osvaldo Fresedo, were placed in the melodic tango camp, while more traditional practitioners cultivated rhythm.[36] De Caro himself shared the notion that tango's roots lay in its rhythm, which, he argued, should be respected by innovators:

"Each of our tangos should be interpreted according to the rhythm appropriate to its essential modality, but the orchestrations, in general, need the contribution of new harmonies."[37] Melody, harmony, instrumentation: these were the areas where tango could be improved; its essential rhythms had to be respected, lest the music lose its essence.

Even as de Caro pursued his symphonic tango, a traditionalist rhythmic revival was under way. Tango fans who rejected the complex harmonic innovations of the New Guard looked increasingly to the genre's past. This pursuit of authentic origins yielded a revival of the *milonga*, a music and dance form that preceded tango and that typically featured a faster tempo and greater syncopation. Beginning in the early 1930s, milongas regained their position on porteño dance floors and on the radio, as orquestas típicas increasingly featured them in their repertoires. Much of the impetus for this renaissance came from a series of popular new milongas composed by Sebastián Piana in collaboration with lyricist Homero Manzi. The two Piana-Manzi compositions that launched the movement were "Milonga Sentimental" (1931) and "Milonga del 900" (1933). Both appeared in the film *¡Tango!* (1933), and both were recorded by Carlos Gardel, among many others. Written from a woman's point of view, "Milonga Sentimental" told a story of lost love in a wistful tone that reinforced the nostalgia implicit in the retrieval of an older musical style. This nostalgic mood was even more firmly established in Manzi's lyrics for "Milonga del novecientos," which explicitly evoke the Buenos Aires suburbios of the previous century. The rediscovery of the milonga reflected a yearning for Argentina's pre-modern, rural past. The milonga, which had long been featured in the repertoire of folksingers, was firmly associated with the rural folk culture of the Pampas.

But even if these rural associations helped produce the nostalgia that Manzi's lyrics cultivated, the milonga of the 1930s was understood to be a new modernized milonga. From the beginning, fan magazines distinguished between the *milonga pampeana* that formed part of the folk music canon and the *milonga tangueada* (or tangoized milonga) that the orquestas típicas were now playing.[38] Similarly, in an interview decades later, Sebastián Piana emphasized the extent of his innovation in transforming the "country milonga," which he associated with the gauchos and payadores of an earlier era, into the *milonga porteña*: "I needed to make milongas that were different, which these were: they maintained the simplicity of the rhythm but with a more defined musical form, as if they were tango songs, but without losing the essence of the milonga."[39] As he put it elsewhere, he respected the "rhythmic spirit" of the original milongas while improving their "monotonous" melodies.[40] Piana saw his own work in much the same terms as Julio de Caro saw the symphonic tango: both sought to introduce melodic or harmonic sophistication to a primitive, rhythmic form.

Milonga's associations with the Pampas were not the only source of authenticity on which the genre's new practitioners could draw. The form was also linked to *candombe*, a music and dance style created by Afro-Argentines and their ancestors during the colonial period. The milonga's African roots may have threatened racist elites for whom the whiteness of Argentine culture was axiomatic, but they were quite helpful to those seeking a primitive music that could serve as the basis for a sophisticated Argentine modernism. Vicente Rossi's book *Cosas de negros* (1926) was among the first to argue that the choreographic origins of tango and milonga lay in the African derived candombe. This idea, widely accepted among scholars today,[41] gained new credence during the 1930s. In *La Historia del Tango*, a lengthy series of lectures given on the radio beginning in 1934 and published two years later, Héctor Bates and Luis J. Bates accepted the notion that the Afro-Argentine candombe had given the tango its essential rhythm.[42] Bernardo Kordon went further in a series of articles he wrote for *Sintonía*, in which he argued that "tango is of pure African origin." Kordon was convinced that tango and Argentine culture more generally had entered a period of decline under the nefarious influence of jazz, which he saw as a commercial music with no cultural value.[43] For him, the recovery of tango's African roots was a way to shore up the music's authenticity, its connection to local folk traditions of long standing. By the end of the 1930s, the recovery of the milonga had been explicitly linked to a renewed interest in the Afro-Argentine culture of the previous centuries. In particular, Homero Manzi had begun to write lyrics with explicitly black themes for milongas by Piana and by Lucio Demare: "Pena mulata," "Negra María," and "Papá Baltasar," to name three of the most well known.

In 1941, *Radiolandia* signaled the importance of this trend within Argentine mass culture, declaring that "the candombe is reborn within Argentine dance." Describing the work of Piana, Manzi, Demare, and others, the magazine was enthusiastic about this "process of re-creating the black Río de la Plata": "We point out these developments with true joy. It is a way to renovate our songbook and open a path for lyricists and composers that will furnish more than one poetic and musical surprise."[44] *Radiolandia* shared Piana's view of the milonga renaissance: it was an effort to rework and improve material from an older, folkloric, and thus authentic tradition. But milonga's connection to the candombe and to Afro-Argentine culture more generally functioned as more than just a guarantee of authenticity. It also anchored and explicated the milonga's reassertion of rhythm. *Radiolandia* situated the new music in the context of an international boom in African-derived musics from Brazil, Cuba, and the United States.[45] The rise of samba, son, and swing in the 1930s represented a "liberation of the drum" throughout the Americas. Even if most orquestas típicas still generally shunned percussion instruments, the milonga's quicker tempo and more syncopated rhythm made it a logical choice for bands looking to compete in this new environment.[46] Like de Caro's symphonic tango, then, the milonga renaissance responded to international trends; it was another product of the transnational marketplace.

The association between Afro-Argentine culture and the milonga's accentuated rhythm reveals the racial logic implicit in the tango debates of the day. De Caro's notion that rhythm provided traditional authenticity while harmony and melody were the natural arenas for innovation and modernization relied on a racial hierarchy that placed primitive Africa below civilized Europe. Nevertheless, proponents of traditionalism were willing to embrace African cultural elements so long as those elements served the purpose of anchoring the tango to the Argentine past. This turn to Afro-Argentine culture was made easier by the fact that it could be depicted as "re-creating" a culture that had "disappeared." Even though, as "El Negro" Ferreyra's nickname demonstrates, some Argentines continued to be identified as the descendants of Africans, Argentina's self-image as a white nation was by now well established.[47]

Within the mass culture of the 1930s, Afro-Argentines figured frequently, most often as symbols of the nation's authentic past. Radio novelas set in the era of Juan Manuel de Rosas invariably featured black characters and ostensibly Afro-Argentine music. For example, the hugely popular *Bajo la Santa Federación* included several "black songs (*canciones de negros*)" including the "Song of the Candombero." A melodrama that explored the illicit love affair between the daughter of a wealthy Rosas loyalist and an opponent of the regime, the radio novela's source of comic relief was "el negro Domingo," the family's frequently drunk household servant. The scripts poked fun at Domingo's stereotypically black speech patterns—the *r*'s pronounced as *l*'s—as well as his unthinking loyalty to Rosas, but they also allowed him to demonstrate his skill as an improvising singer or payador.[48] Since the presence of Afro-Argentine servants, their alleged support for Rosas, and their over-representation among payadores were all well known, Domingo lent this historical reconstruction some much-needed realism. Similarly, tango films set in the seedy arrabales of the turn of the century used black extras in the same way they used old-fashioned clothing: as an easy way to provide a "period" feel. The dance scene that opens the film ¡Tango! features a black woman dancer in the foreground. In her performance of "La morocha" in *Puerta cerrada*, Libertad Lamarque is accompanied not only by a compadrito but also by a couple of Afro-Argentine children playing. In all of these representations, Afro-Argentines were guarantors of authenticity, firmly located in the past. In this context, the blackness of milonga's roots was reassuring.

The debates over rhythmic authenticity and melodic or harmonic innovation preoccupied intellectuals and tango connoisseurs, but in the second half of the 1930s developments in the marketplace seemed to settle the matter. The impressive popularity of Juan D'Arienzo, whose band became a fixture on Radio El Mundo, signaled the commercial triumph of rhythmic traditionalism. The so-called King of the Beat, D'Arienzo self-consciously recovered an earlier musical style associated with tango's Old Guard, one that emphasized a simple, rigid rhythm that made it extremely popular among dancers. D'Arienzo's band played a great many of the older classics of the tango and milonga canon and tended to inspire a happier, more upbeat mood. His success, no doubt, responded to many of the same factors responsible for the milonga renaissance of the same period, even if D'Arienzo did not share Piana's interest in melodic innovation. D'Arienzo gave fans a respite from the mood of sadness and cynicism that had dominated tango lyrics in the early 1930s. For male listeners, D'Arienzo's music also offered reassuring gender associations. Many fans interpreted his traditionalist style as a more virile, ruggedly masculine version of the tango. As one letter writer to *Sintonía* explained, the tango was more macho before New Guard "lyricism" had feminized it: "The tango needs to have that somewhat rustic innocence and that straightforward manliness which was the principal characteristic of the production of years gone by."⁴⁹ As I have argued, the film *Los tres berretines* (1933) drew a sharp distinction between the frivolous feminine consumerism involved in seeing foreign movies and the productive masculinity of domestic mass culture like tango and soccer. Just as the rise of a national cinema could help Argentine men undo their emasculation, D'Arienzo's fans saw his traditionalism as an antidote to the New Guard's sophisticated elaborations, which they heard as overly fancy or even pretty.

The D'Arienzo phenomenon inspired attacks from the partisans of an improved, modernized tango. Referring to D'Arienzo's popularity, one letter writer in *Sintonía* opined that "the current demands of our public represent a step backward of twenty years in the evolution of our tango." In the following issue, *Sintonía* printed a rejoinder from one of its contributors, who criticized innovators like Julio de Caro and Osvaldo Fresedo for having pursued "new forms of tango that may have elevated their musical value but have bastardized their meaning." By contrast, he argued, D'Arienzo was to be complimented for having returned the tango to its "primitive, simple, and genuine paths. He accentuated its rhythm, which had been getting lost among the very musical but not very 'tangoesque' harmonies of cornets and saxes, and he achieved the old novelty of playing a true tango."⁵⁰ This defender of traditionalism accepted the basic association between rhythm and primitive authenticity; he simply argued that the innovations of de Caro and Fresedo had lost that basic rhythmic pulse.

Faced with the success of D'Arienzo, the proponents of improvement reacted defensively. They argued that while tango's rhythm was to be preserved in order to guarantee the music's authenticity, it needed to be kept to reasonable limits. De Caro, whose symphonic tango, in the words of *Antena* "did not have the intense impact that in reality the effort deserved," now sought to inject more rhythm but without going too far: "The restless composer imposes on the band he leads the modality that the public in these times most appreciates, and that is rhythm. . . . He will cultivate rhythm without exaggerations, which are counterproductive, and he will maintain, since everything is compatible, the level he has achieved."⁵¹ *Antena* depicted de Caro's newfound respect for rhythm as a necessary concession to popular tastes but insisted that the orchestra leader would restrain rhythm, keeping it within acceptable limits. *Sintonía* was similarly impressed with de Caro's new effort to balance rhythm and melody, arguing that he had proven it was possible to improve tango without losing its popularity: "He has made the tango an elevated musical expression without thereby eroding the interest the tango has as dance music."[52] Likewise, Osvaldo Fresedo, who continued to pursue innovation through the use of harp and vibraphone and remained a proponent of the "melodic tango," declared that "to dance is not to allow oneself to be carried away by a rhythm. . . . A poet has said that the tango is danced with the soul. And he is right. For that reason, I try to achieve—with my band—that state of the soul in the dancer, preparing his spirit for the melody."[53] Fresedo may have been more willing than de Caro to resist popular trends, but the two men shared a commitment to moderating and containing tango rhythm. This defensive reaction to D'Arienzo's popularity reflected more than just the desperation of musicians worried about losing their audience. De Caro and Fresedo retained the enthusiastic support of the fan magazines because they promised to reconcile primitive authenticity with civilized modernity and commercial success with quality.

Efforts to remake the tango so that it might represent an improved national identity were never more than partially successful. Lunfardo words and plebeian references could be purged from lyrics, vocal techniques improved, tango symphonies composed, and folk traditions elevated with the use of sophisticated harmonies and jazz instrumentation. But all of these "improvements" threatened tango's authentic flavor. Even though improving the tango appealed to many as a way of attracting wealthier consumers, the market seemed to reward the most old-fashioned approaches. Moreover, the most commercially successful forms of tango were inspired not by European high culture or even by modern jazz instrumentation, but by the new emphasis on rhythm visible in the rising popularity of African-derived musical genres throughout the Americas. While this recourse to rhythm smacked of giving in to primitive urges, efforts to improve could easily veer into the terrain of the imitative. Despite the ongoing popularity of jazz in Argentina, many continued to worry that North American influence threatened tango's purity. The protagonist of Manuel Romero's nostalgic film *Los muchachos de antes no usaban gomina* (1937) walks out of a fancy upper-class Buenos Aires club, declaring with disgust, "Here even the bandoneones play in English." The clear implication is that slavish imitation of jazz was part of the elite's desperate attempt to disown the national culture of the masses. Despite all of their efforts, none of the many would-be improvers of tango succeeded in reconciling their visions of cultural elevation with tango's plebeian, even populist, authenticity.

LOOKING FOR THE NATION IN THE INTERIOR

Although many of those who sought to improve popular culture were conservatives, condescension toward the cultural practices of the masses crossed political lines. The Argentine Left had a long-standing interest in spreading high culture to the proletariat. The Socialist Party built libraries in which workers could read the classics of world literature, while turn-of-the-century anarchists militated against carnival celebrations, alcohol consumption, and soccer, and replaced popular tango lyrics with more edifying messages.[54] The leftist artistic and literary movements that emerged in Buenos Aires during the 1920s inherited this distrust of popular culture. The printmakers who formed the so-called Artistas del Pueblo studio produced social realist art aimed at eliciting sympathy for the poor and encouraging workers to fight to improve their lives. More famously, the Boedo group of writers practiced a similar form of social realism, influenced by Zola, Tolstoy, and Gorky as well as the Argentine poet Almafuerte. Rejecting the vanguardism of Borges and the other members of the so-called Florida group, Boedo writers like Elías Castelnuovo, Leónidas Barletta, and Alvaro Yunque wrote fiction aimed at raising the consciousness of the working class. For artists and writers like these, popular culture, particularly in its commercialized mass form, represented a dangerous distraction that lured workers away from revolutionary struggle. As the artist Guillermo Facio Hebequer told his friend Enrique Santos Discépolo, "The tango is the opiate of the masses."[55] There were intellectuals in the 1920s who were drawn to mass culture, such as Enrique González Tuñón, whose stories based on tango lyrics appeared regularly in the popular newspaper *Crítica*, but these writers tended to avoid overtly political messages. González Tuñón sympathized with the milonguitas who chose the life of the cabaret over the soul-killing world of poorly paid factory labor, but he offered no analysis of the causes of such suffering, nor did he suggest any possibility for change.[56] Leftist intellectuals of the 1920s either disdained mass cultural products as counterproductive escapism, or else they embraced mass culture but avoided politics.

In the 1930s, this began to change. In 1935 a group of young Radical Party members rejected the party leadership's decision to participate in electoral politics. These rebels formed the FORJA (Spanish for "forge," the acronym stood for the Radical-Oriented Force of Argentine Youth) to oppose any collaboration with the fraudulent conservative government. Inspired by the writings of Scalabrini Ortiz on the nefarious role of the British in the Argentine economy, FORJA intellectuals like Arturo Jauretche argued that the nation had been colonized by the forces of foreign capital in alliance with the Argentine oligarchy. They believed that liberal constitutionalism served only to entrench the power of this self-serving elite, and they hoped to replace it with a truly popular democracy modeled on Yrigoyenism and on nineteenth-century federalism.[57] Perhaps because of their commitment to liberate Argentines from "mental colonialism," some FORJA members recognized the enormous potential of the mass media. In particular, Homero Manzi, one of the group's founders, emerged as an influential tango lyricist and screenwriter as well as a prolific cultural critic during the 1930s.[58] While Manzi kept overt political messages out of his lyrics and scripts, his cultural production was shaped by a desire to create a new popular nationalism. Like nationalists on the right, Manzi tended to look to rural Argentina as the basis for an authentic Argentine national identity.

Manzi's lyrics and screenplays reflected his desire to produce "a culture of letters for men, not a culture for men of letters." This sentiment betrayed Manzi's populism, but also his desire to improve the quality of popular culture—to raise it to the level of a "culture of letters"—an effort that required a struggle against two forces: the degradation of commercialism and the almost irresistible allure of the foreign. In a series of articles he wrote for the magazine *Micrófono*, Manzi attacked the popular radio novela *Chispazos de Tradición* as superficial and inauthentic. Agreeing with many on the right, he argued that the prominence of low-quality programs of this type demonstrated the need for the state to take over the radio waves.[59] Manzi believed that the capitalist marketplace posed a general threat to Argentine culture, but as a member of FORJA, he was particularly worried about the pervasiveness of foreign cultural influence. In an article in *Antena* published in 1934, he criticized Gardel for making movies abroad, thereby competing directly with local filmmakers while producing inauthentic films set in a "French pampa." Worst of all was Gardel's weakness for Alfredo Le Pera, whose uninteresting plots lacked any "nationalist value."[60] Manzi's hostility to commercialism and to foreign influence shaped his own cultural production. It was apparent, for example, in his long-term collaboration with Sebastián Piana. One of their milongas, "Juan Manuel" (1934), tapped into the popular fad for reconstructions of the Rosas period by evoking the songs of praise sung by blacks loyal to the dictator. On the back of the published sheet music, Manzi and Piana defended the repetition of the phrase *carancuntango* in the chorus by citing Vicente Rossi's book on the Afro-Argentine origins of the tango. But if this amounted to a defense of the song's authenticity, Manzi and Piana also acknowledged that blacks of the Rosas era would have danced a candombe, not a milonga. The song, they said, was "a stylization"; they "looked to the past for an inspirational theme in order to fortify the *porteñismo* of our songs, which is so threatened by foreignism (*extranjerismo*)."[61]

Manzi's attempts to forge a popular national culture entailed a delicate balancing act. He attacked inauthenticity while embracing "stylization." He decried commercialism but defended the "popular." This ambivalence was particularly apparent in his attitudes toward Gardel, Argentina's biggest mass cultural star. In a radio script from 1938, Manzi described Gardel as the perfect synthesis of immigrant and criollo, city and country, and he rested this assessment on the wisdom of popular opinion: "The representative value of an artist is not conferred in the academies nor through the judgment of experts. It is conferred in the assembly of the people." Gardel's popularity, in other words, proved his quality. Yet, just like Julio de Caro, Manzi considered Gardel's repertoire a kind of "folklore" that might serve as "the foundation for the great Argentine music."[62] Elsewhere, Manzi described Gardel as less profound than a singer like Ignacio Corsini: "There are those like Gabino Ezeiza, Gardel, or Maizani, whose art expresses customs, the external . . . what a man wears on the outside . . . in order to hide his true, interior personality . . . But others, like Betinotti and Corsini, penetrating deeper within the human soul, have learned to say what gestures and pretension hide. To express the anxiety . . . of the man in love. The impression that oppresses the superstitious soul of the criollo who crosses the countryside at twilight. The need for companionship that attracts [men] to campfires. Nostalgia for the barrio, love of alleyways. The infinite sadness of memory."[63]

Manzi championed popular culture's capacity to express the deep, emotional truths of a nation, but he worried that an unregulated market would produce more superficial products.

Manzi's own lyrics pursued the goal of authentic nationalist expression by way of elegant poetry, bittersweet nostalgia, and a celebration of masculine toughness.[64] Like his nemesis, Alfredo Le Pera, Manzi tended to avoid lunfardo, preferring an often erudite vocabulary. Yet unlike Le Pera, Manzi rooted his lyrics in the local world, exploring characters and settings drawn directly from Argentine lore:

> Barrio de tango, luna y misterio,
> calles lejanas, ¡cómo estarán!
> . . .
> Barrio de tango, qué fue de aquella,
> Juana, la rubia, que tanto amé.
> ¡Sabrá que sufro, pensando en ella,
> desde la tarde que la dejé!
>
> *Barrio of tango, moon, and mystery,*
> *distant streets, how are they?*
> *. . .*
> *Barrio of tango, what happened to her,*
> *Juana, the blond, whom I loved so much*
> *Does she know that I suffer, thinking of her,*
> *ever since the afternoon I left her!*

In lyrics like this one ("Barrio de tango, 1942), Manzi interweaves tango's classic expression of regret over lost love with a nostalgic longing for the porteño neighborhoods of the past. Similarly, "Milonga del 900" describes the tough knife-wielding man of the suburbio as a relic of an earlier time: "I don't like paved streets / nor do I go for modern life (No me gusta el empedrao / ni me doy con lo moderno)." While the singer describes being abandoned by the woman he loved, he rejects the weepy emotional response of so many other tangos; instead he takes it like a man: "I loved her because I loved her / and so I forgive her. / There's nothing worse than spite / to live embittered." With this tough brand of masculinity, Manzi offered an alternative to the feminized emotionalism elaborated by other lyricists. When Juan D'Arienzo's success in the late 1930s inspired a revival of the older, more primitive tango, Manzi embraced the style precisely because he saw it as "happy" and "virile," in contrast to the "funereal" approach of contemporary tango.[65] In seeking to recover a virile masculinity, Manzi followed his FORJA colleague Arturo Jauretche, who had ridiculed emasculated tango singers for "crying over their unfortunate loves."[66] And like Jauretche, who embraced the tradition of criollismo, Manzi located a more robust masculinity in the rural, pre-modern past: the streets of his Buenos Aires suburbs are unpaved and smell of weeds ("Malena," 1942), and alongside the omnipresent bandoneón, one hears "toads rumbling in the lagoon" ("Barrio de tango").[67] His "country milongas" made this nostalgia for the countryside explicit, in effect relocating tango's stories of lost love and regret to rural settings:

> Llegabas por el sendero,
> delantal y trenzas sueltas.
> Brillaban tus ojos negros,
> claridad de luna llena.
>
> *You used to come by the path,*
> *apron and loose braids.*
> *Your black eyes shone,*
> *light of the full moon.*
>   ("Milonga triste," 1936)[68]

Nostalgia, virility, the countryside: these themes came together in Manzi's cinematic efforts. Manzi had written music for films throughout the 1930s, but his commitment to the cinema grew after 1940 and particularly after he forged a working relationship with a group of film actors and directors who had founded a new studio in 1941. Their company, Artistas Argentinas Asociadas (AAA), aimed to produce higher quality films than those churned out by the dominant Argentine studios. In this, the new company was not unique. That same year, Natalio Botana, the editor of *Crítica*, created the Baires film company in order to produce sophisticated films modeled on foreign cinema, which he hoped might reach an international audience.[69] But whereas Baires and others aimed to raise the quality of Argentine cinema in order to market it abroad, the AAA group envisioned high-caliber films for the Argentine masses. Moreover, they wanted a truly national cinema, one that embraced local themes instead of recycling the plots of foreign movies. According to the actor Francisco

Petrone, one of the founders of the AAA, the goal was "to make cinema that is truly ours."[70] The pursuit of a high-quality, nationalist, commercially viable mass culture perfectly aligned the AAA with the FORJA and with Homero Manzi's dream of "a culture of letters for men."[71]

As a screenwriter for AAA, Manzi's unlikely partner was Ulyses Petit de Murat, a former film critic whose denunciations of the poor quality of domestic cinema bore little trace of the popular nationalism of the FORJA. Yet it was Manzi who suggested that the two write a screenplay based on the modernist poet Leopoldo Lugones's *La guerra gaucha*, a notoriously highbrow collection of twenty-two stories about the battles fought in the northwestern province of Salta during Argentina's war for independence. During the 1920s, Lugones embraced Mussolini's Fascism and became one of the key intellectual architects of Argentina's right-wing, antidemocratic nationalism. But *La guerra gaucha*, written in 1905, belonged to an earlier phase in Lugones's political trajectory, when the poet was a Socialist looking to ground Argentine national identity in the heroic revolutionary struggle for independence from Spain. In order to construct this national myth, Lugones needed to revise long-standing liberal ideas about rural Argentina, and particularly about the figure of the gaucho. Whereas liberals had long imagined violent gaucho outlaws as the major obstacle to nation formation, Lugones saw the independence war as a crucible that transformed the gauchos into an army capable of forging the nation. Lugones did not celebrate the power and agency of the masses. On the contrary, as Juan Pablo Dabove has argued, the hero in this account is the caudillo Martín Miguel de Güemes, the embodiment of Argentine patriotism, who orients rural violence toward the goal of independence and thereby gives it meaning.[72] In Güemes and his army, Lugones saw a deeply hierarchical, patriarchal society that he hoped might form a model for contemporary Argentina.[73] Indeed, Lugones's text reduces the rural population to an anonymous mass; each story features different characters, and many of them are not even named. For Petit de Murat, *La guerra gaucha* offered a means to inspire patriotism and to resist the impact of foreign influences on Argentine cinema.[74] Manzi shared these nationalist aspirations, but he also hoped to democratize and popularize Lugones's patriotic story. Toward that end, he resisted Petit de Murat's efforts to include long passages from the original text, arguing that nobody would understand them.[75]

The film version of *La guerra gaucha* (Demare, 1942), by some accounts the most successful Argentine movie ever, effectively inverted Lugones's elitism.[76] Instead of a paean to the heroic leader, the film offers a group of noble characters who demonstrate self-sacrifice, integrity, and generosity in the patriotic struggle against Spanish oppression: the sexton who passes messages to the patriot army by ringing the church bell in code, the brave captains who lead the struggle in the face of insurmountable odds, the beautiful woman whose love for a captured Spanish lieutenant converts him to the patriotic cause. By weaving one unified narrative out of just a handful of the many stories in Lugones's text, Manzi and Petit de Murat turned anonymous figures into fully developed characters. Similarly, by replacing the poet's difficult modernist prose with a cinematic style that encouraged audience identification, the filmmakers highlighted the active contribution of the poor to the creation of the Argentine nation. The film's final words describe the independence war as a collective struggle: "Like this they lived, like this they died, the nameless, those who fought the gaucho war." Yet in a sense, the film goes further by replacing the "nameless" with vibrant popular heroes. Nevertheless, the screenwriters' reliance on Lugones's text does at least partly undermine the film's democratic message. In particular, the arrival of Güemes to rescue the gaucho army at the end of the movie implies unmistakably that the people need a powerful leader in order to be effective. This verticalism, so central to Lugones's book, stands in tension with the film's otherwise radically democratic vision.

Apart from its reliance on Lugones, *La guerra gaucha* drew on a long tradition of mass cultural representations of gauchos. As we have seen, the criollo circus and criollista literature of the turn of the century packaged the culture of the Pampas for consumption by the urban masses. During the 1910s, the folk music recordings of Gardel and Corsini and the silent film *Nobleza gaucha* brought criollismo to the new media. In the 1930s, *Chispazos de Tradición* ushered in a series of radio plays set in the Pampas, while Gardel's star turn as a gaucho in *Las luces de Buenos Aires* in 1931 inspired domestic filmmakers. Over the next several years, Argentine studios released dozens of criollista films. These movies, both comic and tragic, partake heavily in the conventions of melodrama: the rural poor are represented as noble, generous, and innocent victims, while the villains are either unsavory urban types or rich landowners. In *Los caranchos de la Florida* (de Zavalía, 1938), to cite just one example, the son of a wealthy cattle rancher returns home after completing his education in

Buenos Aires and falls in love with the beautiful daughter of a poor family in town. The hypocritical landowner, who wants the girl for himself, stokes his son's class prejudice in order to convince him that "these people" are beneath him. The film portrays the rural poor in a positive light, but it foregrounds conflict within the family rather than between the classes.[77]

A more incisive, critical approach to the countryside began to appear in the work of the director Mario Soffici, particularly in a series of "social folkloric" films he made between 1937 and 1942. A student of José Agustín Ferreyra, Soffici had directed a handful of forgettable genre films before he began to apply his teacher's social-realist style to stories set in the countryside. Soffici emulated Ferreyra's empathy for the poor as well as his close attention to the details of everyday life, but these films broke new ground by focusing directly on economic exploitation.[78] *Kilómetro 111* (1938) tells the story of a farming community reduced to poverty by wealthy landowners and the British-owned railroad company. While the film embraces the melodramatic opposition between poor and rich, the conflicts it explores are economic, not romantic: a family cannot afford their son's medical treatment because of the low prices the rich landowners pay for their grain. Moreover, unlike typical melodramas, Soffici's film grants the community significant agency. Farmers protest their mistreatment and pool their resources in order to help out one of their own. As in the comedies of Luis Sandrini, *Kilómetro 111* celebrates above all the solidarity and communal spirit of the poor. Considerably less sanguine is *Prisioneros de la tierra* (1939), Soffici's most successful film and, alongside *La guerra gaucha*, one of the acknowledged masterpieces of Argentine cinema. Here, Soffici deepens his critique of economic exploitation by examining the plight of *yerba mate* workers in the remote Misiones region. As Elina Tranchini argues, the film's hero, Podeley, combines a vision of the rural worker as honest and hardworking with an older celebration of masculine courage and violence, drawn from the criollista stories of gaucho rebels like Juan Moreira.[79] When Podeley's girlfriend is murdered by her alcoholic father in a fit of delirium tremens, he takes revenge by murdering the German foreman whose vicious brutality has condemned the workers to a life of despair.

Soffici's films were among the first commercially successful mass cultural works to offer a realistic, explicit depiction of inequality in Argentina. Unlike so many melodramatic films and tango songs, they clearly identified exploitation as the cause of the suffering of the poor. Yet this message was not what earned the films such high praise from critics. Instead, the films were celebrated for having injected authenticity into the domestic cinema. *Sintonía*, for example, praised Soffici's *Viento norte* (1937), *Prisioneros de la tierra*, and *El viejo doctor* (1939), while attacking the bulk of the Argentine film industry for imitating Hollywood: "In order to make a good native film, one must avoid using the false scenery overused on Yankee sets, focusing simply and directly on the social panoramas and typical details of the country. . . . The local cinema faces a difficult challenge. That of competing with the foreign industry and contributing something more than luxurious interiors and the advantages of language. For that we need directors blessed with the broadest vision, who in harmony with skillful camera work and adequate lighting, identify themselves with the goal of creating and sustaining a genuine climate of the country."[80] What *Sintonía* appreciated in Soffici was neither his positive depiction of the poor—a characteristic of virtually all Argentine movies in this period—nor his critique of exploitation, but rather his ability to combine modern filmmaking technique with an authentic "feel" for the nation. Soffici's focus on rural themes made his films authentic, helping him appeal to his audience's nationalism, rather than their consumerist envy of "luxurious interiors."

Nothing like Soffici's critique of economic exploitation appeared in films set in Buenos Aires. The closest the Argentine cinema got to exploring the plight of the urban proletariat was *Chingolo*, the Sandrini comedy about a hobo who resists being corrupted by a greedy industrialist. But *Chingolo* never enters the factory walls or humanizes the suffering of workers. In this era of rapid industrialization, Soffici's depiction of the brutality of rural labor relations reads less as an indictment of contemporary Argentine society than as an authentic representation of the essence of the nation. *El Mundo*'s film reviewer, Calki, praised *Kilómetro 111* as a "truly national" film that exhibits "the thematic orientation that our cinema must take if it wants to come to have its own spirit."[81] Soffici adapted stylistic elements from North American filmmakers like John Ford, but his depiction of rural Argentina also drew on the local, popular cultural tradition of criollismo.[82] This tradition lent the protagonists of his films a certain familiarity, even as it helped locate his stories in a remote time and place. Like *La guerra gaucha*, Soffici's social-folkloric films provided urban audiences with national prototypes drawn from a distant Argentina. His films echoed the nostalgia of Homero Manzi's milonga lyrics by dramatizing the struggles of pre-industrial rural people confronting the damaging impact of modernization.

In the same way that Argentina's urban films featured the tango, Soffici used folk music to lend authenticity to his depiction of the Argentine interior. As a result, these films contributed to a veritable folk revival that began to transform the Argentine popular music scene in the late 1930s. In subsequent years, folk music would attain massive popularity and achieve a centrality in Argentine culture that it retained for decades. As Oscar Chamosa has shown, the rising popularity of folk music as well as its status as a symbol of the nation was the result of a multifaceted "folklore movement." Inspired by European folklorists and by early nationalist writers like Ricardo Rojas, academic folklorists began to study the cultures of Argentina's northern provinces in the early decades of the twentieth century. These efforts were sponsored by diverse groups including Argentine educators, who hoped that an appreciation for the folk cultures of the interior would help assimilate the descendants of immigrants, as well as Tucumán sugar mill owners who believed that folklore research would uncover the Spanish roots of local culture and thereby prove the whiteness of Tucumán sugar workers. Beginning in the 1920s, the efforts of folklorists and educators were reinforced by those of mass cultural entrepreneurs, who recognized the potential of a commercialized folk music.[83]

The success of the criollo circus, criollista pulp fiction, and folk singers like Gardel and Corsini had demonstrated that porteño audiences were attracted to rural culture. These mass cultural commodities repackaged the popular culture of the Pampas region surrounding the capital, but there were also efforts to introduce folk music from the more remote northern provinces. In 1921, Andrés Chazarreta, a composer, musician, and folk song collector from Santiago del Estero, brought his musical troupe to Buenos Aires for a series of performances at the Politeama Theater.[84] Chazarreta packaged the music to appeal to a nationalist vision of the countryside: his musicians and dancers performed on a set made to look like a traditional patio in Santiago del Estero, complete with an elderly Santiagueño couple who provided local color by passing a *mate* throughout the performance. This stagecraft turned professional performers into folk artists, prized less for their creativity or originality than for their authenticity. *Crítica* raved: "Buenos Aires has never seen anything so completely criollo, so traditionally ours."⁸⁵ Yet despite many such positive reviews, the commercial appeal of folk music was limited, and the genre achieved only token representation on the early radio. Tango eclipsed folk music in the 1920s because its modern instrumentation and urban associations allowed it to compete more effectively with jazz.

This commercial calculus began to shift in the deeply nationalist atmosphere of the 1930s. The vogue for gaucho radio programs that began with *Chispazos de Tradición* sparked a revival of interest in rural folk music. The Italian-born composer Félix Scolatti Almeyda, who had composed and arranged folk music for the Gardel-Razzano duo, wrote the music for *Chispazos* as well as for several of the historical radio plays of Héctor Blomberg and Carlos Viale Paz. By 1933 Scolatti Almeyda's "folk orchestra" performed regularly in concert and on the radio.⁸⁶ Meanwhile, the mid-1930s saw the emergence of a new type of radio program built around a narrator who recited criollista verse, with frequent breaks for guitar-based folk music. Perhaps the biggest star to emerge from this type of program was the actor Fernando Ochoa, whose performance on Radio Belgrano was so convincing that one impassioned fan described him as "the greatest gaucho since the times of Juan Moreira!"⁸⁷ Ochoa created several comic characters, including Don Bildigernio, an ancient gaucho prone to confusion, but he was most celebrated for his recitals of gauchesque poetry and his storytelling. In 1941 Radio El Mundo and its national network featured Ochoa's hit program every Tuesday and Thursday evening in the prime time slot of 8:30. Sponsored by the Bayer company's pain medicine Cafiaspirina, the program featured scripts by Homero Manzi. Ochoa, like Manzi and Soffici, earned critical acclaim for contributing to a "revalorization" of Argentina's rural culture by fighting "against indifference and xenophilia, succeeding in demonstrating that in the heart of the country there is a clear accent, a diaphanous melody, equal or superior to that which comes from distant lands overseas."⁸⁸

Such nationalist sentiments produced a steady stream of complaints about the alleged under-representation of folk music on Argentine radio. For example, *Sintonía*'s folk music columnist, Pancho Lucero, regularly bemoaned the quantity and quality of folk programming on the radio, arguing that the few existing programs tended to promote stereotypical styles that were "made in Buenos Aires."⁸⁹ In Lucero's interview with Vice President Ramón Castillo in 1938, both men agreed that radio stations should actively promote authentic Argentine folk music for nationalist ends. As Lucero put it, folk music represented "the logical and efficient means of identifying our people with the most subtle and diverse forms of their sensibility."[90] For many commentators, the music of the rural interior offered a more authentic representation of Argentine national identity than did the tango. Concerned that folk music was "in decline," *Antena* railed against what it saw as the favorable treatment received by urban musicians: "It has been thought that the only thing we need to worry about as far as Argentine music is concerned is the tango. We, and like us a large sector of the public, enjoy the tango and we concede to it the attention and importance that it truly deserves. But the tango, say what you will, does not define in a clear way our true spirit, but rather responds to a local rationale and can in no way be accepted as a faithful translation of the Argentine modality."[91] *Antena*, like many other commentators, celebrated rural musical styles not as products of specific provinces or regions, but as symbols of a national spirit that was threatened by urbanization and foreign influence. Yet such observers seemed to exaggerate the sorry state of folk music on the radio. In fact, folk singers were a staple on the Argentine radio throughout the 1930s, even if they failed to dislodge tango and jazz from their position of prominence. A typical daily radio listing from 1933 included four female folk singers, or *estilistas*, a number that had grown to nine by 1937. By this time, several of these singers had become stars, including Martha de los Ríos, Virginia Vera, and Patrocinio Díaz, a Santiagueña who had debuted in Andrés Chazarreta's troupe. Moreover, the popularity of Ochoa's program and others like it meant that folk music was well represented around the dial. In 1939 one enthusiastic folk music fan listed sixteen duos, bands, and soloists among his favorite radio performers.[92] Radio stations claimed to offer the best of both urban and rural music, and station owners like Jaime Yankelevich bragged of their talent-hunting trips to the northern provinces.[93]

Several factors contributed to the growing presence of folk music on the radio. The decline of agriculture and the intensification of import substitution industrialization during the 1930s provoked significant internal migration, reshaping the porteño radio audience. Between 1937 and 1943, an average of seventy thousand Argentines migrated to greater Buenos Aires each year.[94] Although this figure would be eclipsed by the massive internal migration of the 1940s, it still represented a significant number of listeners who may have hoped to find the music of their native regions on the radio. Likewise, the proliferation of radio networks meant that stations based in Buenos Aires were increasingly broadcasting their programs across the country, and folk music may have offered a means of catering to audiences in the interior. But more important than these changes to the composition of the radio audience was the growing nationalist mood. Folk musicians appeared side by side with tango stars in the fan magazines, and the genres overlapped in performers' repertoires, suggesting that many of the same people who embraced Manzi's milongas and D'Arienzo's traditionalist tangos also enjoyed folk music. These musical trends, as well as films like *La guerra gaucha* and *Prisioneros de la tierra*, reveal the growing commercial appeal of Argentina's rural cultures for the country's urban moviegoers and radio listeners.

As part of the larger, mass cultural turn to the countryside, the folk programs on Argentine radio offered listeners a nostalgic view of their nation's pre-modern past. Proponents explicitly described the preservation of folk music as a bulwark against modernity, "the civilization that advances, represented by the locomotive, the automobile and the radio, destroying the past."[95] Folk music was not immune to the same demands for improvement and innovation that were directed at tango; critics insisted on the need for composers and lyricists in the genre to expand and improve the repertoire.[96] Yet folk musicians were most often celebrated for their authenticity. One of the leading folk acts of the late 1930s and early 1940s was the Tropilla de Huachi-Pampa, a group from the Andean province of San Juan. The group was led by a former journalist and political activist named Eusebio Dojorti, who wrote and performed under the far more criollo-sounding pseudonym Buenaventura Luna.[97] Luna was a poet, songwriter, and storyteller who, as the program's narrator, played much the same role as Fernando Ochoa did on his shows. Magazine reports on the Tropilla inevitably emphasized the group's authentic origins, drawing attention, for example, to the way they preserved their rural customs even as their radio careers required them to live in Buenos Aires.[98] One magazine cover featured a photograph of Luna in the San Juan mountains, dressed in a traditional poncho and tenderly holding a young vicuña.[99] A typical report celebrated the Tropilla for performing the crucial service of assimilating immigrants by disseminating "authentic nationalism" on the radio.[100]

Buenaventura Luna's poetry avoided the critique of exploitation that characterized the films of Mario Soffici as well as the songs of Héctor Chavero, the Communist activist from Tucumán who, as Atahualpa Yupanqui, would become one of the biggest stars in Argentine folk music in the 1950s and 1960s. Nevertheless, Luna's radio program lovingly depicted the world of the simple gauchos, shepherds, and muleteers of the Argentine northwest. According to magazine reports, the musicians in his group had all worked in these humble professions back in San Juan; their authenticity was partly a matter of class. Like *La guerra gaucha*, Luna's poems frequently celebrated the heroic gauchos who fought for Argentine independence with Güemes or San Martín. But they also described the daily suffering and hardship of the rural poor. In the words of one fan, folk groups like the Tropilla de Huachi-Pampa played music "in which each note is the expression of a thousand sacrifices."[101]

Like Homero Manzi, Luna associated rural Argentina with manliness. His poetry and lyrics depicted a world of masculine self-sufficiency, in which wandering muleteers traveled the countryside far from their girlfriends. The all-male lineup of the group, as well as its name—*tropilla* is the gaucho term for a team of horses—reinforced this image of masculinity, as did the name of Luna's most popular Radio El Mundo program: "The Muleteers' Campfire." In many of Luna's songs, gauchos and muleteers gathered around a fire to pass the *mate* or wine, to play guitar and to sing, and to offer male companionship and a spirit of solidarity:

> Quise armar un fogón allá en la sierra
> un fogón que llamara a los andantes
> de todos los caminos y las razas,
> a juntarse al calor de nuestras brasas
> a conversar de cosas trashumantes.
>
> *I wanted to light a campfire up in the mountains*
> *a fire that would call all the wanderers*
> *of all the trails and races,*
> *to come together before the heat of our coals*
> *to talk of migratory things.*[102]

The emphasis on simplicity and genuineness in Luna's lyrics was typical of folk music, which was often represented as an antidote to pretension and materialism. In one interesting layout, the magazine *Antena* featured the folksinger Virginia Vera alongside the tango bandleader Julio de Caro (see

10 Virginia Vera and Julio de Caro, *Antena*, October 28, 1938.

figure 10). While Vera appeared in plain and modest dress, de Caro's slicked-back hair, bow tie, cuff links, ring, and cigarette signaled urban fanciness. In the text that accompanied her photo, Vera described herself as a simple country girl: "Barbecued meat is one of my greatest weaknesses and I have no trouble admitting it, even though to some people my taste might seem vulgar. . . . Perhaps I exaggerate a little, but between a shop window filled with jewels and a well-provisioned rotisserie, I would stay longer in front of the latter. Those criollos who put sauces on their meat make me laugh, as if our ancestors did that. Salt and . . . thank you. That was the only condiment they used. It is the same with *mate* and crackers. I take the former bitter and I do not mind if the latter are a bit hard. To one who likes the country like I do, comforts and refinements are pure luxury."[103] Through the figures of Vera and de Caro, the magazine positioned folk and New Guard tango along an axis of oppositions: rural-urban; traditional-modern; genuine-materialist. By the late

1930s de Caro's sophisticated, modern version of tango stood in contrast to D'Arienzo's rhythmic traditionalism, and this contrast, as we have seen, was often figured in gendered terms. Vera, for her part, subverted gender expectations by choosing meat over jewels and thereby repudiating the feminine consumerism linked to the foppish de Caro. Her disavowal of any interest in jewelry expressed the same gendered prohibition against luxurious display that kept the tango star Azucena Maizani from wearing rings. Folk performers like Luna and Vera offered a wholesome, rural authenticity stripped of any trace of cosmopolitanism or feminine materialism.

From the milongas of Homero Manzi to the films of Mario Soffici and the works of folk artists like Buenaventura Luna, mass cultural representations of rural Argentina offered a national essence uncorrupted by either foreign influence or commercialism and defined in opposition to the pretentious sophistication and materialistic social climbing of the city. This revalorization of rural culture was, in a sense, a riposte to the efforts of Argentina's cultural modernizers. De Caro treated tango as a folk tradition that could provide the basis for a modernized Argentine music, yet his symphonic tango struck many as foreign and overly fancy. But the new vogue for rural traditionalism had its own contradictions. As Virginia Vera's disdain for jewelry suggests, the celebration of rural simplicity posed an implicit criticism of the widespread desire for upward mobility and material comforts. Perhaps more important, by elevating the nation's rural past, these new mass cultural products seemed to get no closer to reconciling Argentine authenticity with modernity.

LA RUBIA DEL CAMINO AND THE FAILURE OF NATIONAL MYTH-MAKING

Both the effort to elevate tango music and the turn toward rural roots constituted attempts to define Argentina's national identity. Yet these efforts tended to reinscribe divisions and therefore to undermine national unity. Stripping the tango of lunfardo lyrics or dressing it up with more sophisticated orchestration might make it a more palatable symbol of the nation, but it also threatened to rob the music of its authenticity by distancing it from its plebeian roots. Similarly, embracing the simple, rustic masculinity of traditional rural folk provided a means to construct a purified national identity, but it also implied a rejection of urban modernity. The contradictions that undermined these attempts at mass-cultural nation building are particularly apparent in the comic films of Manuel Romero, the most prolific and commercially successful Argentine director and screenwriter of the 1930s.[104] Romero had been a tango lyricist as well as a successful director of the musical variety shows known as the *teatro de revistas* before co-writing the screenplay for Gardel's breakout hit *Las luces de Buenos Aires*. Once the Argentine sound film industry took off, he became the principal director for Lumiton studios, where he churned out dozens of lighthearted, formulaic comedies, including some of Luis Sandrini's and Niní Marshall's biggest hits. In contrast to a committed intellectual like Homero Manzi, Romero had purely commercial goals. Instead of seeking to create a "culture of letters for men," he merely aimed to fill the nation's movie theaters. Yet his films were arguably more subversive than anything Manzi ever produced.

Romero's knack for appealing to popular tastes aroused the concern of those who sought to elevate and improve the Argentine cinema. In fact, his films often provoked exasperation among critics, who were dismayed by the immense popularity of what they considered a lowbrow cinematic style. In a review of the film *Gente bien* (1939), *La Razón*'s critic could not hide his condescension as he congratulated Romero for attracting the masses to Argentine cinema: "A few days ago, we referred to Mr. Romero's position in our cinema in order to recognize his contribution to our film industry, as an interpreter of the easy tastes of the masses who attend native films. . . . Although we do not believe that Mr. Romero has attempted anything other than appealing directly to his public, with notes of easy melodrama, in order to tilt the balance in favor of the humble, he has aggressively recharged the depiction of our social circles."[105] That Romero should have provoked such ambivalence among critics anxious to celebrate the progress achieved by the national film industry is, at first blush, paradoxical. As Claudio España has demonstrated, Romero's films typically used happy endings to advance a comforting message of class reconciliation.[106] Yet, as *La Razón*'s reviewer made clear, the problem with Romero had to do with his use of melodrama: not only did the director pander to the "easy tastes" of the masses, but he also did so with melodramatic plot elements that championed the poor and denigrated the rich.

Romero's comedies depict the working poor as a dignified, respectable community held together by strong bonds of solidarity and defined in contrast to the rich. Typically, these films describe this contrast as a question of national identity. That is, the opposition between rich and poor is articulated as an opposition between foreign and national. Romero's movies construct a particular version of the Argentine nation, one that emphasizes conventional morality and conservative values like hard work but also contains a deeply populist message, insofar as it is premised on the exclusion of the rich. The protagonist of *Gente bien* is Elvira, yet another poor girl who is seduced, impregnated, and abandoned by a selfish aristocrat. She is rescued by a group of musicians who give her a home, and since society's prejudice against single mothers prevents her from finding work, they even hire her as a singer. When a judge awards Elvira's child to the wealthy father, the musicians devise a complex scheme that succeeds in restoring the child to Elvira and incorporating her definitively into their community. *Gente bien* offers a stark contrast between the evil rich and the noble poor and locates national authenticity on the poor side of the divide: the musicians prefer to play tangos, but "these days" the wealthy revelers they play for would rather do "gringo" dances like the fox trot. In Romero's films, the poor are not only exemplars of dignity and moral virtue but also the true bearers of Argentine national identity.

In this context, films that tell interclass love stories are particularly interesting. Like the nineteenth-century "foundational fictions" analyzed by Doris Sommer, these films can be read as national romances, efforts to overcome society's divisions by forging a new national family.[107] Many of Romero's comedies include the old melodramatic plot line of the poor girl in love with a wealthy man. But with the release of *La rubia del camino* in 1938, Romero inaugurated a very successful series of films that reversed the typical gender roles of the interclass romance. *La rubia del camino* was followed by *Caprichosa y millonaria* (Discépolo, 1940), *Isabelita* (Romero, 1940), and *Elvira Fernández, vendedora de tienda* (Romero, 1942). Starring Paulina Singerman as a rich young woman who falls in love with a humble working-class man, these films invariably end happily with love and marriage conquering class prejudice (see figure 11). *La rubia del camino* was clearly modeled on Frank Capra's Oscar winner of four years earlier, *It Happened One Night* (1934).[108] In both films, a pampered, rich girl chafes under her father's attempt to control her choice of spouse. She runs away from the family's vacation spot, meets a man of distinctly lower social standing, and travels with him to the big city. They experience a series of

11 Paulina Singerman (right) as a spoiled rich girl in *Caprichosa y millonaria*. Courtesy of Museo del Cine Pablo Ducrós Hicken.

adventures and eventually fall in love. Upon arrival in the city, their union is threatened, but in the end, love overcomes all obstacles. Despite these similarities, however, Romero's film is not merely a remake with a little local color. On the contrary, *La rubia del camino* breaks with its Hollywood precursor in several significant ways. As interclass romances, both films seek to reconcile rich and poor. Yet for Romero, working within well-established Argentine cultural conventions, the elite woman and working-class man reflect a series of binary oppositions that are either muted or absent altogether in Capra's film. In this vision, the rich are also foreign, modern, and urban, while the poor are national, traditional, and rural. These oppositions effectively widen the gulf that separates rich and poor, undermining the film's capacity to generate a unifying national myth.

It Happened One Night, one of the earliest "screwball comedies," promotes the ideal of a classless society. As Kristine Karnick and Henry Jenkins have argued, screwball comedies "explicitly posit work and the work ethic as preferable to a class-based system of inherited wealth, power and status."[109] In these films, the fantasy of interclass romance suggests that class divisions can be overcome, so long as both rich and poor are willing to sacrifice: the rich protagonist must give up her life of privilege in order to struggle alongside the working-class hero, while the working-class character must relinquish his single-minded pursuit of career advancement in order to pursue happiness. In this way, the screwball films exemplified a larger tendency of the Hollywood cinema of these years. The historian Lary May has argued that all the major film genres of the 1930s celebrated an "ethos of interpenetrating opposites." Film protagonists in this era combined the integrity of the heroic citizen with the traits of previously marginal characters like the fallen woman, the comic, and the gangster. These movies generated a vocabulary with which Americans could imagine a more inclusive and pluralistic nation.[110] At the end of *It Happened One Night*, the heiress Ellie Andrews (Claudette Colbert) runs out on her lavish wedding to a wealthy playboy in order to begin a far less luxurious life with the newspaperman Peter Warne (Clark Gable). Peter's initial interest in Ellie is purely opportunistic. Having recently lost his job, the wisecracking reporter offers to help her get to New York in exchange for an exclusive. In the end, though, he also makes a sacrifice; he gives up the scoop in order to get the girl. Successful couple formation requires that both partners learn from each other in order to form a "union of complementary opposites" that models successful national unification.[111]

By contrast, *La rubia del camino*, with its roots in Argentine popular melodrama, presupposes an unbridgeable, moral chasm between rich and poor. Romero's film begins with Singerman's character, Betty, being rude to her servants, playing golf, and snobbishly insulting "the mob (*la chusma*)." Later, when her grandfather instructs her that life is about struggle, she protests: "But I am rich! I don't have any reason to work, to struggle or to suffer." Capra's film pokes fun at Ellie for her sense of entitlement, but it stops short of depicting her as a snob. The contrast between the male protagonists of the two films is even more stark. In Romero's film, Betty encounters not a self-interested reporter, but a simple truck driver, Julián, whose offer to help is purely altruistic, even if a bit paternalist: he is worried about the harm that may befall a woman traveling alone to Buenos Aires. Romero's character is both more clearly working-class and more class-conscious; while Peter pokes fun at Ellie for being spoiled and sheltered, Julián goes further, explicitly denouncing the rich in several scenes. In both films, the rich girl initially despises the male lead, but in Ellie's case, this disdain is at least partly justified by Peter's boorishness. Betty, by contrast, ridicules Julián for his cheap cigarettes and his pedestrian taste in music. Not only is the economic and cultural chasm that separates Betty and Julián deeper, but so is the disparity between their moral characters. Whereas neither Peter nor Ellie begins the film as a paragon of virtue, *La rubia del camino* replicates the depiction of class difference typical of Argentine melodrama: in Betty and Julián, we have, yet again, the hateful rich and the noble poor.[112]

La rubia del camino relates class differences much more explicitly to the question of national identity. In *It Happened One Night*, Peter teaches Ellie a series of comic lessons about popular culture: how to properly dunk a doughnut, how to give a piggyback ride, how to hitchhike. In adapting this basic plot element, Romero transforms it. Instead of doughnut dunking, Julián teaches Betty how to make *mate*, the popular tea. Unlike doughnuts, *mate* is an instantly legible symbol of national identity, associated with Argentina's rural past and with the gaucho. A lesson in *mate* preparation is a lesson in Argentinidad. Peter's mock seriousness about the art of dunking is meant to poke fun at Ellie for being out of touch with the culture of ordinary people, and she understands that she is being teased. By contrast, Julián's analysis of *mate* symbolism—the bitter tea and the sweet sugar represent the two sides of life—is a sincere lesson in folk wisdom; there is no joke to get. The question of Argentine national identity appears in the film in other ways as well. Betty is not simply rich; as both her name and her blond hair suggest, she is also associated with foreignness. She explains her ignorance about *mate* by noting that she was educated in Europe. Julián, by contrast, is unimpeachably Argentine; he rejects her foreign nickname and insists on calling her by her real name, Isabel, instead.

Julián's worthiness as an embodiment of Argentine national identity is reinforced by his roots in a traditional rural world. Reproducing the country versus city binarism that had played such a central role in domestic cinema since *Nobleza gaucha*, *La rubia del camino* associates Buenos Aires with a modernizing elite caught up in slavish imitation of Europe. Betty, at home in the big city and a fish out of water in the country, is repeatedly described as a "frivolous and modern girl." By contrast, the rural interior of the country, represented by Julián, is the locus of Argentine tradition. In this sense, the film fits easily within the larger mass cultural turn to the countryside. Within this logic, class and geography are more important credentials for membership in the nation than even ethnicity. On their trip through the countryside, the couple stops in on some old friends of Julián, including an Italian immigrant and his family. Their rural poverty places them comfortably within the film's imagined community, despite their immigrant status.

Given that Betty begins *La rubia del camino* as the embodiment of a despicable elite, the film's happy resolution requires her to experience a profound transformation. She must unlearn her materialism and her class prejudice, adopt the values of solidarity and generosity associated with the poor, and in fact, embrace her Argentine identity. In other words, she must follow Virginia Vera by choosing barbecued meat over precious jewels. Her transformation from "frivolous and modern girl" to noble Argentine woman and worthy spouse for Julián is heavily gendered. In *It Happened One Night*, Ellie's femininity is both maternal and sexual: she is moved by the sight of an impoverished child, and she successfully hitches a ride by revealing her legs to passing motorists. *La rubia del camino* is quite tame by comparison,[113] and it is Betty's maternal instinct alone that is the key to her transformation. When the couple arrives at the home of Julián's Italian friends, the woman is about to give birth without the benefit of medical attention. The previously useless and selfish Betty rises to the occasion, overseeing the delivery and teaching the men the proper way to wrap a baby. Not only does this scene force Julián to revise his view of Betty, it actually initiates her transformation. In the very next scene, she has suddenly lost her condescending attitude toward the popular music on the radio. When they get a flat tire, she offers to help change it, and when Julián is hungry, she offers him *salamines y pan*, just the sort of working-class meal she had earlier disdained. The emergence of Betty's femininity, her nurturing, maternal instinct, allows her to overcome her shallow arrogance and embrace the music and food of the Argentine masses; gender trumps class, enabling Betty to join the national community. Betty's sudden transformation into a mother figure betrays the film's debt to the moral code of melodrama, within which a more assertive, sexual femininity is transgressive and invariably punished. The nature of her transformation reveals what exactly is wrong with people like Betty: their wealth has corrupted them, perverting their essential (gendered) humanity. In an inversion of Shaw's *Pygmalion*, Romero posits that the rich woman can only discover her true self when she sheds the cultural baggage of wealth under the tutelage of a poor man.

Romero breaks most decisively from Capra's model in the final portion of the film. In *It Happened One Night*, a simple misunderstanding threatens to keep Peter and Ellie apart, but once the confusion is sorted out, nothing stands in the way of their marriage. In *La rubia del camino*, by contrast, class difference remains a powerful obstacle to the formation of the couple. Upon their arrival in Buenos Aires, Betty quickly embarks on an effort to integrate Julián into the materialist and superficial world of Buenos Aires high society, buying him fancy clothes and a manicure. Now it is Julián who is a fish out of water, and he recoils at being treated like a doll. Finally, Julián storms out of town when he suspects Betty of having reunited with her former fiancé. By resisting Betty's efforts to dress him up, Julián retains both his rustic masculinity and his national authenticity. The happy ending is in doubt until Julián drives up to his Italian friends' house and out walks Betty, holding the baby. At this point, hundreds of miles from Buenos Aires and with Betty's maternal instinct restored, the couple's union is definitive. Betty makes interclass romance possible by choosing the authentic Argentine world of the rural poor over the Europeanized, wealthy society of Buenos Aires.

Like those attempts to update the tango without threatening its authenticity, *La rubia del camino* betrays a striking ambivalence about modernity. It is the independence of the "modern girl" that drives the film's plot and enables Betty's transformation. Only by rebelling against her father's authority is she able to escape the morally depraved world of the rich and cross the class line. Romero, in fact, distinguished himself among Argentine filmmakers for his tendency to portray independent women in a positive light.[114] The strong-willed Betty certainly resonated with images of "modern women" that circulated globally in the 1920s and 1930s, and one imagines that the women in the audience must have enjoyed Betty's willingness to stand up to her father.[115] Nevertheless, the film's denouement reinscribes an explicitly anti-modern patriarchy. The reconciliation of Betty and Julián requires not only that she reject her elite urban lifestyle but also that she take on the subordinate feminine role in the couple. In this sense, the movie shares a common gender dynamic with Capra's film: in both, the capricious independent woman is eventually subordinated to the male. But in the melodramatic universe of the Argentine film, this gendered plot line reinforces the triumph of Argentine national identity over foreignness, of the rural over the urban, of the poor over the rich, as well as of tradition over modernity. Betty replaces her father with an even more traditional patriarch, one who presumably will be able to dominate her more effectively. *La rubia del camino*, thus, tries to have it both ways, celebrating the modern woman as the agent of an essentially anti-modern transformation to national authenticity.

As an interclass national romance, *La rubia del camino* is problematic. Unlike in the Hollywood screwball, the formation of the couple does not entail a union of complementary opposites. On the contrary, while Julián nobly resists Betty's efforts to change him, Betty must forsake her previous life and be reborn as Isabel. This rebirth is even more explicit in *Isabelita* (Romero, 1940), the follow-up to *La rubia del camino*, in which Singerman again plays a wealthy heiress who falls in love with a paragon of working-class virtue, in this case a tango singer. Because he despises the rich, she conceals her true identity from him, calling herself Isabel instead of her much fancier real name, Alcida. In the film's climactic wedding scene, after all obstacles to their interclass marriage have been overcome, Singerman embraces her new identity as Isabel, declaring, "Alcida is dead." While these movies hold out hope for the transformation of rich people, they also suggest that the only Argentina worth building is the one associated with the poor. In this sense, the happy endings in the Romero-Singerman films are unconvincing: only the miraculous transformation—even the metaphorical death—of a rich individual makes interclass romance possible. In the melodramatic world of binary oppositions, the formation of the couple reads less as class reconciliation than as the victory of the poor over the rich. National romance can only be forged, these films suggest, through the negation of elite culture. As Betty—now Isabel—drives off with Julián at the end of *La rubia del camino*, they have not forged a new nation. Rather, Betty has joined an already existing national community, one that for all its solidarity, morality, and authenticity remains locked in poverty and anti-modern stasis. Romero's conservative vision of an Argentina defined by tradition, patriarchy, and the virtue of hard work coexists uneasily with his populist condemnation of the other Argentina, a country dominated by a superficial, selfish, Europeanizing elite. As a result, *La rubia del camino* is unable to generate the sort of unifying national myth produced by *It Happened One Night* and other Hollywood movies of the period.

Throughout the 1930s, Argentine mass culture continually reproduced the same basic divisions in the national community. Rising anxieties about national identity as well as the need to compete for consumers of all classes produced a persistent desire to improve mass culture. This desire was visible in the attempts to clean up tango lyrics, the debates between proponents of rhythm and melody, the efforts to forge a sophisticated national art on the basis of folklore, as well as the turn to the countryside as the locus of national authenticity. These projects foundered on a series of oppositions that proved impossible to reconcile: country versus city, tradition versus modernity, authenticity versus cosmopolitanism. Underlying all these divisions, though, was class. The deep populism of mass cultural commodities, itself a reflection of older Argentine popular culture, tended to block efforts at cultural nation building. Stripping the tango of lunfardo and removing it from the lower-class arrabales might make the music less scandalous, but it also made it less Argentine. Celebrating the simplicity and honesty of rural folk might enable a national identity untainted by immigration or materialism, but it also tended to produce a vindication of the poor and a critique of the elite. Imitating Hollywood's screwball comedies might help Argentine filmmakers create a modern cinema, but to make that style their own, they grafted it with the deeply classist brand of melodrama characteristic of local mass culture. The result was hardly a new language for imagining an inclusive nation; it was a reiteration of the basic divisions that already undermined national unity.

5 POLITICIZING POPULISM

Shaped by the forces of transnational capitalism, the Argentine mass culture of the 1930s was deeply divisive. Competing against foreign products, both the tango and the domestic cinema achieved significant market share by combining the signifiers of modernity, including dance rhythms, jazz-inspired orchestration and instrumentation, and Hollywood editing techniques, with markers of authenticity, such as lunfardo, milonguitas, popular melodrama, and recognizable local settings. These gestures of authenticity gave domestic mass culture its populist cast and constructed its audience in opposition to the rich. Despite the many efforts described in the previous chapter, the radio and cinema generally failed to produce unifying national myths. The deep classism of Argentina's mass cultural melodrama meant that the cinema and the radio continued to identify the nation with the poor and to attack the rich as selfish, hypocritical, and anti-national.

The rules of the mass cultural game changed radically in 1943. The military coup of that year inaugurated a new period in which both the radio and the cinema came under the unprecedented scrutiny and influence of the state. The military government enacted laws aimed at censoring certain types of radio programs while promoting others and at protecting the domestic film industry from foreign competition. State intervention in mass culture would expand much further once Juan Perón assumed control of the country in 1946. The Peronist state effectively expropriated the country's most important newspapers and radio stations, cultivated ties to celebrities, enforced systematic censorship and blacklists, and made extensive use of the radio and cinema for the diffusion of propaganda.[1] Nevertheless, in this chapter I will argue that the heavy-handed state intervention of the Perón years did not push mass culture in new directions so much as it reinforced and deepened certain tendencies that were already present. In particular, the populist elements of Perón-era cinema and radio were all developed in the preceding years. They were the result not of a top-down propaganda campaign, but of competition in the mass cultural marketplace.[2]

But the impact of the mass culture of the 1930s went far beyond the nation's radios and movie theaters. In crucial ways, Peronism itself was built from mass cultural raw materials. In the short time between 1943 and 1946, Juan Perón forged a deep connection with the Argentine working class. The strength of this bond and the speed with which it emerged have long puzzled historians. In a now classic account, Daniel James stressed the "heretical" impact of Peronist discourse, which enabled Argentina's long excluded and exploited workers to contest traditional hierarchies. Yet we have only a vague idea of the origins of this heretical language. James has suggested an answer by identifying the tropes of tango songs in Perón's rhetoric use and, more recently, by suggesting that Perón's ability to connect with working-class audiences might have owed something to his use of popular melodrama.[3] In fact, from its beginnings Peronism's debt to Argentine mass culture was profound. The language with which Perón appealed so powerfully to workers was essentially melodramatic; in its Manichean moralism, its attack on the greed and selfishness of the rich, and its tendency to depict the poor as the authentic Argentine pueblo, it bore the unmistakable traces of the movies, music, and radio programs of the 1930s.

In stressing this influence, I am not suggesting that mass culture led inevitably to Peronism. The cinema and radio of the 1930s had a dramatic effect on popular consciousness, but this effect was multivalent and contradictory. Mass culture encouraged both working-class solidarity and the pursuit of individual upward mobility; it denounced the rich even as it encouraged conformism. Moreover, Perón could not merely select which elements of mass culture appealed to him and ignore the others. Contradictions were built into mass cultural discourses at every level. Any attempt to use these discourses politically would require substantial innovation. In the specific conjuncture opened up by the coup of 1943, Perón was able to appropriate elements that circulated in mass culture and refashion them into a powerful political rhetoric. These existing elements did not *cause* Peronism in any sense, but they did help determine the universe of the possible within the political arena of the 1940s. Moreover, Peronism's debt to mass culture helps explain the movement's appeal. Perón's message resonated with the expectations and assumptions of workers who were longtime consumers of domestic radio programs and movies. Just as important, the mass cultural origins of Peronism help account for the movement's deep contradictions. Peronism's tendency to appeal simultaneously to both class envy and class pride and its oscillation between anti-elitism and conformism were inherited from mass culture. Even the movement's profoundly polarizing impact is partly explained by its reliance on the divisive messages of the cinema and radio of the 1930s. In all of these ways, populism in Argentina was not merely a byproduct of industrialization or a reflection of labor politics; it was also the outcome of a particular pattern of mass cultural development.

THE ADVENT OF STATE INTERVENTION

On June 4, 1943, a group of nationalist army officers known as the GOU overthrew Ramón Castillo's government. Tired of the corruption and electoral fraud that had kept conservative governments in power since 1930, these officers were alarmed by the increasing hostility of the United States, which sought to pressure Argentina into declaring war on the Axis. They believed that Argentina's economic future and even its very independence required an aggressive, state-led program of industrialization. At the same time, they were concerned by what they saw as the growing influence of Communism, a threat they believed could only be countered by a powerful state committed to efficiently organizing society along corporatist lines. Over the next two years, Colonel Juan Perón, who served as secretary of labor and vice president, would emerge as the most powerful figure within the military government. Perón embraced both industrialization as the path to economic independence and the corporatist notion of the state as the ultimate guarantor of social justice. But he combined those ideas with a frankly populist defense of the poor and a set of policies that channeled significant material benefits to the organized working class. By 1946 Perón had built a powerful working-class movement, won a presidential election, and accumulated vast quantities of political capital.[4]

For the film and radio industries, the advent of the military government and the rise of Peronism ushered in a new era characterized by unprecedented state intervention. To be sure, the governments of the 1930s had exerted influence on the mass media. The most glaring case, perhaps, was that of Natalio Botana's popular newspaper, *Crítica*. After the coup that overthrew President Yrigoyen in 1930, the paper emerged as a vocal critic of the new military regime led by General José Félix Uriburu. The authorities responded by jailing Botana for three months and then pushing him into exile in Spain. In order to protect his newspaper, Botana transferred ownership of *Crítica* to General Agustín P. Justo, Uriburu's principal rival for power. Publishing under the name *Jornada*, the newspaper now served as a mouthpiece for Justo's presidential campaign. When Justo assumed the presidency in 1932, Botana returned to Buenos Aires and to his position at the helm of *Crítica*, but the paper did not regain its political independence. *Crítica* consistently backed Justo's conservative political alliance, the Concordancia, and Justo himself actively influenced its coverage of politics.[5] Yet notwithstanding the case of *Crítica* and others like it, state intervention in the media was limited in the 1930s. The vast majority of radio stations and film studios remained in private hands throughout the decade, and while these media were subject to meddlesome regulations and occasional censorship, they were never enlisted to serve an official propaganda campaign. Beginning with the coup in 1943, both film and radio would be the target of much more extensive government intervention. By the end of the decade, Perón had replaced Argentina's vibrant capitalist culture industries with a vast media apparatus designed to serve the interests of the state.

In 1943 the Argentine film industry was in crisis. The onset of the Second World War had dramatically transformed the international playing field for Argentine film companies. By effectively closing markets in continental Europe, where Hollywood had done more than a quarter of its business, the war encouraged the North American studios to look to Latin America with renewed interest. Although companies in the United States had long exported films south, since the mid-1930s Argentine filmmakers had steadily increased their share of both the domestic and the Latin American markets. In the early 1940s, Paramount's Buenos Aires office repeatedly complained that Argentine movies posed a threat to sales throughout the region.[6] The Hollywood studios now hoped that the United States government would help them reconquer the Latin American market. At the same time, political considerations also motivated Hollywood to refocus on Latin America. As the global conflict escalated, the U.S. State Department created the Office of the Coordinator of Inter-American Affairs (OCIAA), under the direction of Nelson Rockefeller, in order to counter Axis propaganda in Latin America. Through its Motion Pictures Division, the OCIAA used the cinema as a key component of its efforts to inculcate pro-Allied sentiment. In addition to distributing hundreds of newsreels, the agency encouraged the Hollywood studios to make films with sympathetic Latin American characters and themes and promoted these films abroad.[7]

For American policymakers interested in winning an ideological war against Fascism, the success of Argentine films throughout Latin America was troubling. Under President Castillo, Argentina had committed itself to a policy of neutrality in the war. Although some right-wing nationalists were actively pro-Nazi, the nation's reluctance to join the Allied war effort had other causes. The Smoot-Hawley Act of 1930 increased the already high tariffs that the United States maintained against Argentine imports, generating a strong current of anti-Americanism. This sentiment gained strength after the Lend-Lease Act of 1941, under which the United States began to supply arms to loyal allies, including Argentina's regional rival, Brazil. Meanwhile, at least until Pearl Harbor, Argentina's stance was actively supported by the British, who relied on the import of Argentine foodstuffs. British policymakers recognized that if Argentina abandoned its neutrality, Germany would seek to impede this transatlantic trade.[8] In any case, Argentina's refusal to join the Pan-American alliance and to declare war on the Axis fed United States suspicions about the rise of South American Fascism. Argentina's occasional censorship of Hollywood films at the request of Germany and Spain seemed to justify these concerns, and the OCIAA feared that pro-Axis propaganda might find its way into the Argentine movies that were so popular throughout Latin America.[9] In response, the agency embarked on a concerted effort to weaken the Argentine film industry's position in Latin America while promoting films made in more reliably pro-Allied Mexico. As *Variety* put it in 1943, "Terrific U.S. pressure is being exerted to eliminate Argentina as the world's greatest producer of Spanish language films, and elevate Mexico into the spot."[10] Political and commercial considerations were mutually reinforcing. Since the 1930s, significant United States investment had flowed into Mexican film studios and theater chains. Most famously, RKO joined with the Mexican entrepreneur Emilio Azcárraga to found Churubusco Studio, destined to become Latin America's most important film company in the postwar period. North American investors stood to gain if Mexico replaced Argentina as the dominant supplier of commercial films to the Latin American market.

In this effort, the OCIAA had a potent lever at its disposal. Even as United States investment, loans, equipment, and technical assistance flowed into the Mexican film industry during the war, Washington imposed severe limits on the amount of raw film stock that could be exported to Argentina. Beginning in 1940, Argentine film studios began to experience shortages; in 1943 the United States imposed a formal quota that represented only one-sixth of what the industry required in order to continue to function at its past level. While Mexico enjoyed unlimited imports of raw film, Argentine filmmakers were forced to purchase expensive black market film stock from Brazil and Chile. The results were dramatic. In 1942, Argentine companies released a record 56 films, while the Mexican film industry produced 49; the following year, Argentina produced only 36 films, while Mexico's production soared to 67. The numbers for 1944 and 1945 revealed a dramatic transformation: 157 films were produced in Mexico during those years compared to only 47 in Argentina.[11] By the end of the war, Mexico had definitively replaced Argentina as the dominant producer of Spanish-language cinema for the Latin American market.

While the policy of the United States triggered the rapid decline in the fortunes of the Argentine film industry, other factors were also at work. Compared to its Mexican counterpart, the Argentine film industry was highly inefficient. On the level of production, Argentine companies imitated their Hollywood counterparts by keeping actors and technical workers under contract even when they were not filming. By the end of the 1930s, the studios had to pay steep salaries in order to maintain their exclusive deals with the top talent. Argentina's film distribution system was similarly problematic. Having never managed to secure a percentage of the gross from theater owners, the studios sold their films on a flat-fee basis both in Argentina and throughout Latin America. Domestic exhibitors paid such low prices that Argentina had the longest running film programs in the world: for one inexpensive ticket, a moviegoer could watch four or five features. As a result, the film companies remained chronically undercapitalized. And given the instability and low profit margins that characterized the business, Argentine banks generally refused to provide credit. Even before the OCIAA launched its policy of preferential treatment for the Mexican film industry, Mexican producers had surmounted many of these problems thanks to the active intervention of the state. The Mexican authorities embraced a protectionist policy toward the domestic film industry during the Cárdenas administration (1934–40), a full decade before their counterparts in Argentina. In addition to significant tax exemptions, Mexican filmmakers received 70 percent of their operating budgets in the form of loans from a state institution designed to foment growth in the industry. Likewise, they distributed their films through centralized state agencies, which actively promoted their films abroad and negotiated favorable terms. Argentine filmmakers recognized that in order to compete, they would require the assistance of the state, and in 1940 the Association of Argentine Film Producers requested the suppression of import taxes on raw film and equipment, state bank loans, and a series of other protectionist measures. The request was ignored.[12]

By bringing to power a nationalist government that rejected liberal economic orthodoxy, the military coup of 1943 finally created the conditions for state protection of the Argentine film industry.[13] Confronting the shortage of raw film stock, the studios sought to negotiate better terms from domestic theater chains, and when that effort failed, the conflict was turned over to Perón's Secretariat of Labor and Welfare. Perón responded with a studio-friendly decree establishing a percentage rental system as well as a quota of Argentine films that theaters were required to show. In slightly modified form, this decree would shape the film industry after Perón's election in 1946: a law enacted in 1947 required that domestic films account for 25 percent of screen time in first-run porteño theaters and 40 percent in the rest of the country. At the same time, the Banco de Crédito Industrial began to offer financing to domestic film producers, and film producers were also granted a substantial subsidy generated by a small fee added to ticket prices. Although these measures failed to restore international sales, they did revive film production levels; in 1950 the industry released fifty-six films, finally matching the high it had achieved in 1942. Aggressive state intervention also had a significant effect on the nature of the films produced. Low levels of capitalization combined with the quirks of Argentina's protectionist apparatus encouraged the production of inexpensive films, which stood to receive a greater portion of their financing from the subsidy and which would be guaranteed screen time regardless of their quality. The Peronist government also actively sought to moralize and nationalize the domestic cinema. In addition to direct censorship, the regime used various measures to achieve these aims. While films deemed to be "of national interest" enjoyed preferential access to government credit, the government also centralized the allocation of raw film stock, emulating the OCIAA by doling the material out to producers it favored. By 1949, with the designation of Raúl Alejandro Apold, the former press chief for Argentina Sono Film, as undersecretary of information and press, the regime had created a film industry in which every artistic decision was subject to political control.[14]

Argentine radio entrepreneurs never confronted the sort of crisis faced by their counterparts in cinema. With no foreign competitors and free of any crippling dependence on imported raw materials, radio stations hardly needed the protection of the state. And yet, calls for state intervention were frequent. Many observers felt that the poor quality of radio programming combined with its powerful influence over the masses required state intervention. In the late 1930s, the campaign to "nationalize" the radio gained many adherents who worried about the spread of vulgarity and hoped that radio would promote "the spiritual elevation of the mass of workers and humble people."[15] And the government seemed to agree; a report produced by the Ortiz administration's Commission for the Study and Reorganization of the Radio System in 1939 proposed significant state oversight. Nevertheless, faced with the resistance of broadcasters, the government failed to act on the proposal. Argentine radio, like the nation's film industry, would experience aggressive state intervention only after the coup in 1943 and particularly after the rise of the Perón regime.

The military government's approach to the radio was strongly influenced by the Catholic Church, and particularly by Monsignor Gustavo Franceschi, who sought to moralize and protect Argentine youth by shielding them from the corrupt influence of the tango and teaching them to speak proper Spanish. Within days of assuming power, the government issued a decree against the use of slang on the radio, a measure wholeheartedly endorsed by *La Nación* and other conservative proponents of the effort to clean up mass culture. Over the next three years, the military government decreed that radio stations must be Argentine owned, must provide time for Argentine folk music, and must limit the transmission of radio novelas. Just months before Perón assumed the presidency, the government released a complete set of radio regulations intended to replace the rules put in place in 1933. These enshrined the state's role as that of a "moral guardian" charged with overseeing the contents of radio programs and countering the influence of commercial interests. The new rules dictated that if a network broadcast multiple works of radio theater, at least one must "be related to Argentine history or tradition." No radio novela could be set in a place frequented by criminals or feature prostitutes or alcoholics. Moreover, the rules prohibited certain comic affectations on the radio, including nasal timbres, "effeminate distorsions," or exaggerated shouting. Perhaps most onerous, stations were now required to present a written copy of every work of radio theater, every song, and every advertisement to the Direccion General de Radiodifusión several days before broadcast. This agency would then cut or correct the scripts and lyrics as it saw fit.[16]

The Perón regime maintained this system of censorship essentially unchanged, while dramatically expanding the role of the state in the radio industry. Using its ownership of the airwaves as the ultimate form of leverage, the government pressured station owners to sell their licenses. In July 1947, the transmission of a Perón speech on Radio Belgrano was interrupted by a voice saying "don't believe anything he says; it is all lies." The regime responded by shutting down the station until owner Jaime Yankelevich agreed to sell; in exchange, Eva Perón appointed Yankelevich station administrator. By harassing other station owners with frequent inspections and onerous broadcasting demands, the government forced them to follow suit. By the end of the year, Argentina's vast commercial radio industry had been replaced by two state-owned networks: one built around Yankelevich's network and the other around that of his former competitor, Radio El Mundo.[17] At the same time, the Perón regime used an international newsprint shortage to force the country's major newspapers to sell to its allies. By 1951, when *La Prensa*, the last holdout, was forced to sell, the government had silenced its opposition and assembled a massive official media apparatus under the direction of two agencies: the private holding company Editorial ALEA, run by Perón's personal secretary Carlos Vicente Aloé, which owned the official newspaper chain as well as the El Mundo radio network, and the Undersecretariat of Information and the Press, under the direction of Apold. In a few short years, Argentina's commercial mass media had disappeared, replaced by a lavishly funded propaganda machine.[18]

RUPTURE AND CONTINUITY:
MASS CULTURE UNDER PERÓN

The advent of extensive state intervention in the mass media had a dramatic effect on the lives and creative output of Argentina's musicians, actors, and other popular artists. Lyricists, musicians, playwrights, screenwriters, directors, and radio programmers had to accommodate themselves to the machinery of censorship imposed by the military government and maintained by the Perón regime. The creation of cultural products remained in the hands of independent artists seeking to attract an audience in the commercial marketplace, but these products were now subject to the scrutiny of moralistic and often quite capricious bureaucrats. Among their earliest targets were works that featured lunfardo or slang. The military government banned Niní Marshall's characters Cándida and Catita from the radio for their incorrect Spanish and changed the title and chorus of Discépolo's tango "Yira . . . yira," a lunfardo phrase referring to the aimless walk of a prostitute, to the ridiculously proper "Da vuelta . . . da vuelta." Yet vocabulary was hardly the only issue. Discépolo's "Uno," whose finely wrought poetry was far removed from lunfardo, was one of many tangos banned in 1944, perhaps for its profoundly melancholy mood.[19] Arbitrary censorship persisted under Peronism. In 1949 Apold's staff cleaned up Discépolo's "Cafetín de Buenos Aires," eliminating its use of the slang *vieja* for mother and ameliorating the song's pessimism.[20] According to screenwriter Ulyses Petit de Murat, the authorities intervened in the filming of *Suburbio* (Klimovsky, 1951) to insist that the Peronist actress Fanny Navarro be allowed to wear the latest French fashions, despite the humble origins of the character she was playing.²¹ More significantly, portions of the movie were refilmed in response to Apold's 1950 decree that any film that did not "reflect the elevated cultural state . . . of the Argentine people" would not benefit from the nation's protectionist laws.²²

Even more onerous than censorship were the blacklists that began to circulate as early as October 1946, denying work on the radio, the stage, or the movie set to artists whose loyalty to the regime was suspect. Once again, this punishment was applied capriciously: the lists included both outspoken anti-Peronists and those who may have personally offended Eva Perón or some other high-ranking official. Many of those victimized responded by leaving the country. Most famously, Libertad Lamarque, blacklisted after feuding with the future first lady during the filming of *La cabalgata del circo* (Soffici, 1945), resumed her film career in Mexico. She was joined there by many Argentines, including Niní Marshall, who had returned to the radio and cinema with the rise of Peronism but whose contract with Sono Film was cancelled in 1950 when she was accused of caricaturing Evita (as the first lady was known) in private. Among the many others who left Argentina were the directors Luis Saslavsky, Carlos Hugo Christensen, and Alberto de Zavalía and the actors Paulina Singerman, Delia Gárces, and Francisco Petrone. Several others managed to reconcile themselves with the regime. The jazz singer Blackie, for example, had been blacklisted for her public defense of Socialist political prisoners in 1945, but she was allowed to return to the radio after Fanny Navarro spoke to Evita on her behalf. After Evita died in 1952, artists were subject to the personal whims of Apold, with occasionally perverse results. While Marshall, Singerman, Gárces, and others were allowed to return, Hugo del Carril and Fanny Navarro, both fervent Peronists, found themselves blacklisted.²³

This dramatic transformation in the conditions of mass cultural production undoubtedly affected the content of movies and radio programs. The silencing of dozens of the nation's most important artists and the imposition of official oversight and censorship strongly encouraged cultural producers to police themselves, ensuring that they avoided any contradiction with the "New Argentina" under construction. Nevertheless, it is important to recognize that this was not a "cultural revolution" in which a fully formed official ideology was imposed from the top down. Notwithstanding the many artists who were blacklisted, the Perón regime sought to work with the existing mass cultural industries. The government produced many propaganda films and broadcast its own version of the news on the radio, but the majority of what was heard on radios and seen on movie screens in the Perón era was commercial entertainment aimed at attracting advertisers and ticket-buyers.[24] Eva Perón's career as a radio and film actress gave the regime a wealth of contacts in the entertainment world, which it sought to use to its advantage. Apold himself was a man drawn not from the ranks of nationalist intellectuals but from the film industry. Similarly, Evita's own speechwriter, Francisco Muñoz Azpiri, had written scripts for her during her time on Radio Belgrano. While some artists—del Carril, Navarro, Tita Merello, Discépolo, Homero Manzi—were well-known Peronists, many others—Luis César Amadori, Manuel Romero—were happy to work with the regime. Still others, like the director Lucas Demare, kept their anti-Peronism a secret while continuing to work productively and relatively autonomously.[25] As a result, the subordination of the film and the radio industries to the state had a rather subtle effect, reinforcing certain tendencies that already existed while suppressing others.

Since Domingo Di Núbila published his pioneering history of Argentine cinema in 1959, scholars have tended to view the Perón era as a period of artistic decline for the local film industry. Weakened by the impact of United States foreign policy and then, especially, by the government's heavy-handed interventions, the Argentine studios allegedly abandoned their popular roots, producing "banal" and "anodyne" movies. According to this view, even as Peronism empowered the nation's workers, middle-class filmmakers turned their backs on the social realism of Ferreyra and Soffici.[26] Di Núbila's periodization, which marked 1942 as the end of the "golden era" in Argentine cinema, was likely shaped by the views of the many actors and filmmakers who suffered personally under Peronism. For Petit de Murat, for example, the Perón era was defined by the regime's "contempt (*menosprecio*)" for artistic expression.[27] An examination of the cinema of these years, however, reveals a great deal of continuity with the earlier period. Many of the trends that critics have associated with the Perón era were visible well before 1945: the rise of white telephone films and of light comedies featuring young ingénues, the heavy reliance on melodrama, the fantasy of class reconciliation, the tendency to avoid depictions of the urban working class. By putting more money in workers' pockets, Perón's policies led to a dramatic increase in the size of the Argentine movie audience: in 1952 Buenos Aires cinemas registered an average monthly audience of nearly five million, a threefold increase over the combined theater and cinema audience of 1940.[28] But what these audiences saw on the screen did not represent a dramatic change from what they had seen before. Claudio España and Ricardo Manetti have argued that Peronism did not invent new cinematic forms: "It appropriated existing models without managing to produce forms of representation suited to the popular masses that had supported the political structure."[29] Yet Peronism's reliance on existing cinematic models made perfect sense. These models both reflected the popular aesthetic preferences forged in the previous decade and offered messages that were quite compatible with the regime's populist discourse.

The Perón-era films of Luis César Amadori, who allegedly used his ties to Apold in order to keep Argentina Sono Film in the government's good graces, reveal the essential continuity with the cinema of the previous period. Amadori enjoyed probably the biggest hit of his career with *Dios se lo pague* (1948), a melodramatic adaptation of a comic play by the Brazilian writer Joracy Camargo. The film tells the story of Mario Alvarez, a millionaire by day and a beggar by night. By begging, Alvarez hopes to acquire enough wealth to ruin his former bosses, who cheated him when he was a simple manual laborer. In the end, he and his lover, a high-class woman of the night, are redeemed when they realize that "one must not be ambitious, one must give what one has."[30] Two years later, Amadori enjoyed another commercial success with *Nacha Regules*, another melodrama featuring the same stars as *Dios se lo pague*: the Mexican Arturo de Córdova and the Argentine actress Zully Moreno, who was married to the director. Based on the famous novel published in 1919 by the conservative nationalist Manuel Gálvez, *Nacha Regules* narrated the quest of a wealthy aristocrat to reform a prostitute despite the hostility of his upper-class friends who disdain the poor. The couple are united and morally redeemed at the end of the film, although condemned to a life of poverty. The film critic Néstor (Miguel Paulino Tato) would later attack Amadori for putting Peronist lines in the mouths of Nacha Regules and other characters, and, in fact, the focus on social justice in these movies did seem to echo Peronist rhetoric.[31] Yet Amadori's depiction of the evil, exploitative rich and the noble and long-suffering poor hardly represented a departure from the rules of 1930s melodrama. Likewise, the warning against the moral dangers implicit in upward mobility and in wealth more generally had ample precedent.

From the Manichean worldview long typical of Argentine popular melodrama, it was a small step to ostensibly Peronist messages. In Manuel Romero's *Navidad de los pobres* (1947), a young capitalist rejects his father's exploitative attitude and recognizes the importance of raising wages and improving work conditions for his employees. The wealthy son falls in love with an impoverished, single mother, suggesting the possibility of class reconciliation. The pressures of state intervention are obvious here—in one scene, Niní Marshall's Catita borrows Eva Perón's preferred insult when she denounces "oligarchs"[32]—but the film covers much of the same thematic ground as Romero's earlier films. Juan Perón's vision of a society characterized by class harmony was reflected on movie screens, but this was not much of an innovation. Both before and after 1945, rich characters had to reject hypocrisy and greed in order to achieve moral redemption and make interclass romance possible.

As Clara Kriger has argued, Perón-era films could depict social injustice so long as they made it clear that these problems occurred in the past.[33] For example, when the protagonist of *Dios se lo pague* describes his life as an exploited worker, he clarifies that this mistreatment occurred "when labor protection laws had not yet been invented." The era's most enduring work of social critique was the Peronist Hugo del Carril's *Las aguas bajan turbias* (1951), which revisited the world of exploited *yerba mate* workers first explored in Soffici's *Prisioneros de la tierra*. But unlike the earlier film, del Carril's movie situates the workers' suffering in a pre-modern past, while holding out the promise of a better future. The movie makes this point explicit with its opening statement: "The river is today a path of civilization and progress. But it has not always been this way." The couple at the center of the film rejects the backward family model characteristic of the pre-modern world of the yerba workers, in which authoritarian husbands punish their wives for being raped by foremen. At the end, they go off to find a better life in the urban south where, they have heard, workers are unionized and enjoy better treatment. In its use of an anonymous hero to tell a story of social injustice, del Carril's film had more in common with Italian neo-realism than with the tradition of Argentine *criollismo* that shaped Soffici's work. His protagonist is not a violent rebel like Podeley, the hero of *Prisioneros de la tierra*; instead he is a model worker and supportive husband ready to leave the unjust world of the past and join the utopian modernity being built in the south.[34]

If the advent of Peronism meant that social critiques had to be aimed at the past, it also brought subtle but meaningful changes to film melodrama, which continued to be the dominant genre in domestic cinema. Kriger argues that Perón-era melodramas featured new roles for women. These roles did not break completely with the past: a woman's happiness was still explicitly linked to the home and the family. Yet for many of the melodramatic heroines of this period, "virginity has ceased to be the only good they possess and the virtue that guarantees their happiness."[35] Unlike the passive victims of the past, these characters are strong women who take charge of their own lives. Among the most iconic female stars of the Perón era was Tita Merello, who typically played a humble woman from a poor neighborhood who refuses to submit to male authority (see figure 12). Her characters do not transgress traditional gender roles—they are often hyper-protective mothers—but they do stand up to alcoholic, profligate, or abusive husbands. Moreover, in her successful career as a tango singer, Merello created a distinctive persona that did upend gender expectations. Her low voice and habit of combining singing with talking evoked a more masculine tango style. Even more unusual, she described herself as ugly, thereby explicitly rejecting the stratagem of the milonguita who gets ahead by virtue of attracting men.[36] Merello's signature song, "Se dice de mí," a milonga she performed in the film *Mercado de abasto* (Demare, 1955) is a catalogue of masculine bravado:

> Se dice que soy fiera
> Que camino a lo malevo
> Que soy chueca y que me muevo
> Con un aire compadrón
> . . .
> Si fea soy, pongámosle,
> Que de eso aún no me enteré
> En el amor yo solo sé
> Que a más de un gil, dejé a pie

> *They say I'm ugly*
> *That I walk like a bad guy*
> *That I'm lame and that I move*
> *With a tough guy's attitude.*
> . . .

> If I'm ugly, let's assume it,
> I haven't noticed.
> When it comes to love I only know
> That I have dumped more than one sucker.

Merello's assertiveness certainly resonated with Peronism's tendency to promote a new, public role for women even as it reinforced traditional notions of feminine domesticity.[37] But her persona also drew heavily on earlier mass culture. The working-class pride asserted by Merello's characters is very much in the tradition created by such stars as Carlos Gardel, Luis Sandrini, and Niní Marshall, even if she tended to express that pride more cynically.

Like the cinema, the Argentine radio evolved under Peronism, but without any radical rupture in the content of programming. Despite the heavy censorship of the military government and the forced takeover by the Perón regime, radio stations continued to feature many of the same sorts of programs as they had before. As in the case of the film industry, many of the trends audible on the radio during the Perón years originated in the 1930s. Whereas in 1933, musical programs represented some 62 percent of the offerings on Argentine radio, this proportion had dropped to 42 percent by 1941, with radio theater and, to a lesser extent, news programming taking up the slack. The trend continued over the next few years: in 1946 music, radio theater, and news represented 40 percent, 21 percent, and 15 percent.[38] The continuation of trends was visible within these program categories as well. Beginning in the late 1930s, criollista programs modeled on *Chispazos de Tradición* became somewhat less common, perhaps in part because programs built around gaucho orators like Fernando Ochoa offered a more "authentic" alternative. Yet episodic gaucho dramas retained their appeal well into the Perón period.[39] Alongside the gauchesque, crime stories and romances steadily gained popularity. By the early 1940s, new types of radio novelas emerged, including a growing number of melodramas set in unspecified foreign locales, as well as several adaptations of Hollywood films. Argentine radio-theater companies produced versions of both *Wuthering Heights* (Wyler, 1939) and *Dark Victory* (Goulding, 1939).[40] Perhaps the most innovative radio novela of the Perón period was *Los Pérez García*, which ran on Radio El Mundo throughout the 1940s, 1950s, and into the 1960s. While romantic radio novelas continued to feature love stories between the rich and poor, *Los*

12 Tita Merello. Courtesy of Museo del Cine Pablo Ducrós Hicken.

Pérez García inaugurated a new type of program focused on the daily life of a "model" middle-class family, led by a father who served as breadwinner and a mother who attended to the needs of her spouse and children. According to its writer, the program carefully avoided all social conflict, depicting a world in which "there is always a means of solving problems" and thereby offering listeners a "comforting spiritual rest."[41] This approach may have held special appeal for a middle class that felt besieged by Peronism's tendency to empower those beneath them on the social hierarchy. Yet *Los Pérez García* started its run before Juan Perón began his. The advent of this new middle-class entertainment was not primarily a result of political developments.

Within the field of popular music, the Perón government put the power of the state behind the genre of rural folk music. Official sponsorship of the music began in 1943, when the first radio regulations passed by the military government required that stations broadcast folk music performances. Perón not only extended these requirements, but he also subsidized the academic study of Argentina's folk traditions, featured folk performers prominently in festivals and mass rallies, and mandated that school curricula include the music. Alongside these official developments, folk music and dance became steadily more popular. With the growth of *peñas folklóricas*, both commercial and non-profit venues for listening and dancing to folk music, porteños of all social classes and political affiliations participated in the vogue for the music of the Argentine interior. Since the late 1910s, the commercial potential of folk music had lagged behind that of tango, but this situation began to change in the late 1940s with the emergence of the folksinger Antonio Tormo. Tormo's single, "El rancho 'e la Cambicha" (1950) quickly became the best-selling Argentine record to date. Released at a time when the Argentine population numbered only sixteen million, the record allegedly sold some five million copies.[42]

Although the policies of the Perón government clearly helped expand the popularity of folk music, the commercial viability of the genre was not primarily the result of official sponsorship, nor did it represent a radical break with recent trends. As I have described, folk music had steadily gained prominence on the radio during the late 1930s as part of a larger trend toward nationalist depictions of the countryside. Matallana's statistics confirm that folk music became a significant component of radio programming before the advent of state intervention. Having accounted for 6 percent of musical programs in 1936, the genre more than doubled its share to 13 percent by 1941, two years before the military coup and the first of the new radio regulations.[43] These numbers suggest that the rise of folk music responded to commercial prerogatives more than to the dictates of the state. "El rancho 'e la Cambicha" was very much a product of these market trends. Tormo had performed on the radio since the late 1930s as a member of Buenaventura Luna's Tropilla de Huachi-

Pampa. As a professional musician embarking on a solo career, Tormo was interested in selling records, not advancing a nationalist intellectual program. His performance of "El rancho 'e la Cambicha" was hardly an exercise in authenticity. The song was a *rasguido doble*, a version of the *chamamé* rhythm particular to northeastern Argentina, but Tormo, like the rest of Luna's group, was from the distant Andean province of San Juan. The idea that he should record a chamamé, a rhythm that he had never performed before, came from his recording company, RCA Victor.[44]

The rise of commercial folk music in the 1940s and 1950s partly reflected the vast internal migration of those years. For the thousands of rural Argentines who had moved to Buenos Aires in pursuit of jobs in the growing industrial sector, the music of artists like Tormo may have been a welcome reminder of home. Tormo was vilified by middle-class porteños precisely because they saw him as the musical representative of the hordes of Peronist *cabecitas negras* invading their city. And this was an association that Tormo himself accepted, describing himself years later as "the mouthpiece of the cabecitas."[45] Nevertheless, as Oscar Chamosa has argued, Tormo's huge sales figures indicate that his popularity, and that of folk music more generally, extended beyond the internal migrants. As Natalia Milanesio has shown, the insult *cabecita negra* became synonymous with "Peronist," blurring ethnic and class-based identities. While the term explicitly invoked the migrants' mestizo features—their dark hair and skin color—it came to signify class and political affiliation as well.[46] Given the existence of folk music peñas for the middle and upper classes, anti-Peronist scorn for Tormo was more an expression of hostility to the working class than a rejection of the cultural practices of the countryside. In any case, for most of Tormo's fans, his music was not part of their cultural patrimony. Outside of the northeastern provinces of Santiago del Estero, Entre Ríos, and Corrientes, most Argentines, whether they lived in urban or rural settings, would likely only have heard a chamamé on the radio. As a professional radio performer, Tormo differed from earlier artists like Andrés Chazarreta, who collected and disseminated "authentic" folk music to connoisseurs. Tormo's music was aimed at as broad an audience as possible. Toward that end, he played simple, accessible rhythms, and incorporated lyrics that resonated with Argentine popular culture. Several of his hits, for example, included melodramatic lyrics that described social inequalities in ways that would have been familiar to Argentine film audiences. The lyrics of "El rancho 'e la

Cambicha," although peppered with Guaraní words and phrases typical of the northeast, also sought to connect the song with a musical form to which urban audiences would have been more accustomed: "I'll dance a tango-ized chamamé in little steps / a milonga-ized chamamé in Uruguayan style / slowly trotting as they dance it in Entre Ríos."[47] Through these references to tango and milonga, the lyrics introduced a novel musical form to a diverse Argentine audience.

According to some scholars, the rise of folk music during the Perón years coincided with the decline of the tango. Blas Matamoro argues that tango lost its creative spark because its largely middle-class creators felt alienated from Peronism and were therefore unable to create a tango style appropriate to the New Argentina.[48] For Pablo Vila, tango lost popularity because it did not speak as effectively as folk music to the internal migrants who supported Perón.[49] These explanations may contain elements of truth, but they exaggerate the extent to which Peronism forced a radical rupture in the history of Argentine popular music. The first years of Peronism were hardly a moment of crisis for tango; if anything, the new regime's policies produced a tango boom. As populists, the Peróns embraced the culture of the masses whenever possible, and tango was no exception. The regime lifted the military government's prohibition on lunfardo, cultivated the support of prominent tango stars, recruited tango bands to play at public events, and even created a national prize for the tango to be awarded every year on October 17, Peronism's most important holiday. More important, the dramatic rise in working-class living standards produced by Peronist policies, as well as the regime's sponsorship of myriad opportunities for popular recreation, produced an explosion in popular dance. The milonga renaissance and the rise of Juan D'Arienzo's band had already sparked a dance revival in the late 1930s and early 1940s. Peronism reinforced the trend. Cabarets thrived downtown and in every barrio, while sports and social clubs throughout the city turned their meeting spaces and soccer fields into tango dance floors on a nightly basis.[50] The neighborhood of Villa Crespo alone had at least seven social clubs that regularly featured tango bands.[51] In addition to D'Arienzo, dozens of bandleaders enjoyed success, including Aníbal Troilo, Carlos Di Sarli, Osvaldo Pugliese, Horacio Salgán, Pedro Laurenz, and Miguel Caló, just to name a handful of the best known. Beyond the dance floor, tango continued to find space on the radio and, as Tita Merello's career indicates, on the screen. As the singer Edmundo

Rivero recalled of the late 1940s, "Everywhere the king was the tango. Even when it occasionally shared the stage with bands of other genres, these could not come close to it in audience or applause."[52]

Although some artists connected to the tango world found their way onto Peronist blacklists and many others resented the regime's perceived assault on their own middle-class interests, many of tango's pre-eminent artists and poets embraced Peronism. In addition to Hugo del Carril, who recorded the definitive version of the "Marcha peronista," the movement's famous fight song, the tango bandleader Francisco Lomuto was an outspoken Peronist. But the tango performer who seemed to fit Peronism best was singing star Alberto Castillo, probably the most successful tango singer of the 1940s and 1950s. Although he was a physician from a middle-class family, Castillo cultivated a populist persona. The lyrics to his hit "Así se baila el tango" (1942) were peppered with lunfardo and proudly insisted on the genre's connections to the poor: "¿Qué saben los pitucos, lamidos y shushetas, qué saben lo que es tango, qué saben de compás? (What do rich boys and fops know, what do they know about tango, what do they know about rhythm?)." On stage, Castillo punctuated this line by throwing punches like a boxer, celebrating the aggressive masculinity of his popular audience, and symbolically knocking out the rich. The song's commercial success, which preceded the rise of Perón, highlighted the classism implicit in the tango's plebeian associations. Later, Castillo performed in the gaudy ties and wide lapels of a *divito*, proudly embracing a déclassé sartorial style associated with Perón's followers. Since according to some accounts, many of those who dressed as divitos were internal migrants, Castillo's populist persona likely appealed across ethnic lines.[53] By drawing on tango's long-standing pride in its popular origins, Castillo demonstrated that the genre was perfectly compatible with the class message of Peronism.

During the Perón era, Alberto Castillo became a deeply polarizing figure within the tango world, revealing a growing class division in Argentina's mass cultural audience. The radio journalist Jorge Conti, who was a young boy in the 1940s, remembered scandalizing his mother by imitating Castillo's wardrobe and singing style. As Conti later realized, Castillo's outfits and mannerisms, as well as the lyrics of many of his biggest hits, represented a deliberate rejection of "good manners," a "snide provocation" to "sanctimonious" conservatives. In this way, the singer inspired a revival of the sort of moral outrage that tango had provoked at the turn of the twentieth century.⁵⁴ For the Argentine writer Julio Cortázar, Castillo was symptomatic of the immorality and impertinence that had taken hold of Buenos Aires under Perón. In a piece written two years after his decision to leave Peronist Argentina for France, Cortázar attacked Castillo for ruining the tango of Carlos Gardel: "The simple delight in bad taste and in resentful meanness (*canallería resentida*) explains the triumph of Alberto Castillo."⁵⁵ Like Antonio Tormo, Castillo became a symbol of the Peronist masses and an object of scorn for the anti-Peronist middle class.

Argentine mass culture had long attracted a multiclass audience, even if consumers of different backgrounds enjoyed the same products for different reasons. We have seen, for example, how some fans of Niní Marshall's Catita enjoyed laughing at one of their social inferiors while others saw the character as a vindication of their own class position. In the 1940s, these two audiences were beginning to develop distinct preferences. Some tango bands, like D'Arienzo's and Castillo's, appealed primarily to working-class audiences while others had a more middle-class following. The Villa Malcolm Club of Villa Crespo, whose members were primarily white-collar employees and professionals, hosted both kinds of bands. But the club's leaders imposed a strict dress code and rules banning lasciviousness on the dance floor. When one band's fans behaved inappropriately, the club rescinded its contract.⁵⁶ The rise of Peronism facilitated a tango boom, but it also lent political significance to the populist performance of artists like Alberto Castillo. In so doing, it encouraged a deepening middle-class anxiety about the cultural practices of the poor.

Peronism did not transform the tango. Just as the regime did with cinema, it appropriated existing models, encouraged certain tendencies, and added minor bits of rhetoric. Apold's office censored tangos deemed incompatible with the New Argentina, but neither the government nor its allies created a Peronist tango per se. The tango bands that thrived in the 1940s drew heavily on the existing repertoire, including the tangos of Discépolo and Manzi, the "golden era" songs of Flores, Cadícamo, and Contursi, as well as the Old Guard classics of Villoldo and others. Most tangos written during the Perón years avoided any explicitly Peronist message. Perhaps the most enduring masterpiece of the period was Manzi's "Sur" (1948), set to music by the legendary bandoneonist and bandleader Aníbal Troilo. In Manzi's characteristic poetry, the song offers a wistful portrait of the romantic, tango-esque neighborhoods of the southern part of Buenos Aires:

> La esquina del herrero, barro y pampa,
> tu casa, tu vereda y el zanjón,
> y un perfume de yuyos y de alfalfa
> que me llena de nuevo el corazón.
>
> . . .
>
> Nostalgias de las cosas que han pasado,
> arena que la vida se llevó,
> pesadumbre de barrios que han cambiado
> y amargura del sueño que murió.
>
> *The blacksmith's corner, mud and pampa,*
> *your house, your sidewalk, and the ravine,*
> *and a scent of weeds and alfalfa*
> *that fills my heart all over again.*
>
> . . .
>
> *Nostalgias for things that have past,*
> *sand that life swept away,*
> *sorrow for barrios that have changed,*
> *and bitterness for a dream that died.*

Manzi's evocation of old neighborhoods that seem to exist in a borderland between urban and rural space echoes the nostalgia and the hostility to modernization that characterized his earlier works like "Barrio de tango" and "Milonga del 900." Manzi embraced the Perón regime, arguing that its commitment to nationalism and social justice represented the historical fulfillment of Hipólito Yrigoyen's vision.[57] Yet his enthusiasm for the New Argentina did not have a discernible impact on his lyrics, which continued to express a powerful longing for the past. Similarly, Cátulo Castillo and Enrique Santos Discépolo, who along with Manzi were among the most prominent tango lyricists of the period, were also outspoken Peronists, yet neither allowed Peronist ideology to shape their tangos.

The case of Discépolo is particularly interesting because it reveals the tango's imperviousness to Peronist ideology. Despite his irritation at Apold's censorship and his awareness of the limits that the regime had imposed on the freedom of expression, Discépolo was moved by the sincere concern for social justice that seemed to motivate Juan and Eva Perón. When the regime asked for his help during the months leading up to the presidential elections of 1951, Discépolo agreed. Between July and November, he delivered extremely effective propaganda in the form of a regular radio show called "I think . . . and I say what I think!" That Discépolo expressed his support for the government in a monologue rather than a tango lyric reflected his sense that tango's nostalgia as well as its internal contradictions made it unsuitable as Peronist propaganda. As he told his imaginary anti-Peronist interlocutor, "You only knew the barrio of tangos when an orchestra dressed in smoking jackets played them . . . that is why that parade of dignified little houses [built by the government] cannot move you like they do me." Here, Discépolo criticizes the middle class for indulging vicariously in the culture of poor people without doing anything to address their poverty. Elsewhere, he exchanged tango's nostalgia for Peronism's clear distinction between the bad old days and the New Argentina: "The suburb of yesterday was nice to read about, but not to live in."[58] While tango's nostalgia, melancholy mood, and tendency to indulge in fantasies of individual upward mobility made it ill-suited as Peronist propaganda, the genre's populism—its celebration of the world of the urban poor—fit well with the new regime and allowed it to thrive.

It was during the 1950s that tango's long reign as Argentina's most popular musical form finally came to an end.[59] The principal factors in its decline were economic and transnational. The postwar bonanza that Perón had overseen began to dry up by the late 1940s. As the agricultural export sector declined and trade imbalances grew, the economy stagnated. Real wages fell by 20 percent between 1948 and 1952.[60] In this context, the popular dance craze of the preceding years could not be sustained. Lower wages meant fewer paying customers and a reduced nightlife. Cabarets and other dance spaces closed, and bandleaders could no longer afford to maintain large orquestas típicas. In their place, the 1950s saw the emergence of much smaller ensembles playing tango for smaller audiences who paid to sit and listen rather than to dance. Eventually, this development would lead to the cerebral "new tango" of Astor Piazzolla and others. These trends almost perfectly replicated events in the United States, where changing tastes and the difficult economic conditions of the immediate postwar years led to the decline of the big jazz bands and the fall of swing music. With the rise of bebop, jazz lost its status as commercial dance music, as smaller bands played for reduced audiences of connoisseurs.[61] This transformation in North American popular music was itself a key factor in the decline of tango. As I have argued, tango's commercial success occurred in a unique transnational context. Tango thrived because it was the Argentine genre best suited to offer listeners an alternative modernism patterned on the sophisticated dance music of jazz bands. With the decline of big band jazz, tango lost its dance partner. The standard bearers of musical modernity, as defined by North American tastes, were now pop singers like Frank Sinatra and, by the mid 1950s, Elvis Presley and rock 'n' roll. Although more research remains to be done on the Argentine music scene of the 1950s, it seems reasonable to suggest that in this new context, tango no longer seemed very modern. As *La Razón* lamented with only slight exaggeration in 1956: "Sadly, the tango finds itself increasingly replaced in popular preferences by North American rhythms. First, dancers left it behind and now those who only like to listen to music are forgetting it.... On the radio dial, it takes work to find a tango program, most of which are relegated to non-commercial time slots."[62] Well suited to compete with the fox trot, the tango was no match for the new musical imports from the North.

Under Perón, the state exercised control over a vast mass cultural apparatus that had previously been governed by the laws of the market. The regime erected a massive propaganda machine and carefully controlled what was played on the radio and in movie theaters. Nevertheless, Peronism's impact in this area was less than transformative. The popular genres of the period—film melodramas, radio soap operas, folk music, tango—were all popular in the period before 1943. More important, these genres saw only modest changes in their thematic content and in their relative popularity: folk music gained more prominence; tango declined after 1950; filmmakers were careful to situate social injustice in the past, while female characters were allowed more agency. In fact, Perón appears to have been far more interested in borrowing from mass culture than he was in transforming it, a wise political strategy given the legitimacy and popularity of commercial styles forged in a competitive marketplace. The strategy also made sense because the mass culture of the 1930s and early 1940s already contained within it a strong current of populism that was well suited to Perón's political project. Stars such as Tita Merello, Antonio Tormo, and Alberto Castillo, who in different ways seemed to embody Peronist discourse almost perfectly, emerged from the commercial trends of the previous period rather than from any official cultural program. Perón did not need to create such icons of popular anti-elitism, because they already existed.

THE PERONIST APPROPRIATION OF MASS CULTURAL MELODRAMA

The Peronist movement appeared almost overnight. In June 1943, when the GOU overthrew the government of Ramón Castillo, Juan Domingo Perón was an obscure army colonel. Little more than two years later, his policies and rhetoric had made him so popular among the Argentine working class that his colleagues in the military government arrested him rather than allow him to gain any more power. On October 17, 1945, thousands of Argentine workers flooded the Plaza de Mayo in downtown Buenos Aires to demand Perón's release from jail, refusing to disperse until Perón addressed them from the Casa Rosada, the presidential palace. On this symbolic birthday of the movement, workers linked their futures to Perón's and, in so doing, began to construct and inhabit a Peronist identity. After he won the presidential election of 1946, Perón's enormous charisma—seconded in crucial ways by that of his wife, Eva—enabled him to disband the Labor Party, a coalition of unionists that had helped bring him to power, and to forge a more personal bond with the working class. Although no phenomenon in Argentine history has attracted as much scholarly interest, the roots of Peronism's mass appeal remain mysterious. The commercial mass culture analyzed in this book represents a crucial piece of this puzzle. In the foundational period between 1943 and 1946, Perón's rhetoric was deeply influenced by mass culture, a phenomenon that went far beyond the occasional use of lunfardo or of a tango-esque turn of phrase. In speech after speech, Perón spoke the language of popular melodrama, as it had been reworked on the radio and in the cinema of the 1930s. This language shaped Peronist discourse in fundamental ways, enabling it to resonate powerfully for workers whose consciousness was partially formed in dialogue with Argentine popular music, radio theater, and movies.

Historical analyses of Peronist rhetoric have stressed the essential binarism at its heart. Juan and Eva Perón explained their political project through a series of basic oppositions: national versus anti-national, pueblo versus anti-pueblo, workers versus oligarchs. Moreover, the logic that the Peróns used to make these distinctions between us and them was always deeply moralistic; by opposing sacrifice to egotism, austerity to frivolity, solidarity to treachery, and hard work to idleness, Peronism depicted class struggle in essentially moral terms. Perón frequently denounced the exploitation of the working class, but he described it as part of a historic contest between good and evil.[63] In a speech before the railroad workers union in 1944, Perón, then labor secretary, described his agenda as a "revolution of the poor. . . . The country was sick of important men; it is necessary that the days of simple, working men arrive." He then denounced his opponents as representatives of "the eternal forces of egotism and avarice, that make the pocket into man's only sentient organ."[64] Here, the conflict between bourgeoisie and proletariat is initially described as a battle between rich and poor, "important men" and "simple, working men," before being boiled down to a struggle against a particular form of immorality, namely greed. As Eduardo Elena has demonstrated, Perón's promise to control the cost of living was central to his political rise. And when he turned from the sphere of production to that of consumption, Perón continued to operate within the discourse of moralism and binary oppositions. As he put it in another 1944 speech, "We are a dignified and proud country; and none of its children should have to tolerate ever again that Argentine workers be converted into shabby people (*gente astrosa*) so that a group of privileged individuals can hold onto their luxuries, their automobiles, and their excesses." According to Perón, rising prices, like capitalist exploitation, were the product of immorality, in this case the selfish greed of merchants and speculators.[65]

As many scholars have noted, Perón rejected class conflict and promised to achieve not the triumph of the proletariat but a state of harmony between labor and capital. Conflict and struggle characterized the past; Perón would bring about "the union of all the Argentines so that that struggle is transformed into collaboration and cooperation, so that we can create new values and not destroy uselessly, in a sterile struggle, values and energies that are the only forces capable of making men happy and nations great."[66] In order to create this harmonious national unity, Perón promised to do two things. First, he aimed to reduce the gap between the haves and the have-nots or, as he put it in a speech in Rosario in 1944, to "equalize a little the social classes so that there will not be in this country men who are too poor nor those who are too rich."[67] But redistribution of wealth was not enough. Class reconciliation and social harmony also required a process of moral education and rehabilitation. The rich had to learn to behave morally, to renounce their greed and egotism and embrace the spirit of cooperation and solidarity. Perón described this learning process in a speech in 1946: "Our doctrine is simpler. I can now explain it with an example given to me by five boys in Paraná. Our doctrine embraces that first great humanitarian principle. They were in the port, and one of them had no boots. From on board, we threw him five pesos, which fell into the hands of one who was well dressed. The four boys who witnessed the scene said: 'No, that's not for you; that's for him, who's barefoot.' And the boy gave the five pesos to the barefoot kid. This is our doctrine; we want one of those great gentlemen (*grandes señores*) to learn how to give to those who have no boots. We want that one day those who have everything sympathize with their fellow man, so that there are no more barefoot people and so that our children learn to smile from the moment they are born."[68] Rich people had to be taught generosity and selflessness, and for this, the best teachers were those beneath them on the socioeconomic ladder. Throughout Perón's speeches, one finds constant praise for the noble, dignified poor as "simple," "humble" people without pretension. In this discourse, the socially inferior are morally superior; national unity and class reconciliation can only occur when the rich learn to follow the example of the poor. The idea of the poor as teachers of the rich is one aspect of Peronism's heretical inversion of hierarchy and part of a broader anti-intellectualism characteristic of the movement.[69]

If Perón's major goals included defending the poor and achieving national unity, he made those promises through a rhetoric filled with the vocabulary of work and production. According to a recent linguistic analysis, "politics is work" is the one "major metaphor" that Perón introduced to Argentine discourse. His repeated use of verbs such as to build, to construct, to employ, to produce, and to earn extended this basic metaphor.[70] This language clearly had resonance for those Argentines who earned a living through manual labor. It lent concreteness and familiarity to abstract concepts like progress and justice. But the power of this discourse lay above all in its moral connotations. Perón pledged to "humanize capital" and to "dignify labor."[71] If the rich would be taught the virtues of solidarity and generosity, the poor would be publicly recognized as dignified, virtuous, and respectable. Honest, hard work was, in fact, the ultimate proof of moral superiority: "We struggle so that labor may be considered with the dignity that it deserves, so that we all may feel the desire and the impulse to honor ourselves by working, and so that no one who is able to work may live only to consume."[72] For Perón, the hardworking poor were not just admirable; they were the most authentic representatives of the nation. In announcing his resignation from the army in the highly charged atmosphere of October 17, 1945, Perón made this vision explicit: "I leave, then, the honorable and sacred uniform given to me by the fatherland in order to put on the coat of a civilian and join with that suffering and sweaty mass that produces with its labor the greatness of the country.... This is the people; this is the suffering people that represents the pain of the mother earth, which we must vindicate. It is the people of the fatherland (*Es el pueblo de la patria*)."[73] Here as elsewhere, Perón equated the Argentine nation with the people and the people with workers.

In its binary moralism, its emphasis on class harmony and national unity, as well as its depiction of the poor as authentic representatives of the nation capable of teaching the rich to overcome their egotism, Peronism reproduced the central themes of the mass culture of the 1930s. Whether in the films of Libertad Lamarque or the tangos of Celedonio Flores, mass cultural melodrama presupposed a Manichean world in which poverty was proof of virtue and wealth functioned as a sign of malice. The story of the milonguita, so often repeated, contrasted the safe, moral world of the humble barrio with a seductive, dangerous downtown filled with selfish rich kids and frivolous playboys. The comic films of Luis Sandrini as well as the packaging of tango stars like Carlos Gardel celebrated the essential goodness of the poor and expressed pride in their cultural practices and aesthetic preferences. Poor rural folk were depicted as paragons of simplicity and authenticity and contrasted with consumerist urban sophisticates. In the films of Manuel Romero, interclass romance was only possible when the poor character taught the rich one to exchange her egotism and condescension for solidarity and generosity. In all of these cultural products, the moral categories used to distinguish poor and rich were essentially the same as those taken up by Perón: the rich are greedy and frivolous, while the poor are hardworking practitioners of sacrifice and solidarity. When he celebrated the moral superiority, dignity, authenticity, and cultural inventiveness of the poor and attacked the egotism and avarice of the rich, Perón was drawing on the well-established melodramatic tradition that permeated 1930s mass culture.

Of course, the discursive affinities between Peronism and 1930s mass culture do not prove that Perón self-consciously imitated the movies and radio programs of the previous decade. The moral superiority of the poor was an idea that circulated within the larger cultural milieu that Perón shared with Argentine filmmakers and radio programmers. Catholic social thought, in particular, offered one possible source for this notion as well as for Perón's rejection of individualism and bourgeois materialism. Catholic intellectuals had played an important role in the elaboration of right-wing, nationalist ideology.[74] Perón was initially supportive of Catholic goals, and several prominent Catholic nationalists, including Oscar Ivanissevich and Virgilio Filippo, attained important positions in the government. Yet even if there were other possible sources for some of Perón's language, there is reason to believe that the echoes of mass cultural melodrama in his rhetoric reflect purposeful borrowing. Perón's concerted effort to cultivate and eventually control the media suggests that he recognized the political potential of mass culture, as does his decision to grant his actress wife a key role in his administration. As early as 1944, Eva Duarte put her radio stardom at the service of her future husband's political project via a twice-weekly propaganda program aimed at a largely female audience.[75] But regardless of his sources or intentions, Perón's message certainly resonated with the meanings already widely disseminated in movies, music, and radio theater, and this resonance helps account for the power of his appeal. What I am suggesting is that one reason workers responded so enthusiastically to Peronism is that it was built out of discursive raw materials with which they were very familiar. As fans of tango and folk music and as longtime consumers of popular melodrama, working-class Argentines were already likely to see the world through the Manichean, moralistic lens that Perón used.

As Juan Perón began building his mass movement in the wake of the coup in 1943, he confronted a public that had been shaped by the explosion of mass culture in the previous couple of decades. Needless to say, other developments had been important as well: industrialization, migration, the resurgence of the labor movement, the political frustrations of the *década infame*. But the entertainment offered on the radio and in the movie theater had become a significant part of the everyday lives of Argentines of all classes. It would be an exaggeration to say that this mass culture had prepared working-class Argentines for populism. As I have tried to show, mass culture was ideologically ambivalent, oscillating between conformist and heretical messages. Neither can one claim that Peronism was a straightforward case of selective appropriation, that Perón simply adopted the subversive elements that circulated in mass culture while leaving aside its conservative aspects. On the contrary, Perón's political success was due to his ability to overcome some of the central contradictions reproduced by 1930s mass culture. In order to do that, he could not take mass cultural populism as he found it; in politicizing commercial culture, he transformed it. At the same time, Perón did not manage to overcome all of mass culture's contradictions. Peronism was a profoundly ambivalent movement, its discourse marked by numerous points of tension. Many of these ambivalences originated in the commercial culture of the previous period.

Part of Perón's achievement lay in his ability to appropriate melodrama's moralistic binarism while rejecting its fatalism. He managed, in other words, to depict society as divided between the noble poor and the evil rich, while simultaneously suggesting that workers need not accept the status quo. Perón appropriated the discourses of authenticity that made the poor central to Argentine national identity. Yet in mass culture, this vision of authenticity tended to lock the poor in a position of stasis. Since poverty was a sign of moral virtue and true Argentinidad, upward mobility and progress itself were problematic goals. Both the absence of factory workers in the movies and the omnipresence of nostalgia reflected a deep disjuncture between authenticity and modernity. If jazz was the music of modernity, then tango was authentic to the extent that it remained focused on the past. Argentine mass culture depicted the poor as authentically Argentine by virtue of their affinity with either the rural past of the gauchos or the turn-of-the-century urban underworld of the tango. This authenticity served to compensate the poor for their fatalistic acceptance of subordination.

Perón overcame this fatalism by articulating mass culture's discourses of authenticity with a modernizing discourse of industrialization and economic nationalism. These commitments were hardly unique to Peronism. Calls for economic independence were central to both left- and right-wing nationalism in the 1930s, and by 1943 virtually every political party accepted the need for a state-led program of industrialization.[76] But by combining these arguments with a melodramatic interpretation of society, Perón positioned the poor as the primary beneficiaries of industrialization. Economic nationalism and the promise of industrialization gave him a way of connecting the poor to a particular vision of modernization. He could appropriate melodrama's Manichean worldview without its fatalism. In effect, by fusing these very different discourses, drawn from very different sources, Perón managed to articulate authenticity and modernity more successfully than Argentine cultural producers ever had.[77]

Another of Peronism's key innovations involved placing workers, and particularly urban workers, at the center of its melodramatic vision of Argentine society. As we have seen, the mass culture of the 1930s tended to erase urban workers. The cinema of social critique concentrated on the plight of the rural poor, while the protagonists of popular melodramas were far more likely to be tango singers than factory workers. Perón appropriated melodrama's depiction of a society divided between noble poor and hateful rich, but he applied this vision to the travails of actual contemporary workers. Just as important, through the prominence of Eva Perón, Peronism granted new visibility and legitimacy to women workers.[78] By persistently invoking the suffering and pain of Argentina's workers, Peronism lent mass cultural melodrama greater specificity and relevance.

Perón's focus on workers was part of a collective mode of address that helped him begin to reconcile the pursuit of upward mobility with the celebration of working-class identity. As I have argued, mass culture catered both to working-class pride and to envy of the rich. White telephone films enabled poor viewers to feel morally superior even as they fantasized about wealth. Carlos Gardel was a hero for having achieved fame and wealth, yet tango lyrics condemned social climbing as petty and doomed to fail. In this way, mass culture promoted both the pursuit of individual achievement and the defense of collective interests. It attacked the rich for their selfishness and greed, even as it indulged the popular desire to experience the good life. Perón sought to avoid this contradiction by offering an upward mobility that was fundamentally collective. By addressing workers not as individuals, but as members of a social class, he suggested they could attain a higher standard of living without acting selfishly. By organizing in unions and supporting Perón, they could enjoy the benefits of a more egalitarian distribution of wealth. Useful in this regard was the Peronist concept of the state as the guarantor of social justice. In Daniel James's words, Peronist rhetoric envisioned the state as "a space where *classes*—not isolated individuals—could act politically and socially with one another to establish corporate rights and claims."[79]

Perón constantly trumpeted the state's capacity to provide the poor with a comfortable standard of living and to enable them to enjoy material benefits previously reserved for the rich. Perón thus appropriated from mass culture both the rags-to-riches fantasy and the idea of the moral superiority of the poor, but his capacity to use these discourses politically required creative reworking. In particular, he combined them with a corporatist vision of society and with the concept of an activist state, both more likely drawn from Italian Fascism than from Argentine movies and radio.[80]

Nevertheless, individualism and consumerism persisted. Despite Peronism's rejection of elite materialism and its celebration of the generosity of the poor, the tension between class pride and class envy never quite disappeared. James has suggested that one of Peronism's advantages over traditional leftist parties was precisely its ability to express workers' desires for expensive consumer goods. In particular, he argues, the figure of Eva Perón provided working-class women with a model that legitimized their feelings of envy and resentment.[81] Building on this argument, Barbara Weinstein has contrasted the Argentine case with that of São Paulo, Brazil. The working-class Brazilian women she studied were unable to generate any alternative to the dominant ideal of respectable femininity embodied in the middle-class housewife. By contrast, the image of Evita as a lower-class woman who snubbed Argentina's rich society ladies while dressing in Christian Dior enabled women workers to feel that they too could be beautiful and glamorous.[82] Similarly, Peronism's annual coronation of a "working-class beauty queen" entailed a rejection of the long-standing idea that manual labor made women ugly. This vision amounted to a resignification of femininity but one that was limited, in that it did not challenge conventional forms of beauty. As Mirta Lobato, María Damilakou, and Lizel Tornay point out, contestants in Peronist pageants were judged beautiful to the extent that they approximated ideals depicted in glossy fashion magazines.[83] Similarly, Eduardo Elena has demonstrated that the Peronist magazine *Argentina* catered to workers' desire to emulate bourgeois or elite aesthetic preferences, enabling its readers to go "window shopping," indulging the fantasy of luxury and wealth.[84] As Evita herself put it, responding to those who argued that the houses she built for the poor were too luxurious, "I want them to be luxurious. Precisely because a century of miserable asylums cannot be wiped out except by another century of 'excessively luxurious' homes. Yes, excessively luxurious. . . . I wish [the poor] to accustom themselves to live like the rich . . . to feel worthy to live among the greatest riches. For when all is said and done, everyone has the right to be rich on this Argentine soil . . . and in any part of the world. The world has sufficient available riches for all men to be rich. When justice is done, no one will be poor, at least no one who does not want to be."[85] Eva Perón offered working-class women a utopia in which they might acquire what had previously only been available to the rich: beauty, expensive clothes and jewelry, fancy homes. Even as it celebrated working-class culture, Peronism publicly acknowledged working-class envy.

Peronist expressions of envy, consumerism, and even materialism reflect the movement's mass cultural roots. After all, poor people's resentment of the rich—visible, for example, in the tango singer's complaints about the bacán whose wealth enables him to steal the singer's girl—drove much of Argentine melodrama. Azucena Maizani dressed in fur and Carlos Gardel performed in black tie to allow their working-class fans to fantasize about attaining wealth. Niní Marshall's Catita thrilled her audience both by rejecting elite notions of good taste and by aggressively pursuing the things that the rich could afford. The notion that poor women might aspire to beauty and glamour was hardly a Peronist invention; it was implicit in the career of Libertad Lamarque and so many other actresses who played *bellas pobres*, poor, honest, and selfless women from the barrios, whose beauty enabled them to attract the leading man. As a poor girl from the interior who had attained unimaginable status and prestige in the big city, Eva Perón embodied and expressed the fantasy of the milonguita. The Peróns' debt to this tradition distinguished their brand of populism from a more orthodox leftist appeal. Peronism appropriated mass cultural discourses that expressed both the popular resentment over social inequality and the popular desire for the trappings of wealth. This discursive framework imposed limits on the utopias Peronism might imagine. Thus, Peronism often endorsed bourgeois standards of propriety and conventional models of beauty. It also reproduced the contradiction between working-class pride and envy, a contradiction that resurfaced whenever economic conditions prevented the state from delivering on its economic promises to workers.[86] In a sense, these limits were the consequence of Perón having built his movement out of melodrama rather than Marxism.

Several of mass culture's other contradictions persisted within Peronism. For example, at the heart of Peronism was the contradiction between liberation and control, between mobilization and authoritarianism. The movement invited workers to play an active role in history, but it also asked them to obey their leaders and to stay off the streets. It represented both a heretical challenge to hierarchy and a self-conscious attempt to discipline the masses. Obviously, these different faces of the movement responded to the exigencies of different historical moments. When he was seeking power, Perón emphasized mobilization and heresy. Once in control of the state, he reverted to discipline and social control. Yet here too one finds the traces of mass culture. It seems reasonable to suggest that the contradiction between conformism and populist heresy so central to the cinema and radio of the 1930s represents one source of Peronism's ambivalence. Argentine mass culture disseminated a visceral anti-elitism, even as it depoliticized class conflict and suggested the futility of social transformation. Peronism's simultaneous commitment to a frontal assault on the oligarchy and to social harmony and class reconciliation betrays its origins in melodramatic mass culture.

Another of Peronism's contradictions was its deeply polarizing impact. A regime that claimed to pursue class harmony and national unity excoriated its enemies, defining them as selfish, corrupt, and anti-national oligarchs. Juan and Eva Perón's vituperative language was matched only by that of their political opponents, who denounced "the dictatorship" and heaped scorn on "that woman." Perón tried to build a multiclass coalition but failed. Instead, his regime produced a fundamental schism in Argentine political culture that would last for decades. This division reflected in part the material effects of Peronist policies. For example, even though factory owners stood to benefit from Perón's nationalist economic policies, the leading association of industrialists joined the opposition once it became clear that Perón's support for unions would dramatically alter the balance of power on the factory floor.[87] Yet the emergence of a rabidly anti-Peronist opposition was not simply the result of rational economic calculation. The advent of Peronism provoked a powerful reaction from white-collar workers, clerks, professionals, and other middling groups. Many of these groups benefited from Perón's expansion of the public sector as well as his support for unions, but they suffered profound status anxiety in the face of the new rights and benefits enjoyed by those beneath them on the social hierarchy. They deeply resented the invasion of Buenos Aires by what they saw as a dark-skinned, lower-class rabble from the interior.[88] A deep-seated, middle-class, anti-Peronist identity thus emerged within only a couple of years of Perón's rise to prominence.

Perón's discursive debt to mass culture helps explain his failure to win over these middling groups. Seeking to enlarge his base of support beyond the labor unions, Perón convoked three huge rallies in 1944 aimed explicitly at the middle class. Yet his speeches on these occasions reveal his inability to appeal to middle-class concerns. Although he praised the middle class as essential to the progress of any modern nation, he called on its members to overcome their "inferiority complex" and their individualism, to emulate workers by organizing themselves in unions, and to "sacrifice for the common good."[89] The appeal to self-sacrifice and solidarity and the condemnation of middle-class social striving echoed 1930s mass culture. Films and tango lyrics indulged rags-to-riches fantasies but criticized the more mundane pursuit of upward mobility. Mass culture celebrated the working-class kid who struck it rich as a tango star but generally skewered the idea of education and self-improvement as a respectable path to a better standard of living. Having inherited and endorsed this critique of selfishness and egotism, Perón had little to offer the middle class. He could tolerate and even encourage working-class envy, but he had no patience for the middle-class pursuit of status. By appropriating the populist message of mass culture and linking it to actually existing workers, Perón alienated middle-class Argentines, for whom even mass cultural populism suddenly seemed threatening. Antonio Tormo and Alberto Castillo, whose populist appeal hardly constituted a novelty in the worlds of folk music and tango, now appeared as scandalous symbols of the Peronist mob.

If Peronism was unable to forge a unified nation, it was in part because the mass culture it drew on was itself fundamentally polarizing. It is not only that the melodrama so central to Argentine radio and movies was premised on an irreconcilable division between rich and poor. It was also that Argentine popular music, radio theater, and movies were profoundly populist. In Ernesto Laclau's terms, these mass cultural commodities presented popular culture as "an antagonistic option" against the elite. As I have argued, efforts to purge tango of its illicit and lowbrow associations or to treat it as primitive, folkloric raw material for a sophisticated art form failed, as did the attempts to forge a national identity on the basis of Argentina's rural cultures. Insofar as these images were stripped of their plebeian associations, they lost their capacity to represent the nation. In the same way, Manuel Romero could emulate Hollywood directors like Frank Capra, but he could not reproduce Capra's national myths. The work ethic might conquer class prejudice and enable interclass romance in Hollywood, but in Argentina, the rich woman would have to reject her class in order to be with her working-class lover. Argentine mass cultural commodities contained divisive class messages. In a very real sense, tango *meant* identifying with the barrio boy who loses his girl to the aristocrat; folklore *meant* celebrating the simplicity and generosity of the rural poor against the materialism and selfishness of the rich; and films like Romero's *meant* siding with the culture of the working poor rather than with that of the cosmopolitan elite. Weinstein points out that the working-class model of femininity enabled by Eva Perón was premised on the denigration of elite women and therefore precluded a cross-class feminist alliance.[90] But Evita's hostility simply recapitulated dozens of mass cultural representations of scornful, condescending elites: the wealthy mothers who rejected Libertad Lamarque's characters as too common for their sons, to cite just one example.

Perón's use of mass culture was innovative, but his innovations did not include the introduction of class hostility; that element was already present. In his early efforts to win over the middle class, Perón tried to forge class reconciliation, but like the mass cultural reformers of the 1930s, he failed. The melodramatic moralism that Perón appropriated from mass culture helped inject a populist divisiveness into his rhetoric. In the relatively unfettered, transnational marketplace for mass culture, the radio and film producers of the 1930s reworked existing popular cultural forms into powerfully populist genres and styles. Perón then appropriated these, articulating them with other ideological elements and reconfiguring them in the process. James argues that Peronism's "heretical power" derived from its ability to articulate workers' private, previously unnamed experiences of exploitation and mistreatment.[91] Yet in an important sense, these experiences, as well as the values and assumptions through which they were interpreted, had been publicly named already; they were named every day on movie screens and radios. Through these mass entertainments, the Argentine poor had already been interpellated as the noble, dignified, long-suffering, and authentic *pueblo*. What Perón did was take this message and make it the basis of politics and policy. This gesture helped him attract legions of working-class followers, but it also alienated elite and middle-class Argentines. In other words, the populist images of the nation that circulated in mass culture were deeply polarizing. Perón's use of those images helps account for the divisiveness of his appeal.

EPILOGUE: THE RISE OF THE
MIDDLE CLASS, 1955–1976

The mass culture explored in this book constructed an image of Argentina that did not accurately reflect reality. By the mid-1920s, Argentina was a dynamic, mobile society that had apparently left behind the fierce class conflicts of earlier decades. In the expanding barrios of Buenos Aires, a heterogeneous population pursued the opportunities that economic development provided. While there were of course many poor people who struggled to survive in the city and beyond, a sizable and growing segment of the population lived in the broad middle ground between rich and poor. Yet domestically produced mass culture depicted Argentine society as fundamentally bipolar. In tango lyrics, radio plays, and films of all genres, an honest, dignified, and long-suffering pueblo confronted condescending and egotistical aristocrats. One of my central claims is that this disjuncture between reality and representation was produced by the dynamics of Argentina's transnational cultural marketplace. Another is that over time the representation came to exert a powerful influence on reality. Mass cultural images gave Argentines a powerful language for understanding their society and their place in it.

Nevertheless, Argentine audiences did not simply become the characters they saw on the screen. Mass culture was polysemic; there was more than one way to relate to the images of Argentine society it disseminated. Many consumers must have identified with the plight of the humble girl seduced and abandoned by a wealthy playboy. They surely embraced mass cultural versions of national identity that identified Argentineness with the cultural practices of the urban and rural poor. Yet other members of the audience may have responded more to the recurring images of conspicuous consumption and to the fantasy of rapid upward mobility. For these Argentines, the celebration of rural folk may have offered a means of locating the roots of national identity in a comforting past, rather than a vindication of actually existing poor people. Some saw themselves in the pushy materialism of Niní Marshall's Catita, while others simply enjoyed laughing at her. Cultural producers attempted to construct unifying national myths in order to expand the market for their products, but their efforts generally failed to overcome the deep classism of popular melodrama. As a result, contradictory messages persisted.

When Juan and Eva Perón appropriated and politicized the populist discourses that circulated in mass culture, the audience began to split. For the first time, a substantial number of Argentines now came to consider themselves members of the middle class. And they constructed this middle-class identity in explicit opposition to newly empowered Peronist workers.[1] Mass culture did not cause this sudden division between working-class and middle-class Argentines; Peronism did. But as I have tried to show, Peronism was in many ways built out of the discourses that circulated on the radio and in the cinema, and it inherited their class contradictions. Peronism thus failed to build a cross-class, nationalist movement. Instead, it polarized the nation. Over the next several decades, this rift hardened into an unbridgeable fault line. A political conflict rooted in irreconcilable class identities intersected with Cold War ideologies and a growing generational divide, producing severe instability and culminating in the brutal dictatorship of 1976–83. Throughout these years, mass culture continued to reproduce the social divisions that undermined national unity.

Perón's ouster in 1955 ushered in the so-called Revolución Libertadora, a nearly three-year military dictatorship whose first priority was the "deperonization" of Argentine society. Activists and officials were arrested; the Peronist party was banned; and the visible signs of the regime were eradicated from public space. Peronist holidays were abolished, school textbooks burned, and public monuments destroyed.[2] For many artists and producers associated with the deposed regime, the transfer of power had dramatic consequences. Antonio Tormo, who was widely seen as "the voice of the cabecitas" despite never having publicly endorsed Peronism, had his radio and recording contracts summarily cancelled in the wake of the coup.[3] The actor Hugo del Carril spent two months in jail, alongside the director Luis César Amadori and the film producers Atilio and Luis Angel Metasti, allegedly for the illegal exportation of films to Uruguay, but in fact for having collaborated with the Perón government. Del Carril would not make another film until the end of the dictatorship in 1958. Many artists, among them Tita Merello, left the country so as to be able to continue working, while others, such as Fanny Navarro, were unable to resurrect their careers.[4] Still others suffered no direct persecution at the hands of the new authorities but nevertheless struggled to adapt to the new environment. Alberto Castillo was a casualty of the commercial decline of tango. Having starred in ten films between 1946 and 1956, he would make only one more movie, in 1958.[5] Niní Marshall, back from her exile in Mexico, resurrected her most famous character for *Catita es una dama* (Saraceni, 1956). A box-office failure, the film marked the beginning of an eight-year hiatus from the Argentine cinema for Marshall and the end of the line for Catita. After the defeat of Peronism, there were very few Argentines who felt like laughing either at or with a working-class striver. Marshall did have success on the radio with a new character, a wealthy snob named Mónica Bedoya Hueyo de Picos Pardos Sunsuet Crostón, but she never recaptured her earlier stature.[6]

Notwithstanding these career reversals, there were many signs of continuity in the mass culture of the late 1950s.[7] Like the rise of Peronism ten years earlier, the fall of the regime did not occasion a cultural revolution from above so much as a deepening of certain tendencies that were already visible. For example, both the rising commercial viability of folk music and the relative decline of tango proceeded apace. Within the folk milieu, the blacklisting of Antonio Tormo seems to have been a unique case. Although the military government discontinued the official sponsorship that folk music had enjoyed under Perón, and many clubs and festivals were forced to downsize, most folk performers who had benefited from Peronism were allowed to resume their careers. At the same time, several newer acts became major recording and radio stars, including Los Cantores de Quilla Huasi, Los Fronterizos, Los Chalchaleros, and Los Huanca Huá. In fact, the genre would achieve its commercial high point in the period between 1959 and 1966, a phenomenon known as the "folklore boom."[8]

Folk music had clearly benefited from state sponsorship during the Perón years; laws requiring the inclusion of the genre on the radio and in live venues, as well as direct financial subsidies, were major factors in the consolidation of the genre. Nevertheless, Argentine folk music was primarily a commercial genre and had gained a significant and growing presence on the radio before the advent of official support. It is no surprise, then, that the music was able to retain its audience after 1955. Oscar Chamosa points out that despite its support for the genre, Peronism never established its own "brand" of folk music. There were no Peronist folk lyrics and, with the exception of the work of Atahualpa Yupanqui, very few in this period that even expressed an explicit concern for social justice. As a result, Chamosa argues, folk music offered a source of Argentinidad that was attractive to a middle class that had rejected Peronist versions of national identity.[9] The most commercially successful folk music of the boom years featured rich vocal harmonies and romantic lyrics. Roberto Cambaré's *zamba* "Angélica," a hit for several different folk groups, was typical:[10]

> Angélica, cuando te nombro,
> me vuelven a la memoria
> un valle, pálida luna en la noche de abril,
> y aquel pueblito de Córdoba.
>
> *Angélica, when I say your name,*
> *a valley, a pale April moon,*
> *and that little town in Córdoba*
> *come back to my memory.*[11]

In its romanticism and its nostalgic evocation of rural life, this version of folklore recalled Homero Manzi's "country milongas" of the 1930s. Middle-class consumers embraced it wholeheartedly.

During the late 1950s and early 1960s, the rise of the middle class decisively reshaped Argentine mass culture. Middle-class Argentines took to the streets in support of the Revolución Libertadora, and by the time the dictatorship ended, they had become the primary target of new political appeals. Arturo Frondizi, who assumed the presidency in 1958, emerged as "the Perón of the middle class." Embracing the doctrine of "developmentalism," Frondizi aimed to achieve economic growth through a combination of industrial policy and foreign investment, while building a cross-class alliance that would assure social integration and stability. Within this project, Frondizi carved out an especially prominent role for the middle class, becoming the first Argentine president to defend that sector's interests explicitly. Having staked its claim to both politics and public space, the middle class now constituted an inviting market for cultural producers. In addition to folk music, a host of other programming was aimed at these consumers. Programs featuring model middle-class families proliferated on television, which was introduced in Argentina in 1951. One classic of the genre was *La Famila Falcón*, launched in 1962, the same year that its sponsor, the Ford Motor Company, introduced its new sedan to the Argentine market. In reassuring programs like this one, middle-class porteño families encountered a series of challenges and conflicts, but all was happily resolved by the end of each episode thanks usually to the wisdom of the father.[12]

Like the decline of tango and the boom in folk music, the development of mass cultural products depicting happy middle-class families began before 1955. As early as 1933, *Los tres berretines* featured a respectable family led by an immigrant shop owner, although, as I have argued, that film was quite ambivalent about the patriarch's middle-class values. *Así es la vida* (Múgica, 1939), a film adaptation of another sainete by the authors of *Los tres berretines*, betrayed less of this ambivalence.[13] The movie follows one prosperous family over thirty years, presenting a series of generational conflicts that pit old-fashioned parents against children with modern ideas. In the inevitable happy ending, the parents adapt, and the family survives. By 1940 *Los Pérez García* had begun its long run on Radio El Mundo, following the quotidian struggles of a middle-class family. In sharp contrast to the melodramatic mass culture that was so dominant in the 1930s, these films and programs depicted a world in which class divisions were easily overcome. Interclass romance, for example, no longer required that a rich person embrace working-class values. In *Así es la vida*, the father is happy to marry his daughters off to his employees, so long as they are not Socialists or atheists. In *Los Pérez García*, the family's only son married the maid in an episode from 1955 that was a major event for the program's fans.[14] Rather than challenge the middle-class characters in any way, the marriage offered the poor servant an easy and unproblematic route to upward mobility. As they became more and more common on the radio and television, shows like *Los Pérez García* and *La Familia Falcón* began to transform the dominant image of national identity, holding out the contented middle-class porteño household as the quintessential Argentine family.

The growth of mass culture about and for the middle class was a transnational phenomenon, in which influences from the United States were particularly important. These influences partly reflected the growing role of North American capital in the Argentine mass media. Immediately after the coup of 1955, the military authorities had dismantled the Peronist radio networks. As they prepared to relinquish power three years later, they sought to prevent the reemergence of media oligopolies run by Perón allies. In a public auction closed to Peronists and designed to outlaw networks owned by a single entity, many individual radio stations were sold to private owners. Similarly, just three days before turning the government over to the Frondizi administration, General Pedro Aramburu granted television licenses to three private companies with no connection to Peronism. But unlike radio, commercial television was new in Argentina. The new license holders lacked the necessary capital to produce programs that could compete with the state-owned Canal 7. For help, they turned to the North American television networks, NBC, CBS, and ABC. Each network created a production company that generated programs for one of the Argentine stations. Not only did this system allow the North American companies to evade the legal prohibition against foreign ownership of stations, it also enabled the elaboration of de facto networks. By 1970 the production company PROARTEL, co-owned by CBS and Time-Life, had acquired seventeen affiliates throughout Argentina.[15] Although charting the precise impact of these corporations is beyond the scope of this book, the direct involvement of networks based in the United States in the production of Argentine television represented an important channel for North American influence.

In the 1950s, Argentines remained enthusiastic consumers of mass culture from the United States, including the films of James Dean and Marilyn Monroe, the rock 'n' roll of Elvis Presley and Bill Haley, as well as dubbed television programs like *Highway Patrol* and *The Cisco Kid*.[16] There is little doubt that mass cultural depictions of harmonious middle-class families were constructed in dialogue with North American images. Television programs like *Father Knows Best* offered obvious models. Beyond the realm of mass culture, North American imports provided middle-class consumers with opportunities for distinction. Peronism had dramatically increased the purchasing power of the working class, expanding that sector's consumption of household appliances and other amenities. By the late 1950s, refrigerators, blenders, washing machines, television sets, and stereos were symbols of modernity. For middle-class consumers, North American brands like Osterizer, General Electric, and RCA Victor carried the most prestige.[17] Similarly, during the early 1960s, Argentine young people of all classes began to wear blue jeans. But while working-class teenagers wore domestically manufactured *vaqueros* that evoked North American associations through the brand name "Far West," middle-class youth bought the real thing: Lee and Levi's.[18]

As the example of blue jeans suggests, foreign influence had a great deal to do with the emergence of youth as the nation's newest and fastest growing marketing category. Imitating international trends, local producers developed a series of mass cultural commodities aimed specifically at young people. In 1962, RCA Victor and local television station Canal 13 inaugurated *El Club del Clan*, a weekly musical program featuring a cast of clean-cut, well-dressed teenagers. With each performer specializing in one particular genre, the show offered rock 'n' roll in the style of Elvis Presley, international pop music, *cumbia*, bolero, and tango, alongside lighthearted comic sketches. Gradually, an emphasis on songs in English and Spanish-language covers of North American hits gave way to original compositions. In terms of both aesthetics and morality, *El Club del Clan* offered only the gentlest sort of rebellion. The show was apolitical to a fault, suggesting that while teenagers had their own tastes, they had no deeper critique of the adult world. Similarly, in the television program *La Nena*, an independent-minded teenage girl caused her middle-class father an unending series of headaches. Like *Los Pérez García*, each episode of *La Nena* ended happily. In this comforting vision, the middle-class family was strong enough to withstand generational conflict.[19] The omnipresence of this sort of programming constituted a middle-class takeover of mass culture, an echo of that sector's new political dominance. The proscription of the Peronist party combined with this mass cultural transformation to reduce the space for the expression of working-class values and aesthetics in the public sphere.

The 1960s witnessed the political radicalization of significant segments of Argentine society. The coup that overthrew the Frondizi government in 1962 demonstrated that politics had become an "impossible game": the military refused to countenance the participation of the Peronists, who continued to enjoy the support of a majority of Argentines.[20] Frustrated by this political stalemate and inspired by the example of the Cuban Revolution of 1959, many Argentine young people joined the revolutionary Left. This radicalization was a response to developments in domestic and international politics, but for middle-class youth it also involved the reworking of identity through consumption. Blue jeans, which had been marketed as "dynamic, joyful, and sexy," now became a countercultural symbol and the typical uniform of young radicals.[21]

Mass culture played a significant role in the leftward drift of Argentine society and particularly middle-class youth. In the late 1960s, the apolitical music of the folklore boom gave way to the protest songs of the Nuevo Cancionero movement. New singers like Mercedes Sosa drew on the legacy of Atahualpa Yupanqui as well as the example of Chilean singers like Violeta Parra to create a politicized folk music that provided the soundtrack to leftist militancy. At more or less the same time, the Beatles inspired a generation of young rock musicians in Argentina. Luis Alberto Spinetta, Litto Nebbia, and many others elaborated multiple versions of what would come to be called *rock nacional*.[22] The emerging rock scene—with its sexual freedom and drug use—scandalized the older generation but also horrified young leftists, for whom the new music represented both sterile escapism and cultural imperialism. Eventually, as Sergio Pujol points out, this rift would be inadvertently healed by the brutality of a military dictatorship that made no distinction between "Marxist subversives" and "hippie drug addicts."[23]

In the context of this generalized radicalization, disaffected middle-class youth forged a powerful, if short-lived, alliance with Peronist workers. Persecuted and shut out of politics by the Revolución Libertadora and subsequent governments, labor activists steadily moved to the left. Workers forged the so-called Peronist Resistance in the late 1950s, using sabotage, strikes, and factory takeovers to combat the anti-popular policies of the military. The proscription of the Peronist party as well as workers' exclusion from the public sphere deepened their attachment to the exiled Perón.[24] At the same time, Peronism became attractive to many middle-class leftists. The coup of 1966, which installed the repressive military dictatorship of Juan Carlos Onganía, increased the appeal of Marxism for middle-class young people. For many, including a sizable percentage of those who joined armed revolutionary groups, Peronism represented an Argentine variant of international anti-imperialism. These two trends came together in a series of rebellions, the most important of which was the "Cordobazo" of 1969, in which radical university students made common cause with combative, left-wing unions in the city of Córdoba, the epicenter of the country's automotive industry.[25] In a sense, this alliance reflected a temporary intersection of class-based and generational polarization. When the military finally legalized Peronism and allowed Perón himself to return to Argentina in 1973, the movement could no longer withstand its internal divisions: as a huge crowd assembled at the airport to greet the returning leader, right-wing, anti-Communist Peronists opened fire on the Peronist left.[26] After three more years of persistent instability, the military, with substantial middle-class support, responded with yet another coup, repressing both Peronist workers and those middle sectors suspected of radicalism with unprecedented brutality.

The mass culture of the 1950s, 1960s, and 1970s broke in three important ways from the patterns established in the 1920s and 1930s. First, whereas the radio and cinema of the earlier period addressed its audience as a popular mass defined in opposition to the rich, post-Perón-era mass culture spoke primarily to the middle class, a class that had coalesced in opposition to the Perón regime. Second, the marketing of mass cultural products specifically to young people was also novel. Finally, the intense politicization of the 1960s and 1970s had no equivalent in the earlier period. In the 1930s, consumer choices—whether to listen to tango, folk, or jazz, for example—did not tend to indicate specific political preferences, as similar choices later would.

Nevertheless, there were also significant continuities. The Argentine mass cultural marketplace remained—and remains—fundamentally transnational. In both periods, Argentines consumed substantial amounts of foreign, particularly North American, mass culture. Likewise, in both periods, this imported culture offered more prosperous Argentines a means of achieving distinction: those who disdained local films in favor of the latest Hollywood releases prefigured middle-class porteños who insisted on wearing Levi's jeans. Domestic mass culture—whether it was tango music or rock nacional, radio theater or television—reflected a dialectical process in which producers both emulated and sought to distinguish their output from prestigious, ultra-modern imports. The resulting genres constituted alternative modernisms through which Argentines reconfigured national identities. The vocabulary and imagery disseminated by mass culture were available for political mobilization and, as a result, had real effects in the world. As I have tried to show, the deep divisions so visible in the 1950s and beyond were the results of a political process that was itself made possible by mass culture. By appropriating and repackaging the populist messages that coursed through mass culture, Peronism generated a profound chasm that would divide the Argentine working and middle classes for the rest of the twentieth century. This chasm looked quite different from the one depicted in so many melodramatic movies and songs, but it was every bit as deep.

NOTES

INTRODUCTION

1 Arlt, *Crónicas periodísticas* (www.elaleph.com), 53. All translations are mine unless otherwise noted. Arlt's comment was part of a debate with the Communist Party leader Rodolfo Ghioldi. See Saítta, "Entre la cultura y la política," 405.
2 Gutiérrez and Romero, *Sectores populares, cultura y política*. The "popular sectors" argument has become something of a historiographical consensus. For a summary, see González Leandri, "La nueva identidad de los sectores populares," 201–37.
3 For example, Karl Hagstrom Miller has recently demonstrated how the music industry in the United States shaped racial perceptions and associations in the early twentieth century. See Miller, *Segregating Sound*.
4 Hall, "Culture, Media and the 'Ideological Effect,'" 315–48.
5 Adorno and Horkheimer, *Dialectic of Enlightenment*.
6 For a useful account of this trend in cultural studies, see Storey, *Inventing Popular Culture*, 48–62.
7 Levine, "The Folklore of Industrial Society," 1373.
8 Habermas, *Legitimation Crisis*.
9 Lipsitz, *Time Passages*, 39–75. Lipsitz's recovery of the possibility of alternative working-class readings of television programs echoes the conclusions of other

cultural historians from the United States. Michael Denning, for example, reveals the subversive meanings contained in the nineteenth-century dime novel. See Denning, *Mechanic Accents*.

10 Hansen, *Babel and Babylon*, 60–125.
11 Sarlo, *Una modernidad periférica*, 28.
12 Miller, *In the Shadow of the State*, 3. For another formulation, see García Canclini, *Hybrid Cultures*.
13 Orlove and Bauer, "Giving Importance to Imports," 1–29. See also Bauer, *Goods, Power, History*, 150–52.
14 O'Brien, *The Revolutionary Mission*.
15 Moreno, *Yankee Don't Go Home!* For an account that stresses the influence of North American products, see Pérez, *On Becoming Cuban*. In the Argentine context, Ricardo Salvatore shows how the advertising agency J. Walter Thompson appropriated Argentine nationalism in order to sell mass consumer goods. See Salvatore, "Yankee Advertising in Buenos Aires," 216–35.
16 McCann, *Hello, Hello Brazil*, 137–45.
17 Zolov, *Refried Elvis*. Other recent works that examine the complex uses to which Latin Americans put North American mass culture include Seigel, *Uneven Encounters*; Alberto, "When Rio Was *Black*," 3–39.
18 On the evolution of consumption in Argentina, see Rocchi, "La americanización del consumo," 131–89. On film imports, see 151. For the number of radio stations and movie theaters, see chapter 2.
19 Hansen, "Fallen Women, Rising Stars, New Horizons," 10–22.
20 Bigenho, *Sounding Indigenous*, 18. On efforts to market authenticity in Brazil, see McCann, *Hello, Hello Brazil*, 96–128.
21 Turino, "Nationalism and Latin American Music," 193–94. For a similar account, see Vianna, *The Mystery of Samba*.
22 Chamosa, *The Argentine Folklore Movement*.
23 Several recent accounts of Latin American musical nationalism stress the role of the market alongside that of intellectuals and the state. See McCann, *Hello, Hello Brazil*, 34–40; Velázquez and Vaughan, "*Mestizaje* and Musical Nationalism in Mexico," 107.
24 Even that most elitist of Argentine observers, Domingo Faustino Sarmiento, seemed to recognize as much when he argued in 1845 that a truly national Argentine literature would have to focus on the savage countryside, rather than on the civilized, urban world of the Europeanized elite. Sarmiento, *Facundo*, 59–60.
25 This historiography is discussed in Agnew, "Coming Up for Air." The Susman essays are in Susman, *Culture as History*. For consumerism as a cause of labor militancy in the 1930s, see Rosenzweig, *"Eight Hours for What We Will,"* 226–28. For a recent account of the way consumption and citizenship became linked in the United States, see McGovern, *Sold American*.
26 May, *The Big Tomorrow*, 55–99.

27 Erenberg, *Swingin' the Dream*.
28 Sklar, *Movie-Made America*, 195–214. The quote is from 196. For an account that emphasizes both the progressive and conservative elements in the Hollywood films of the 1930s, see Gary Gerstle's discussion of Frank Capra in *American Crucible*, 170–75.
29 Joseph, Rubenstein, and Zolov, "Assembling the Fragments," 16. For an early overview of this scholarship, see Stern, "Between Tragedy and Promise," 32–77. For examples from Argentine historiography, see Karush and Chamosa, eds., *The New Cultural History of Peronism*.
30 Hall, "Encoding/Decoding," 128–38.
31 Laclau, "Towards a Theory of Populism," 173.
32 This is far too large a historiography to summarize here. For one recent summary, see Karush and Chamosa, Introduction, *The New Cultural History of Peronism*, 3–8.

I CLASS FORMATION IN THE BARRIOS

1 The recording is almost certainly the Duke Ellington band in an improvisational passage. A stuttering, screaming trumpet follows a wild bass clarinet solo, a near cacophony that matches the images of urban chaos.
2 Sandrini played the role of Eusebio in the stage version of *Los tres berretines*. Sensing his star power, the filmmakers expanded his role when they adapted the script for the movie. See España, "El modelo institucional," 41.
3 As Pablo Alabarces has pointed out, the film underscores the power of popular sport by casting a star forward, Miguel Angel Lauri, in the role of the soccer-playing son. Alabarces, *Fútbol y patria*, 60. But this casting choice also made it even more likely that Sandrini, an experienced comic actor, would steal the show.
4 Rocchi, *Chimneys in the Desert*.
5 Johns, "The Urbanisation of a Secondary City," 489–513.
6 Szuchman, "The Limits of the Meliting Pot in Urban Argentina"; Baily, "Marriage Patterns and Immigrant Assimilation in Buenos Aires."
7 Moya, *Cousins and Strangers*, 292.
8 Baily, *Immigrants in the Lands of Promise*, 194.
9 Míguez, Argeri, Bjerg, and Otero, "Hasta que la Argentina nos una," 804–7.
10 Moya, *Cousins and Strangers*, 180–82. On Italian immigrants' dispersion throughout the city, see Baily, *Immigrants in the Lands of Promise*, 123–24.
11 On the occupational distribution of Italian and Spanish immigrants in Buenos Aires, see Baily, *Immigrants in the Lands of Promise*, 100–102; Moya, *Cousins and Strangers*, 205–19.
12 Germani, *Política y sociedad en una época de transición*, 197–210.
13 Rock, *Politics in Argentina*, 166–67.
14 *Crítica*, June 4, 1928, 9.

15 On Cocoliche, see Cara-Walker, "Cocoliche," 37–67; Seigel, "Cocoliche's Romp," 56–83. As Samuel Baily puts it, "Popular nativism . . . was inclusive of the immigrant." Baily, *Immigrants in the Lands of Promise*, 82.
16 Moya, *Cousins and Strangers*, 373–74. On anti-immigrant humor in the sainete, see Donald Castro, "The Image of the Creole Criminal in Argentine Popular Culture."
17 Rock, *Politics in Argentina*, 220. By 1936 two-thirds of the population of the city of Buenos Aires was native-born. Walter, *Politics and Urban Growth in Buenos Aires*, 152.
18 Rock, *Politics in Argentina*, 232.
19 Little, "The Social Origins of Peronism," 162–78.
20 Shipley, "On the Outside Looking In."
21 Rocchi, *Chimneys in the Desert*, 51.
22 On the development of the streetcar system and the concomitant urbanization of the north and west, see Scobie, *Buenos Aires*, 160–207. On the growth of the barrios in the 1920s and 1930s, see Walter, *Politics and Urban Growth in Buenos Aires*, 152, 258; González Leandri, "La nueva identidad de los sectores populares," 213–15.
23 Gutiérrez and Suriano, "Workers' Housing in Buenos Aires," 38.
24 Walter, *Politics and Urban Growth in Buenos Aires*, 84.
25 Gutiérrez and Suriano, "Workers' Housing in Buenos Aires," 40.
26 Horowitz, *Argentina's Radical Party and Popular Mobilization*, 65–94.
27 Moya, *Cousins and Strangers*, 216–18; Baily, *Immigrants in the Lands of Promise*, 93–120.
28 Moya, *Cousins and Strangers*, 274–75.
29 Fernando Devoto, *Historia de los italianos en la Argentina*, 372–78.
30 Rocchi, *Chimneys in the Desert*, 160–62.
31 On the zoning ordinance of 1914 see Scobie, *Buenos Aires*, 199. On industrial expansion in the barrios, see Walter, *Politics and Urban Growth in Buenos Aires*, 235–36.
32 Cited in González, "Lo propio y lo ajeno," 97.
33 Cited in Gutiérrez and Romero, "Sociedades barriales y bibliotecas populares," *Sectores populares, cultura y política*, 87.
34 The notion of conference attendance as a "desirable lifestyle" that could produce upward mobility is from ibid., 91. See also González Leandri, "Lo propio y lo ajeno," 111.
35 Gorelik, *La grilla y el parque*, 277–306. See also Silvestri and Gorelik, "San Cristóbal Sur entre el Mataadero y el Parque."
36 Gutiérrez and Romero, "Sociedades barriales y bibliotecas populares," *Sectores populares, cultura y política*, 92–96.
37 Privitellio, "Inventar el barrio," 122–24.
38 Historians of ethnic mutual-aid associations in Argentina have identified a similar phenomenon: leadership by a small, wealthy elite coexisted with

formal equality within the institutions and with a rhetoric that emphasized ethnic unity across class lines. Devoto and Fernández, "Mutualismo étnico, liderazgo y participación política," 140.

39 On the CHADE affair, see de Privitellio, *Vecinos y ciudadanos*, 149–82. Walter, *Politics and Urban Growth in Buenos Aires*, 173–75.
40 De Privitellio, "Inventar el barrio"; González Leandri, "La nueva identidad," 223–25.
41 González Leandri, "Lo propio y lo ajeno," 103–5.
42 *Canción Moderna* 1, no. 4 (April 16, 1928).
43 Rocchi, *Chimneys in the Desert*, 50.
44 The shoe industrialist Luis Pascarella, cited in ibid., 62. The translation is Rocchi's.
45 Rocchi, "La americanización del consumo," 155–56. The work cited is Loncán's *Mirador porteño: Nuevas charlas de mi amigo*.
46 *Canción Moderna* 8, no. 299 (December 11, 1933).
47 Horowitz, *Argentina's Radical Party and Popular Mobilization*; Karush, *Workers or Citizens*, 91.
48 Yrigoyen, *Mi vida y mi doctrina*, 137–38.
49 On non-pluralist democracy and on the efforts of pro-labor Radicals in the city of Rosario, see Karush, *Workers or Citizens*. On the avoidance of class-based appeals and on the similarities between Radicalism and Socialism in Buenos Aires, see de Privitellio, *Vecinos y ciudadanos*, 87–99, 208–9. On Yrigoyen's use of *obrerismo*, see Horowitz, *Argentina's Radical Party and Popular Mobilization*, 115–47. See also Persello: *El Partido Radical*.
50 Romero: "El apogeo de la sociedad de masas," http://www.efdeportes.com/efd50/romero.htm; Rocchi, "La americanización del consumo," 154.
51 Rocchi, *Chimneys in the Desert*, 62.
52 De Privitellio, "Inventar el barrio," 116.
53 Adamovsky, *Historia de la clase media argentina*, 135–216. See also Adamovsky, "Acerca de la relación entre el Radicalismo argentino y la 'clase media' (una vez más)," 209–51. Enrique Garguin agrees with Adamovsky's periodization. See Garguin, "'Los Argentinos descendemos de los Barcos,'" 161–84. Peru and Brazil represent contrasting cases. See Parker, *The Idea of the Middle Class*; Owensby, *Intimate Ironies*.
54 Míguez, "Familias de clase media," 21–45.
55 Rocchi, "La americanización del consumo," 177–80.
56 Míguez, "Familias de clase media," 38–42.
57 Falcón, "Izquierdas, régimen político, cuestión étnica y cuestión social en Argentina," 378–87.
58 Thompson, "The Limitations of Ideology in the Early Argentine Labour Movement," 81–99; Korzeniewicz, "The Labour Movement and the State in Argentina," 25–45.
59 Jeremy Adelman argues that the pragmatism of Argentine workers reflected

the fact that as immigrants, they lacked "a heritage of opposition to the capitalist designs of the dominant class." Adelman, "The Political Economy of Labour in Argentina," 16.

60 Rock, *Politics in Argentina*; Horowitz, *Argentina's Radical Party and Popular Mobilization*.

61 Adelman, "The Political Economy of Labour in Argentina," 21.

62 Munck with Falcón and Galitelli, *Argentina*, 100–102. On the strikes of 1928 in Rosario, see Karush, *Workers or Citizens*, 180–95; and Korzeniewicz, "The Labor Politics of Radicalism," 1–32.

63 Korzeniewicz, "Labor Unrest in Argentina," 9.

64 On the rise of the new industrial unions, see Durruty, *Clase obrera y peronismo*; Korzeniewicz, "Labor Unrest in Argentina," 7–40. On the success of the Communists, see also Tamarin, *The Argentine Labor Movement*, esp. 152.

65 Carrera, *La estrategia de la clase obrera—1936*. On the location of strike incidents, see 84–85.

66 Adamovsky, *Historia de la clase media argentina*, 135–76.

67 Horowitz, *Argentine Unions, the State and the Rise of Perón*, 79–84, 105–9, 165–68.

68 Saítta, *Regueros de tinta*, 49, 73.

69 Ibid., 117.

70 Ibid., 55–90.

71 Ibid., 65–79.

72 Rivero, *Una luz de almacén*.

73 *Los tres berretines*, originally a sainete by Arnaldo Malfatti and Nicolás de las Llanderas, belongs to a tradition of Argentine theatrical works about the middle class. Adamovsky traces the origins of this tendency to the plays of Gregorio de Laferrère, Florencio Sánchez, and Federico Mertens written in the first decade of the twentieth century. See Adamovsky, *Historia de la clase media argentina*, 219–26. There are other films that belong to this tradition—*Así es la vida* (Múgica, 1939), also based on a play by Malfatti and de las Llanderas, is a well-known example—but they are far outnumbered by the melodramatic films discussed in chapter 3. As I argue in the epilogue, the 1950s and 1960s would witness the full flowering of this tradition.

2 THE TRANSNATIONAL MARKETPLACE

1 Appadurai, *Modernity at Large*, 32.

2 Hansen, "Fallen Women, Rising Stars, New Horizons," 10–22.

3 On Argentine enthusiasm for the culture of the United States in this period, see Sheinin, *Argentina and the United States*, 60–62.

4 Silguer, "El primer sueldo de Max Glücksmann: cincuenta pesos mensuales," *Atlántida*, July 16, 1931, reprinted at: http://www.todotango.com/spanish/biblioteca/cronicas/gluucksmann.asp. On Glücksmann and the early years

of the Argentine recording industry, see Pujol, *Valentino en Buenos Aires*, 180–85. For a biographical account of Glücksmann as well as an analysis of his connections to the Jewish community, see Lewis, "Con Men, Cooks, and Cinema Kings," 170–83.

5 Collier, *The Life, Music, and Times of Carlos Gardel*, 49.
6 On Glücksmann's contests see Sierra, *Historia de la orquesta típica*, 87–89; Pinsón, "Los concursos de Max Glücksmann."
7 Pujol, *Jazz al sur*, 43. In Brazil, too, Whiteman was a much bigger star than the swing bands led by African Americans like Duke Ellington and Count Basie. According to Bryan McCann, this perception resulted from the local success of the Hollywood Whiteman vehicle *King of Jazz* (Anderson, 1930). See McCann, *Hello, Hello Brazil*, 138. However, by the mid-1930s Ellington in particular had begun to attract the attention of Argentine jazz aficionados. See, for example, *Sintonía* 3, no. 98 (March 9, 1935).
8 *Canción Moderna* 1, no. 4 (April 16, 1928). In the mid-1920s advertisements for Max Glücksmann's Discos Dobles Nacional invariably featured recordings of jazz and tango by the same artists. See, for example, *Caras y Caretas* (January 17, 1925), 17. On Firpo's jazz recordings, see Pujol, *Jazz al sur*, 20–21.
9 *Canción Moderna* 1, no. 6 (April 30, 1928).
10 Ibid. 7, no. 289 (October 2, 1933).
11 *Sintonía* 3, no. 101 (March 30, 1935).
12 Ibid., no. 91 (January 19, 1935). For another letter criticizing local radio stations for playing too much jazz, see *Sintonía* 6, no. 261 (April 21, 1938).
13 Pujol, *Jazz al sur*, 33–35; Héctor Angel Benedetti, "Adolfo Carabelli," http://www.todotango.com; Néstor Pinsón, "Orquesta Típica Victor," http://www.todotango.com.
14 Groppa, *The Tango in the United States*, 93–97. Nudler, "Osvaldo Fresedo."
15 Kenney, *Recorded Music in American Life*, 63.
16 Thompson, *Tango*, 174–75.
17 On the transition from Old Guard to New Guard, see Labraña and Sebastián, *Tango*, 45–49.
18 For one tango historian's take on de Caro, see Sierra, *Historia de la orquesta típica*, 97–99. One contemporary critic does link de Caro's innovations to jazz, comparing him to Duke Ellington: Nudler, "Julio De Caro," 45–48. On de Caro's "violin-cornet," see de Caro, *El tango en mis recuerdos*, 51–52.
19 *Sintonía* 5, no. 228 (September 2, 1937).
20 De Caro, *El tango en mis recuerdos*, 98.
21 *Sintonía* 3, no. 97 (March 2, 1935); *Sintonía* 5, no. 228 (September 2, 1937). Similarly, another member of the New Guard, the "master of the modernist tango," Juan Carlos Cobián, was said to have brought back innovations from a trip to North America. *Canción Moderna* 1, no. 15 (July 2, 1928).
22 *Sintonía* 3, no. 115 (July 6, 1935).

23 Sierra, *Historia de la orquesta típica*, 51–53.
24 On the musical origins of tango, see Thompson, *Tango*, 48–167; Collier, "The Tango Is Born," 18–64; Bates and Bates, *La Historia del Tango*, 19–27.
25 On the history of the bandoneón, see Zucchi, *El tango, el bandoneón, y sus intérpretes*.
26 Collier, *The Life, Music, and Times of Carlos Gardel*, 50–52.
27 On the Magaldi-Noda duo, see Amuchástegui, *Agustín Magaldi*, 53–66. Amuchástegui notes that the vogue for folk duos might have been inspired by popular Mexican acts of the period.
28 On criollista literature, see Prieto, *El discurso criollista en la formación de la Argentina moderna*. On the criollo circuses, see Chasteen, *National Rhythms, African Roots*, 51–70.
29 Collier, *The Life, Music, and Times of Carlos Gardel*, 43.
30 The tangos of Agustín Bardi and José Martínez stand out for their criollista lyrics, as does the early classic of Villoldo and Saborido, "La morocha."
31 Canaro, *Mis bodas de oro con el tango y mis memorias*, 42–44.
32 Castro, "The Massification of the Tango," 94.
33 Garramuño, *Modernidades primitivas*.
34 A useful account of the international tango craze is Cooper, "Tangomania in Europe and North America," 67–104.
35 Savigliano, *Tango and the Political Economy of Passion*, 111. On the reception of tango in Europe, see also Matallana, *Qué saben los pitucos*.
36 To cite just one of many examples, Osvaldo Fresedo, a modernizing tango bandleader born and raised in the city of Buenos Aires, was pictured in the *New York Times* in 1930 dressed as a gaucho. See *New York Times* (March 30, 1930), XX12.
37 On the impact of Valentino in Argentina, see Pujol, *Valentino en Buenos Aires*, 107–10.
38 Garramuño, *Modernidades primitivas*, 223.
39 Lugones, *El Payador*.
40 *Sintonía* 3, no. 115 (July 6, 1935).
41 Ibid. 5, no. 208 (April 15, 1937).
42 *Canción Moderna* 7, no. 295 (November 13, 1933).
43 *Sintonía* 5, no. 208 (April 15, 1937). Ellipses in original.
44 *Crítica*, March 18, 1925, 7.
45 Ibid., June 13, 1928, 2. See also ibid., June 9, 1928, 12.
46 *Canción Moderna* 7, no. 297 (November 20, 1933).
47 *Sintonía* 3, no. 101 (March 30, 1935).
48 Ibid. 6, no. 266 (May 26, 1938).
49 Ibid., no. 269 (June 16, 1938).
50 The price of records and phonographs as well as the 4.5 percent figure are from Castro, "The Massification of the Tango," 94. The wage information is from *Anuario "La Razón,"* 219.
51 On the early years of radio, see Claxton, *From Parsifal to Perón*, 10–12; Gallo,

La radio, vol. 1; Ulanovsky et al., *Días de radio,* 16–22; Sarlo, *La imaginación técnica,* 109–22.
52 Claxton, *From Parsifal to Perón,* 147.
53 Writing in 1936, Edmundo Taybo estimated that there were 1.5 million receivers in Argentina. Cited in Castro, "The Massification of the Tango," 94. In 1940 the U.S. Department of Commerce reported its best guess as "1,000,000 to 1,050,000" but also claimed that some 200,000 sets were sold in the country each year (*World Radio Markets,* 26). Claxton cites two estimates of roughly 1.2 million for 1934. See Claxton, *From Parsifal to Perón,* 146, 149. The population of Argentina in 1930 was 12,046,000.
54 U.S. Department of Commerce, *World Radio Markets,* 25.
55 Claxton, *From Parsifal to Perón,* 106.
56 Schwoch, *The American Radio Industry and Its Latin American Activities,* 134–40.
57 Ibid., 137–38; Claxton, *From Parsifal to Perón,* 91–92.
58 *La Nación,* September 14, 1923, 12. On the Firpo-Dempsey fight, see also Gallo, *La radio,* vol. 1, 41.
59 See, for example, the ad for the locally produced Pekam receivers in *La Nación,* September 13, 1923, 16.
60 Ibid.
61 On the evolution of radio regulation in Argentina, see Claxton, *From Parsifal to Perón,* 160–64; Andrea Matallana, "Locos por la radio," 39–52.
62 Starr, *The Creation of the Media,* 363–67.
63 Claxton, *From Parsifal to Perón,* 73.
64 Gallo, *La radio,* vol. 2, 62–71.
65 Dirección General de Correos y Telégrafos, *Reorganización de los servicios de radiodifusión,* 21.
66 Claxton, *From Parsifal to Perón,* 32.
67 Finkielman, *The Film Industry in Argentina,* 112–14.
68 *Sintonía* 9, no. 399 (July 9, 1941), 28; *Caras y Caretas,* January 25, 1936. On Yankelevich, see also Matallana, *"Locos por la radio,"* 81–90; Claxton, *From Parsifal to Perón,* 16, 31.
69 Lary May, *The Big Tomorrow,* 58–59; May, *Screening Out the Past,* 169–76.
70 De Paoli, *Función social de la radiotelefonía,* 43–51; "La Torre de Babel," *Sintonía* 7, no. 303 (February 8, 1939).
71 *Radiolandia* 11, no. 538 (July 9, 1938). See also *Sintonía* 10, no. 425 (July 8, 1942).
72 *Radiolandia* 11, no. 538 (July 9, 1938).
73 Simari, *Mi historia la escribo yo,* 61–66. See also the tremendous attendance of fans anxious to bid farewell to Vermicelli, when Simari, dressed as his most popular character, left for Europe. *Canción Moderna* 7, no. 302 (December 30, 1933).
74 Monte, "Chispazos de tradición," 47.
75 *Sintonía* 5, no. 231 (September 23, 1937).

76 Matallana, "Locos por la radio," 83–84.
77 On the wild popularity of *Chispazos de Tradición*, see Ulanovsky et al., *Días de radio*, 73–80. On the use of *Chispazos* scripts in the schools, see *Canción Moderna* 7, no. 290 (October 9, 1933).
78 See *Canción Moderna* 7, no. 300 (December 18, 1933); ibid., no. 301 (December 23, 1933).
79 On one contest on Radio Stentor, see ibid., no. 296 (November 20, 1933).
80 *Caras y Caretas*, December 28, 1935. Dirección General de Correos y Telégrafos, *Reorganización de los servicios de radiodifusión*, 343.
81 *Caras y Caretas*, December 19, 1936, 150.
82 *Sintonía* 1, no. 23 (September 30, 1933), 89–91.
83 Matallana, "Locos por la radio," 101.
84 Ibid., 95. These proportions hardly wavered between 1936 and 1941. Matallana emphasizes heterogeneity in her account of radio programming, but as these numbers suggest, this heterogeneity existed on the margins of a programming core that was quite similar up and down the dial.
85 For advertising rates, see Office of Inter-American Affairs, *Data and Rates of Radio Stations in the Other American Republics and Puerto Rico*, 15–18. On the program offerings of Radio Splendid and Radio Excelsior, see Claxton, *From Parsifal to Perón*, 36–39.
86 *Sintonía* 3, no. 100 (March 23, 1935).
87 De Paoli, *Función social de la radiotelefonía*, 22. *Sintonía* 3, no. 135 (November 23, 1935).
88 *El Mundo*, November 29, 1935, 10.
89 Ibid., November 30, 1935, 8. For a description of the station's programming plans, see ibid., November 28, 1935, 8. A couple of weeks after Radio El Mundo's inauguration, *Caras y Caretas* applauded the station as "a guarantee of good taste and technical progress." *Caras y Caretas*, December 7, 1935, 132.
90 *Sintonía* 3, no. 135 (November 23, 1935).
91 "La torre de Babel," *Sintonía* 7, no. 300 (January 18, 1939).
92 *Sintonía* 6, no. 298 (January 4, 1939), 38. Dirección General de Correos y Telégrafos, *Reorganización de los servicios de radiodifusión*, 259–64.
93 Sarlo, *La imaginación técnica*, 114–15.
94 *Canción Moderna* 11, no. 401 (November 23, 1935).
95 *Radiolandia* 11, no. 538 (July 9, 1938).
96 Claxton, *From Parsifal to Perón*, 69–72.
97 Starr, *The Creation of the Media*, 367.
98 Chamosa, "Indigenous or Criollo," 90. On the dominance of the networks in the Interior, see Dirección General de Correos y Telégrafos, *Reorganización de los servicios de radiodifusión*, 260–61.
99 On early Argentine experiments in film, see Finkielman, *The Film Industry in Argentina*, 5–11.
100 Sarlo, *La imaginación*, 125–28.

101 Di Núbila, *La época de oro*, 11–50. Barnard, "Popular Cinema and Populist Politics," *Argentine Cinema*, 18–24.
102 López, "'A Train of Shadows,'" 161–62. Di Núbila, *La época de oro*, 17–19.
103 As one scholar has recently argued, Latin American filmmakers of the silent era produced a "criollo aesthetic" that combined elements drawn from sources at home and in the United States and Europe in order to insert their nations into a "Euro-American modernity." Rodríguez, "Latin American Silent Cinema," 36.
104 Thompson, *Exporting Entertainment*.
105 Ibid., 78–79.
106 Schnitman, "The Argentine Film Industry," 51–52.
107 Thompson, *Exporting Entertainment*, 79.
108 Barnard, *Argentine Cinema*, 147.
109 Schnitman, "The Argentine Film Industry," 63.
110 Ibid., 34.
111 Ibid., 65–68.
112 Interview with Luis Moglia Barth in *Reportaje al cine argentino*, ed. Calistro et al., 264–72; Di Núbila, *La época de oro*, 71–76; Manetti, "Argentina Sono Film," 162–65.
113 Of course the influence likely went both ways: John Alton had an extensive and influential career in Hollywood *after* spending his formative years in Argentina. On Alton, see España, "John Alton," *Cine Argentino*, vol. 1, 220–21. Another American cinematographer who enjoyed a long career in Argentina was Bob Roberts.
114 Schnitman, "The Argentine Film Industry," 61–62. For one call for more Spanish-language films, see *Sintonía* 1, no. 15 (August 5, 1933), 79.
115 Finkielman, *The Film Industry in Argentina*, 166–84.
116 In 1910, for example, blue-collar workers constituted almost three-quarters of the audience for movies in New York City. Rosenzweig, "Eight Hours for What We Will," 194.
117 Ibid., 198–204; Cohen, *Making a New Deal*, 120–27.
118 May, *Screening Out the Past*, 22–95. Ross, *Working-Class Hollywood*, 173–77. On the earlier working-class genre of spectacular melodrama, see Singer, *Melodrama and Modernity*.
119 On Classical Hollywood style, see Bordwell, Staiger, and Thompson, *The Classical Hollywood Cinema*. On the standardization of reception, see Hansen, *Babel and Babylon*, 76–89.
120 Maranghello, "Cine y estado," 24–159 and "Orígenes y evolución de la censura," 160–83.
121 Cited in Maranghello, "Cine y estado," 27.
122 *El Mundo*, May 28, 1939, 14.
123 Ibid., September 7, 1934, 15. The film under review is the Carlos Gardel vehicle *Cuesta Abajo* (1934). See also ibid., May 23, 1935, 28, in which Néstor

congratulates the film *Monte Criollo* for avoiding "any base and distasteful notes, without concessions and with laudable dignity." In a letter to *Sintonía*, one reader attacked Néstor's persistent negativism in patriotic terms: "He does not do anything but speak ill of our national films. It is impossible to believe that this man is Argentine." *Sintonía* 5, no. 232 (September 30, 1937).

124 Cited in España, "El modelo institucional," 48.

125 To cite just one example, in its review of the Argentine films of 1935, *Caras y Caretas* denounced "plots from the slums, lunfardo expressions, and actors pulled from the theater where certain successes are achieved with dangerous ease." *Caras y Caretas*, January 1, 1936.

126 *La Razón*, May 25, 1939, 15.

127 Arlt, *Notas sobre el cinematógrafo*, 82. On the masculine fear of foreign movie stars like Rudolph Valentino, see Pujol, *Valentino en Buenos Aires*, 107–10. Frustration over the inability to attain the lifestyles depicted in Hollywood films was a common reaction among moviegoers throughout the world in the 1920s. For the cases of the United States and Cuba, see Rosenzweig, "Eight Hours for What We Will," 221; and Pérez, *On Becoming Cuban*, 290–353.

128 See *Sintonía* 5, no. 226 (August 19, 1937); *Sintonía* 5, no. 221 (July 15, 1937).

129 *Radiolandia* 13, no. 595 (August 12, 1939).

130 *La Razón*, July 7, 1938, 10. The film under review is *Mujeres que trabajan* (Romero, 1938).

131 Garramuño, *Modernidades primitivas*, 216–18.

132 U.S. Department of Commerce, *Motion Pictures in Argentina and Brazil*, 15.

133 Golden, *Review of Foreign Film Markets during 1936*, 176.

134 Golden, *Motion Picture Markets of Latin America*, 23.

135 *El Mundo*, June 29, 1939, 30–31, 34.

136 On Pompeya's movie theater, see Romero, "Nueva Pompeya, libros y catecismo," 176.

137 Golden, *Motion Picture Markets of Latin America*, 23–24. Average daily wage rates are listed on 19.

138 Cited in Tranchini, "El Cine Argentino y la construcción de un imaginario criollista."

139 Golden, *Motion Picture Markets of Latin America*, 24.

140 See, for example, the descriptions of *Riachuelo* (Moglia Barth, 1934) and *Ayúdame a vivir* (Ferreyra, 1936) in *El Heraldo del Cinematografista*, July 11, 1934, and September 2, 1936. The U.S. Commerce Department commented in 1944 that "not so long ago" Argentine films were shown in only one first-run house in Buenos Aires.

141 I arrived at these numbers by cross-referencing the listings in *El Mundo*, June 29, 1939, 30–31, 34, with Manrupe and Portela, *Un diccionario de films argentinos*.

142 See chapter 5, below.

143 The forty-nine Argentine movies released in 1940 represented just 10 percent of the total number of films shown in the country that year.

3 REPACKAGING POPULAR MELODRAMA

1 Brooks, *The Melodramatic Imagination*, 21, 15.
2 See Singer, *Melodrama and Modernity*, 131–48; Walkowitz, *City of Dreadful Delight*, esp. 85–87.
3 Martín-Barbero, *Communication, Culture and Hegemony*, 167. See also Oroz, *Melodrama*.
4 Monsiváis, "Se sufre, pero se aprende," 7–19.
5 Bourdieu, *Distinction*.
6 Williams, "'Something Else besides a Mother,'" 320. On the "radical ambiguity" in melodrama, see Elsaesser, "Tales of Sound and Fury," 47. Feminist film theorists have emphasized the structural instability of melodrama, even if they have disagreed over the extent to which particular films enable readings that question patriarchal ideology. See, for example, E. Ann Kaplan's more skeptical interpretation of *Stella Dallas* (Vidor, 1937) in Kaplan, *Motherhood and Representation*, 149–79. Laura Podalsky has extended this sort of analysis to the Mexican "revolutionary melodrama." Podalsky, "Disjointed Frames," 57–71.
7 Pellettieri, *Cien años de teatro argentino*, 15–18; Chasteen, *National Rhythms*, 51–56; Cara-Walker, "Cocoliche," 41–43.
8 On the broad, cross-class appeal of the zarzuela in Buenos Aires, see McCleary, "Popular, Elite *and* Mass Culture," 1–27.
9 On the transition from the Spanish sainete to the Argentine version, see Pellettieri, "El sainete español y el sainete criollo: géneros diversos," *Cien años del teatro argentino*, 27–36; Pellarolo, *Sainete criollo/Democracia/Representación*, 95–107. On the authors' rights law of 1910, see McCleary, "Life Is a Cabaret?"
10 Mazziotti, "Bambalinas," 74–75.
11 The poem is "Antífona Roja," and the translated excerpts are from James, *Doña María's Story*, 253. See Szmetan, "Enigmas sobre aspectos de la vida, y la relación con su obra, de Almafuerte," 219–30.
12 Armus, "Tango, Gender, and Tuberculosis in Buenos Aires," 103–10; García Jiménez, *Estampas de tango*, 85–86.
13 Collier, *The Life, Music, and Times of Carlos Gardel*, 61; McCleary, "Life Is a Cabaret?," 21.
14 Armus, "Tango, Gender, and Tuberculosis in Buenos Aires," 115.
15 Collier, *The Life, Music, and Times of Carlos Gardel*, 65–66; for the performance record of *El cabaret de Montmartre*, see McCleary, "Life Is a Cabaret?," 22.
16 Mazziotti, "Bambalinas," 73. On Vaccarezza's *Tu cuna fue un conventillo*, see Pellettieri, *Historia del Teatro Argentino en Buenos Aires*, 14–15.
17 Borges, *Evaristo Carriego*, 79, 134, 146–47.
18 Romano, "Prólogo," *Las letras del Tango*, 8.
19 As Miriam Hansen suggests, commodification renders popular traditions

"politically ineffective," and yet counter-hegemonic readings remain possible. Hansen, *Babel and Babylon*, 92.
20 Savigliano, *Tango and the Political Economy of Passion*, 61. My analysis of the milonguita theme in tango lyrics draws on Ulla, *Tango, Rebelión y Nostalgia*, 33–44.
21 All tango lyrics are from Romano, *Las letras del Tango*, unless otherwise noted, and all English translations are mine unless otherwise noted.
22 Guy, *Sex and Danger in Buenos Aires*, 152.
23 Archetti, *Masculinities*, 152–55. The phrase "doubting masculinity" comes from one of Archetti's informants. See 157.
24 Armus, "Tango, Gender, and Tuberculosis in Buenos Aires," 111.
25 *Canción Moderna* 1, no. 9 (May 21, 1928).
26 Lyrics cited in Matamoro, *Ciudad del tango*, 117.
27 Savigliano, *Tango and the Political Economy of Passion*, 65–66.
28 Matamoro, *Ciudad del tango*, 136.
29 *Sintonía* 6, no. 298 (January 4, 1939).
30 Ibid. 1, no. 10 (July 1, 1933).
31 *Canción Moderna* 7, no. 294 (November 6, 1933).
32 On the symbolism of seamstresses and tuberculosis in Argentine popular melodrama, see Armus, "Tango, Gender, and Tuberculosis in Buenos Aires."
33 Amuchástegui, *Agustín Magaldi*, 76.
34 Matamoro, *Ciudad del tango*, 116–46; Pablo Vila accepts Matamoro's analysis of tango fatalism in part, but he argues that Matamoro fails to appreciate the significance of the social recognition that tango granted the popular sectors and that he ignores those tango lyrics which contested elite hegemony. Vila, "Tango to Folk," 113–21.
35 Matamoro, *El Tango*, 49–52.
36 Viladrich, "Neither Virgins nor Whores," 272–93.
37 Calistro et al., *Reportaje al cine argentino*, 238.
38 Néstor Pinsón, "Rosita Quiroga."
39 *Sintonía* 1, no. 10 (July 1, 1933).
40 *Sintonía* 7, no. 329 (August 9, 1939).
41 Sarlo, *El imperio de los sentimientos*.
42 Ibid., 169.
43 Ibid., 63.
44 Ibid., 135.
45 Gledhill, "The Melodramatic Field," 34.
46 Couselo, *El Negro Ferreyra*. Ferreyra's article is cited on 112. See also Falicov, "Argentine Cinema and the Construction of National Popular Identity," 66–68.
47 Calistro et al., *Reportaje al cine argentino*, 77.
48 Kohen, "Estudios Cinematográficos Argentinos SIDE," 265–67.
49 Lamarque, *Libertad Lamarque*, 149–50.

50 Ibid., 135. Elsewhere, Lamarque contrasted her own appeal to that of Tita Merello, who specialized in depicting women from the arrabales. Calistro et al., *Reportaje al cine argentino*, 97.

51 On the trilogy of tango operas Lamarque and Ferreyra made for SIDE, see Couselo, *El Negro Ferreyra*, 79–87; Kohen, "Estudios Cinematográficos Argentinos SIDE," 267–71; Di Núbila, *La época de oro*, 133–40.

52 Kohen, "Estudios Cinematográficos Argentinos SIDE," 274–76. On Hollywood's reliance on cutting and seamless continuity editing, see Bordwell, Staiger, and Thompson, *The Classical Hollywood Cinema*, 55–59.

53 On the popularity of the tango among elite Argentines, see Matallana, *Qué saben los pitucos*, 19–20.

54 Paladino, "Libertad Lamarque, la reina de la lágrima," 69. On elite consumption of tango, see Matamoro, *La ciudad del tango*, 96–103.

55 Todo Tango, *Diccionario Lunfardo*, http://www.todotango.com/spanish/bblioteca/PalabraLunfarda.aspx?p=pimpollo.

56 Oroz, *Melodrama*, 171 (italics in original).

57 España, "El modelo institucional," 134. On *Stella Dallas*, see the works cited in note 6, above.

58 Laclau, "Towards a Theory of Populism."

59 Arlt, "Ayer ví ganar a los argentinos."

60 *Crítica*, June 4, 1928, 9.

61 Quinziano, "La comedia," 129–46.

62 Calistro et al., *Reportaje al cine argentino*, 152; Di Núbila, *La época de oro*, 72. *La Prensa*'s reviewer commented on Sandrini's tendency to play the same role in every film: "Is his repertoire the same? Does he keep repeating his old character from *Los tres berretines*? Certainly." *La Prensa*, January 21, 1937, 16. See also Pelletieri, "El ultimo actor popular," 91–99.

63 A clear precedent for the character of the lovable thief is the criollo criminal celebrated in the sainete. See Castro, "The Sainete Porteño," 46.

64 As María Valdez points out, Sandrini's image as a "buenazo del barrio," always willing to "jugarse por un amigo" is central to all his film characters. Valdez, "Luis Sandrini," 45.

65 *La Nación*, September 19, 1940, 15.

66 Marshall and D'Anna, *Niní Marshall*, 72–73.

67 Moya, *Cousins and Strangers*, 225–27, 371–72.

68 Marshall, *Las travesuras de Niní*, 28.

69 Pauls, *Lino Palacio La infancia de la risa*, 51–55.

70 Posadas, *Niní Marshall*, 113.

71 Marshall and D'Anna, *Niní Marshall*, 75.

72 Ibid., 64; Posadas, *Niní Marshall*, 23–24.

73 Marshall and D'Anna, *Niní Marshall*, 76–77.

74 Posadas, *Niní Marshall*, 51–52.

75 According to *Sintonía*'s radio reviewer, Marshall had managed what no one

else had: she appealed to "every category of listener." *Sintonía* 6, no. 266 (May 26, 1938). In light of the enormous success of *Divorcio en Montevideo*, *El Mundo* declared Marshall the biggest box-office star in Argentina: *El Mundo*, June 13, 1939, 25.

76 *La Prensa*, July 7, 1938, 18.
77 Marshall and D'Anna, *Niní Marshall*, 77, 81.
78 *Sintonía* 7, no. 326 (July 19, 1939).
79 Ibid. 7, no. 330 (August 16, 1939).
80 Ibid. 7, no. 326 (July 19, 1939).
81 The term "white telephone film" comes from the Italian cinema of the 1930s, in which these escapist movies set among the wealthy proliferated. See Hay, "Placing Cinema, Fascism, and the Nation in a Diagram of Italian Modernity," 115–37.
82 Posadas, *Niní Marshall*, 69.
83 The Legrand twins would go on to star as "innocent girls" (ingénues) in dozens of similar comedies: Di Núbila, *La época de oro*, 336–37.

4   MASS-CULTURAL NATION BUILDING

1 Guy, *Sex and Danger in Buenos Aires*, 142–44. Analogous to this crackdown on the tango were elite attempts to enforce good sportsmanship among working-class soccer players. See Frydenberg, "Prácticas y valores en el proceso de popularización del fútbol, Buenos Aires," 7–29.
2 Finchelstein, *Transatlantic Fascism*. See also Spektorowski, *The Origins of Argentina's Revolution of the Right*; Deutsch, *Las Derechas*; Buchrucker, *Nacionalismo y Peronismo*.
3 Quattrocchi-Woisson, *Los males de la memoria*.
4 Sarlo, *Una modernidad periférica*, 215–46.
5 Martínez Estrada, *La cabeza de Goliat*, 202.
6 One example is Linyera's tango "Boedo" (1927), which juxtaposes the quintessential tango barrio with the more pretentious Florida neighborhood: "¿Qué quiere hacer esa fifí Florida? / ¡Si vos ponés tu corazón canyengue / como una flor en el ojal prendida / en los balcones de cada bulín!" (What can that fancy Florida do? / If you put your workingman's heart like a flower in a boutonniere / in the balconies of every guy's pad). Linyera's real name was Francisco Bautista Rímoli.
7 *Canción Moderna* 1, no. 6 (April 30, 1928).
8 Collier, *The Life, Music, and Times of Carlos Gardel*, 196.
9 Ulla, *Tango, rebelión y nostalgia*, 76–79.
10 Matallana, *"Locos por la radio,"* 53–60. See also Maranghello, "El espacio de la recepción," 51.
11 *Canción Moderna* 7, no. 295 (November 13, 1933).
12 Ibid., no. 289 (October 2, 1933).
13 *Radiolandia* 11, no. 545 (August 27, 1938).

14 Ibid., no. 536 (June 25, 1938).
15 Ibid., no. 533 (June 4, 1938).
16 Ibid., no. 538 (July 9, 1938).
17 Ibid., no. 537 (July 2, 1938).
18 In 1933 *Canción Moderna* argued that lyricists like Alfredo Le Pera should be praised for avoiding lunfardo, but five years later, the magazine insisted that improving tango lyrics did not require doing away with the porteño argot: *Radiolandia* 11, no. 545 (August 27, 1938).
19 *Sintonía* 3, no. 94 (February 9, 1935).
20 Ibid., no. 101 (March 30, 1935).
21 Ibid., no. 90 (January 12, 1935).
22 Ibid., no. 92 (January 26, 1935).
23 *Sintonía* 1, no. 10 (July 1, 1933).
24 Ibid. 3, no. 100 (March 23, 1935).
25 *Antena* 8, no. 397 (October 1, 1938).
26 *Sintonía* 6, no. 271 (June 30, 1938).
27 Ibid.
28 *Canción Moderna* 7, no. 297 (November 27, 1933).
29 De Caro, *El tango en mis recuerdos*, 99.
30 *Sintonía* 6, no. 228 (September 2, 1937). Dajos Bela, who was Jewish, led a successful dance band in Berlin before the rise of the Nazis. In 1935 he relocated to Buenos Aires.
31 Ibid. 5, no. 208 (April 15, 1937).
32 *Radiolandia* 11, no. 538 (July 9, 1938); ibid., no. 545 (August 27, 1938).
33 *Canción Moderna*, October 12, 1935.
34 De Caro, *El tango en mis recuerdos*, 35. Blas Matamoro stresses de Caro's position as a member of the "middle class with status pretensions." Matamoro, *La ciudad del tango*, 108.
35 Sierra, *Historia de la orquesta típica*, 99.
36 *Radiolandia* 11, no. 538 (July 9, 1938).
37 *Sintonía* 6, no. 228 (September 2, 1937).
38 For example, the folk pianist Argentino Valle's "Pampita" is described as a milonga pampeana in ibid. 3, no. 98 (March 9, 1935), while Ciriaco Ortiz's version of "Soy porteño" is described as a milonga tangueada, played with authentic porteño flavor, in ibid., no. 125 (September 14, 1935).
39 Barrese and Piana, "El último reportaje a Sebastián Piana. Reprinted at http://www.todotango.com/spanish/biblioteca/cronicas/entrevista_piana.asp. In this interview, Piana gives equal credit for the creation of the new milonga to Pedro Maffia.
40 Interview with Piana in Göttling, *Tango, melancólico testigo*, 88.
41 The most recent and most exhaustive account of Tango's African origins is Thompson, *Tango*.
42 Bates and Bates, *La Historia del Tango*, 19–27.
43 For Kordon's articles on the African origins of tango, see *Sintonía* 6, no. 226

(August 19, 1937), ibid. 5, no. 211 (May 6, 1937), ibid., no. 212 (May 13, 1937), among others. For Kordon's denunciation of jazz, see ibid., no. 210 (April 29, 1937).

44 *Radiolandia* 15, no. 690 (June 7, 1941).
45 According to Robert Farris Thompson, Piana himself was inspired by these international musical trends. See Thompson, *Tango*, 131.
46 "Liberation of the drum" is a phrase coined by Ned Sublette in *Cuba and Its Music*, 433.
47 Andrews, *The Afro-Argentines of Buenos Aires*.
48 Blomberg and Paz, *Bajo la santa federación*.
49 *Sintonía* 7, no. 305 (February 22, 1939).
50 Ibid. 6, no. 270 (June 23, 1938). *Sintonía*'s editors signaled their partial disagreement with this piece by printing it alongside photos of de Caro and Fresedo, with extremely flattering captions. Incidentally, tango historians often emphasize the differences between de Caro, whose music always featured polyphony and rhythmic counterpoint, and Fresedo, who pursued melody and harmony. See, for example, Labraña and Sebastián, *Tango*, 49. But as the piece from *Sintonía* indicates, at the time the two were commonly lumped together as melodic and harmonic innovators, defined in opposition to the "King of the Beat," Juan D'Arienzo.
51 *Antena* 8, no. 394 (September 10, 1938). *Antena* frequently praised de Caro for having achieved the perfect balance between rhythm and melody: "The genre that Julio De Caro's band now cultivates is in perfect accord with the tastes of the public, which enjoys rhythm but also appreciates when the melodic concept is not forgotten." Ibid. 8, no. 396 (September 24, 1938).
52 *Sintonía* 6, no. 265 (May 19, 1938).
53 *Radiolandia* 11, no. 538 (July 9, 1938).
54 Suriano, *Anarquistas*, 145–73.
55 On the Artistas del Pueblo, see Frank, *Los Artistas del Pueblo*. The quote from Facio is cited and translated on page 172. On the Boedo group, see Leland, *The Last Happy Men*, 38–44, 57–66.
56 Saítta, *Regueros de tinta*, 105–8.
57 Spektorowski, *The Origins of Argentina's Revolution of the Right*, 142–50.
58 On Manzi's participation in FORJA, see Salas, *Homero Manzi y su tiempo*, 155–70.
59 Ford, *Homero Manzi*, 36–37.
60 Reprinted in Manzi, *Sur*, 97.
61 Ibid., 116–17.
62 Cited in Ford, *Homero Manzi*, 84.
63 Cited in ibid., 79. The ellipses are in Ford. On Manzi's ambivalent view of Gardel, see Salas, *Homero Manzi y su tiempo*, 126–30.
64 On Manzi's lyrics, see Ulla, *Tango, rebelión y nostalgia*, 122–29; Salas, *Homero Manzi y su tiempo*, 120–24, 134–46, 171–81.
65 Ford, *Homero Manzi*, 82.

66 Cited in Sarlo, *Una modernidad periférica*, 210.
67 Manzi's nostalgia for rural Argentina may have reflected his memories of the small town of Añatuya in the province of Santiago del Estero, where he lived as a child before moving to the Buenos Aires barrio of Pompeya. See Alén Lascano, "Homero Manzi," 8–27.
68 Manzi, *Sur: Barrio de tango*, 148.
69 Félix-Didier, "Soñando con Hollywood," 77–103.
70 Maranghello, *Artistas argentinos asociados*, 34.
71 Ibid., 17.
72 Dabove, *Nightmares of the Lettered City*, 229–40. On Lugones's political trajectory, see Spektorowski, *The Origins of Argentina's Revolution of the Right*, 67–77.
73 Fürstenberger, "Güemes y los de abajo," 1109–19; Gramuglio, "La primera épica de Lugones," 157–63.
74 *Sintonía* 10, no. 425 (July 8, 1942).
75 Maranghello, *Artistas argentinos asociados*, 49. On the collaboration between Manzi and Petit de Murat, see Salas, *Homero Manzi y su tiempo*, 198–207.
76 Maranghello, *Artistas argentinos asociados*, 67. On the success of the film, see Di Núbila, *La época de oro*, 392. See also Lusnich, *El drama social-folklórico*, esp. 178–83; Félix-Didier and Levinson, "The Building of a Nation," 50–63.
77 *Los caranchos de la Florida* is based on the novel of the same name by Benito Lynch (1916). Like his contemporary Ricardo Güiraldes, Lynch was a criollista novelist who depicted the gaucho as a domesticated peon, lacking the rebelliousness and proclivity to violence that defined the gaucho in nineteenth-century literature. Slatta, *Gauchos and the Vanishing Frontier*, 191–92.
78 On Soffici's social-folkloric films, see Falicov, "Argentine Cinema and the Construction of National Popular Identity," 68–72; Tranchini, "El Cine Argentino y la construcción de un imaginario criollista," 131–35; Lusnich, *El drama social-folklórico*, 182–86.
79 Tranchini, "El Cine Argentino y la construcción de un imaginario criollista," 134–35.
80 *Sintonía* 9, no. 400 (July 23, 1941), 78. *Prisioneros de la tierra* won an Argentine critics' poll as the best domestic film of 1939. See *El Heraldo del Cinematografista* 10, no. 44 (January 17, 1940), 8.
81 *El Mundo*, September 1, 1938, 21.
82 On Ford's influence on Soffici, see Di Núbila, *La época de oro*, 264.
83 Chamosa, *The Argentine Folklore Movement*.
84 Alén Lascano, "Cuando el folklore llegó a Buenos Aires," 64–75.
85 Cited in ibid., 68.
86 *Canción Moderna* 7, no. 294 (November 6, 1933).
87 *Sintonía* 7, no. 309 (March 22, 1939).
88 Ibid. 10, no. 431 (December 30, 1942). On Ochoa's Cafiaspirina program, see the ad in *Radiolandia* 15, no. 693 (June 28, 1941).

89 See, for example, *Sintonía* 6, no. 261 (April 21, 1938); *Sintonía* 7, no. 298 (January 4, 1939).
90 Ibid. 6, no. 263 (May 5, 1938).
91 *Antena* 11, no. 570 (January 22, 1942).
92 *Sintonía* 7, no. 314 (April 26, 1939).
93 *Radiolandia* 11, no. 526 (April 16, 1938).
94 Lattes, "La dinámica de la población rural en la Argentina."
95 *Sintonía* 1, no. 22 (September 23, 1933), 7.
96 *Radiolandia* 11, no. 526 (April 16, 1938).
97 On Luna, see Almeida de Gargiulo, de Yanzi, and de Vera, *Buenaventura Luna*.
98 *Sintonía* 6, no. 260 (April 14, 1938).
99 *Antena* 8, no. 397 (October 1, 1938).
100 *Sintonía* 9, no. 402 (August 20, 1941).
101 *Sintonía* 7, no. 314 (April 26, 1939).
102 Almeida de Gargiulo, de Yanzi, and de Vera, *Buenaventura Luna*, 52.
103 *Antena*, October 29, 1938. The second ellipsis is in the original.
104 On Romero's film career, see Insaurralde, *Manuel Romero*; Mallimacci and Marrone, eds., *Cine e imaginario social*.
105 *La Razón*, June 29, 1939, 13. Romero's films repeatedly inspired this sort of critical condescension. In *El Mundo*, Calki summed up his review of *Gente bien* as follows: "Easy spectacle, with straightforward techniques, aimed at the broadest popular sector." *El Mundo*, June 29, 1939, 17. Reviewing another Romero film, *La vuelta de Rocha*, *La Prensa* echoed this elitism: "Perhaps because it is aimed at the popular, it carries the plot to vulgar terrain and plays rude notes . . . Precisely for those reasons, in popular theaters its success is guaranteed." *La Prensa*, September 9, 1937, 16.
106 España, "Los muchachos de antes no usaban gomina," 229.
107 Sommer, *Foundational Fictions*. Of course, *Birth of a Nation* (Griffith, 1915) is the paradigmatic case of a cinematic national romance.
108 That *It Happened One Night* provided the inspiration for *La rubia del camino* is a matter of scholarly consensus. See, for example, Di Núbila, *La época de oro*, 190–92; Insaurralde, *Manuel Romero*, 24; Valdez, "El reino de la comedia," 286–87. Contemporary critics frequently cited the Hollywood influences visible in Romero's films. As *La Nación* commented in its review of *Mujeres que trabajan*, "The frequent moviegoer must recognize . . . the atmosphere, the heart and even the details of foreign films." *La Nación*, July 7, 1938, 14.
109 Karnick and Jenkins, "Introduction: Comedy and the Social World," 277. See also Karnick, "Comedy and Reaffirmation in Hollywood Romantic Comedy," 123–46. Although Robert Sklar argues that *It Happened One Night* ought not to be considered a screwball comedy, most film critics do apply that label. Sklar, *Movie-Made America*, 207.
110 May, *The Big Tomorrow*, 55–99.

111 For the idea of couple formation in the screwballs as a "union of complementary opposites," see Lent, "Romantic Love and Friendship," 314–31.
112 María Valdez has noted that *La rubia del camino* differs from its Hollywood model in that the repartee is entirely one-sided; Julián, unlike Peter, does not participate in the wisecracking. Valdez, "El reino de la comedia," 287. Clearly, Julián's seriousness results from the melodramatic logic of the film: as the embodiment of the poor, he is a study in nobility and dignity, not a character who is particularly apt to express sarcasm or lighthearted humor.
113 The recurring joke in *It Happened One Night*, in which Peter erects "the walls of Jericho"—a blanket hung on a string—between his bed and Ellie's has no counterpart in *La rubia del camino*, which shies away from this sort of erotic tease. This prudishness likely had multiple causes, but it follows logically from the identification of Julián—and poor people more generally—as the essence of moral rectitude.
114 Romero's celebration of working women is most explicit in *Mujeres que trabajan* (1938). The contrast with Libertad Lamarque's films is striking. In both *Besos brujos* and *Puerta cerrada*, Lamarque promises to give up her artistic career upon marriage.
115 See Hershfield, *Imagining la Chica Moderna*.

5 POLITICIZING POPULISM

1 On Perón's mass media policies, see Ciria, *Cultura y política popular*; Sirvén, *Perón y los medios de comunicación*. On the expropriation of the newspapers, see Cane, *The Fourth Enemy*.
2 Luis Alberto Romero has pointed out that Peronism disseminated existing cultural models, rather than inventing new ones, but he emphasizes the traditionalism implicit in those models, rather than the populist current I have identified. See Romero, *Breve historia contemporánea de la Argentina*, 160–62.
3 James, *Resistance and Integration*, 26–27; James, *Doña María's Story*, 255.
4 On the coup of 1943, see Spektorowski, *The Origins of Argentina's Revolution of the Right*, 173–77; Potash, *Perón y el GOU*. On the rise of Perón, see, among many others, Torre, *La vieja guardia sindical y Perón*.
5 Cane, *The Fourth Enemy*, 62–69.
6 Falicov, "Hollywood's Rogue Neighbor," 259.
7 Falicov, *The Cinematic Tango*, 17–19.
8 Rock, *Politics in Argentina*, 242–47; Escudé, *Gran Bretaña, Estados Unidos, y la declinación Argentina*.
9 Falicov, "Hollywood's Rogue Neighbor," 245–60. The best-known case of such censorship was the banning of Charlie Chaplin's *The Great Dictator* in 1941. The film was not shown in Buenos Aires until 1945.
10 Cited in Falicov, "Hollywood's Rogue Neighbor," 256.
11 Schnitman, "The Argentine Film Industry," 84.

12 Ibid., 81–90; Barnard, "Popular Cinema and Populist Politics," *Argentine Cinema*, 39–40.
13 On the advent of cinematic protectionism after 1943, see Kriger, *Cine y peronismo*, 27–55.
14 Maranghello, "Cine y estado," 56–100; Schnitman, "The Argentine Film Industry," 91–106; Barnard, "Popular Cinema and Populist Politics," *Argentine Cinema*, 41–43.
15 Cited in Matallana, *Locos por la radio*, 174.
16 Ibid., 48–51; Donald Castro, *The Argentine Tango as Social History*, 209–15.
17 Sirvén, *Perón y los medios de comunicación*, 116–18.
18 Cane, *The Fourth Enemy*, 199–232.
19 Castro, "The Massification of the Tango," 104–5; Pujol, *Discépolo*, 315.
20 Pujol, *Discépolo*, 354–55.
21 Petit de Murat, *Este cine argentino*, 55.
22 Maranghello, "Cine y estado," 96.
23 Maranghello, "Los exilios," 170–72. For Lamarque's version of her notorious run-in with Eva Perón, see Lamarque, *Libertad Lamarque*, 211–18; For the story of Hugo del Carril's falling out with Apold, see Nudler, "La gran marcha," 52.
24 On Peronist propaganda films, see Kriger, *Cine y peronismo*, 111–33.
25 On the efforts of Amadori and Argentina Sono Film, the studio that hired Apold, to ingratiate themselves with the Perón regime, see Manetti, "Argentina Sono Film," 189–205.
26 Di Núbila, *Historia del cine argentino*, vol. 2; Falicov, "Argentine Cinema and the Construction of National Popular Identity," 66; Barnard, "Popular Cinema and Populist Politics," *Argentine Cinema*, 43–49. "Banal" is Alberto Ciria's term, while "anodyne" is the judgment of Claudio España and Ricardo Manetti. See Ciria, *Cultura y política popular*, 259; España and Manetti, "El cine argentino, una estética especular," 269. Only very recently has the notion of Perón-era cinema as pure escapism begun to be challenged, most notably in Kriger, *Cine y peronismo*.
27 Petit de Murat, *Este cine argentino*, 55.
28 Milanesio, "Peronists and *Cabecitas*," 59.
29 España and Manetti, "El cine argentino, una estética especular," 274.
30 On *Dios se lo pague*, see Kriger, *Cine y peronismo*, 217–22; Paranaguá, "Populismo y hibridación," 331–54.
31 España, *Luis César Amadori*, 38.
32 Posadas, *Niní Marshall*, 67. On *Navidad de los pobres*, see also Kriger, *Cine y peronismo*, 209–12.
33 Kriger, "El cine del peronismo, una reevaluación," 136–55.
34 Kriger, *Cine y peronismo*, 189.
35 Kriger, "El cine del peronismo, una reevaluación," 151–55.
36 Viladrich, "Neither Virgins nor Whores," 281–85; D'Addario, "Tita Merello," 49–51.

37 Ramacciotti and Valobra, eds., *Generando el Peronismo*.
38 Matallana, "*Locos por la radio*," 101.
39 Romano, "Apuntes sobre cultura popular y peronismo," 48–54.
40 Gueñol, "Evocación del radioteatro," 70–71.
41 Grau, *Los Pérez García y yo*, 10. See also Cosse, "Relaciones de pareja a mediados de siglo en las representaciones de la radio porteña," 131–53.
42 This brief account of the history of folk music in the Perón era is drawn from Chamosa, "Criollo and Peronist," 113–42.
43 Matallana, "*Locos por la radio*," 95.
44 Tormo, "Chamamé de sobrepaso, charla entre Antonio Tormo y León Gieco."
45 Vitale, "Fui vocero de los cabecitas."
46 Milanesio, "Peronists and *Cabecitas*," 53–84.
47 See Vila, "Tango to Folk," 127–28. Vila argues that Tormo's principal audience was composed of internal migrants, a point of view shared by Eduardo Romano. See Romano, "Apuntes sobre cultura popular y peronismo," 46–48.
48 Matamoro, *Ciudad del tango*, 215–21.
49 Vila, "Tango to Folk," 124–32.
50 Pujol, "El baile en la Argentina de los 40," 75–84.
51 Gálvez, "El tango en su época de gloria," 6.
52 Rivero, *Una luz de almacén*, 84.
53 The divito style was named for the cartoonist Guillermo Divito, who sought to make fun of the poorly dressed. As Natalia Milanesio points out, the style was based on the outfits that turn-of-the-century compadritos would wear, and thus already had an association with tango. See Milanesio, "Peronists and *Cabecitas*," 68–69. Ernesto Goldar affirms that many tango fans dressed as divitos: Goldar, *Buenos Aires*, 60. On Castillo's use of the divito style and his embodiment of working-class Peronist identity, see Salas, "Relaciones tango y política," 133. On Castillo's performance of "Así se baila el tango," see Aresi, "Alberto Castillo, el cantor de los milongueros (El tango es danza de rango)."
54 Conti, *Aguafuertes radiales*, 127–29.
55 Cited in Salas, *El tango*, 297.
56 Gálvez, "El tango en su época de gloria," 7–13.
57 On Manzi's relationship with Peronism, see Salas, *Homero Manzi y su tiempo*, 241–70.
58 On Discépolo's radio show, see Pujol, *Discépolo*, 372–85; Vila, "Tango to Folk," 128–30. For the scripts themselves, see Discepolín, *¿A mí me la vas a contar?*
59 See, for example, Goldar, *Buenos Aires*, 138–43. Goldar points out that even Alberto Castillo's big hits of the 1950s were no longer tangos.
60 Rock, *Politics in Argentina*, 301.
61 Erenberg, *Swingin' the Dream*, 211–18; Stowe, *Swing Changes*, 180–220.
62 Cited in Horvath, *Esos malditos tangos*, 159.

63 Sigal and Verón, *Perón o muerte*, 72–74; Bianchi and Sánchis, *El Partido Peronista Feminista*. Caimari and Plotkin, *Pueblo contra antipueblo*.
64 Perón, *El pueblo quiere saber de qué se trata*, 238.
65 Elena, "Peronist Consumer Politics and the Problem of Domesticating Markets in Argentina," 111–49. The quotation is from 118, and the translation is Elena's.
66 Quoted in Sigal and Verón, *Perón o muerte*, 66.
67 Quoted in James, *Resistance and Integration*, 24. The translation is his.
68 Perón, *Obras completas*, 24.
69 On Peronist anti-intellectualism, see James, *Resistance and Integration*, 22.
70 Berhó, "Working Politics," 65–76.
71 Perón, *El pueblo quiere saber*, 10–11.
72 From Perón's speech on Labor Day, May 1, 1944. Ibid., 49. On the centrality of working-class respectability within Peronism, see Gené, *Un mundo feliz*.
73 Quoted in Sigal and Verón, *Perón o muerte*, 50.
74 On the Catholic Nationalist intellectuals of the 1930s, see Finchelstein, *Transatlantic Fascism*, 118–37; Spektorowski, *The Origins of Argentina's Revolution of the Right*, 109–23; Zanatta, *Del estado liberal a la nación católica*.
75 Ehrick, "'Savage Dissonance,'" 86–87.
76 Spektorowski, *The Origins of Argentina's Revolution of the Right*, 128–32, 181–83.
77 Nevertheless, Mariano Plotkin's analysis of Peronist textbooks reveals the persistence within Peronism of a tension between tradition and modernization. Plotkin, *Mañana es San Perón*, 189–92.
78 As Valeria Manzano has argued, the cinema of the earlier period tended to depict femininity and labor as mutually exclusive. See Manzano, "Trabajadoras en la pantalla plateada," 267–89.
79 James, *Resistance and Integration*, 18. The emphasis is his.
80 On Perón's debt to, and reformulation of, Fascism, see Finchelstein, *Transatlantic Fascism*, 163–71.
81 James, *Doña María's Story*, 240–41.
82 Weinstein, "'They Don't Even Look like Women Workers,'" 161–76.
83 Lobato, Damilakou, and Tornay, "Working-Class Beauty Queens under Peronism," 171–207.
84 Elena, "Peronism in 'Good Taste,'" 209–37.
85 Perón, *My Mission in Life (La razón de mi vida)*, 144–45.
86 During the economic decline of the early 1950s, Perón criticized Argentine consumers for living beyond their means. See Elena, "Peronist Consumer Politics and the Problem of Domesticating Markets in Argentina," 138.
87 James Brennan and Marcelo Rougier demonstrate that even though Perón faced the opposition of the owners of well-established, large industrial firms who dominated the Unión Industrial Argentina, other segments of the incipient "national bourgeoisie" did support him. Brennan and Rougier, *The Politics of National Capitalism*, 17–40.

88 Milanesio, "Peronists and *Cabecitas*."
89 Adamovsky, *Historia de la clase media argentina*, 245–47.
90 Weinstein, "'They Don't Even Look like Women Workers,'" 173.
91 James, *Resistance and Integration*, 30.

EPILOGUE: THE RISE OF THE MIDDLE CLASS

1 Adamovsky, *Historia de la clase media argentina*, 364–78. Adamovsky emphasizes the "anti-plebeian" character of Argentine middle-class identity. See also Garguin, "'Los Argentinos descendemos de los Barcos,'" 161–84.
2 Seveso, "Political Emotions and the Origins of the Peronist Resistance," 242–43.
3 Chamosa, *The Argentine Folklore Movement*, 293.
4 Maranghello, "Cine y estado," 152; Maranghello, "Los exilios," 172.
5 "Alberto Castillo," http://www.cinenacional.com/personas/index.php?persona=4027.
6 Posadas, *Niní Marshall*, 96–98.
7 Pujol, "Rebeldes y modernos," 289–93.
8 Chamosa, "The Folklore Movement in Tucumán, from Perón to the Revolución Libertadora"; Gravano, *El silencio y la porfía*, 116–41.
9 Chamosa, "The Folklore Movement in Tucumán, from Perón to la Revolución Libertadora." On Yupanqui's lyrics, see Orquera, "Marxismo, peronismo, indocriollismo," 185–205.
10 Gravano, *El silencio y la porfía*, 133. Horacio Guarany, Los Cantores de Quilla-Huasi, Los Fronterizos, and Los Chalchaleros all recorded the song between 1957 and 1962.
11 Zaldívar, *La zamba*, 38.
12 Adamovsky, *Historia de la clase media argentina*, 327–403. La Familia Falcón was the brainchild of the advertising agency J. Walter Thompson. See Ulanovsky, Itkin, and Sirvén, *Estamos en el aire*, 181–82.
13 Both plays were written by Arnaldo Malfatti and Nicolás de las Llanderas.
14 Adamovsky, *Historia de la clase media argentina*, 395. As Adamovsky points out, the wedding took place in the middle of the coup of 1955.
15 Fox, *Latin American Broadcasting*, 102–3; Mastrini, "Los orígenes de la televisión privada"; Ulanovsky, Itkin, and Sirvén, *Estamos en el aire*, 92–103.
16 Goldar, *Buenos Aires*, 125–27, 157; Pujol, "Rebeldes y modernos," 289. On the Argentine reception of Bill Haley, see Manzano, "The Blue Jean Generation," 660.
17 Goldar, *Buenos Aires*, 77–79; Podalsky, *Specular City*, 66.
18 Manzano, "The Blue Jean Generation," 661–62.
19 Pujol, "Rebeldes y modernos," 308–10.
20 The term "impossible game" was coined by O'Donnell, *Modernization and Bureaucratic-Authoritarianism*, 166–92.
21 Manzano, "The Blue Jean Generation," 667–69.

22 Alabarces, *Entre gatos y violadores*.
23 Pujol, "Rebeldes y modernos," 311–12. See also Pujol, *La década rebelde*.
24 The best account of the evolution of working-class consciousness in this period remains James, *Resistance and Integration*.
25 On the Cordobazo and its aftermath, see Brennan, *The Labor Wars in Córdoba*.
26 Moyano, *Argentina's Lost Patrol*, 35–36.

BIBLIOGRAPHY

FILMOGRAPHY

The following films were consulted for this book:
Las aguas bajan turbias (del Carril, 1951)
Alma de bandoneón (Soffici, 1935)
Así es la vida (Múgica, 1939)
Ayúdame a vivir (Ferreyra, 1936)
Besos brujos (Ferreyra, 1937)
Cándida (Bayón Herrera, 1939)
El canillita y la dama (Amadori, 1938)
El cañonero de Giles (Romero, 1937)
Caprichosa y millonaria (Discépolo, 1940)
Los caranchos de la Florida (de Zavalía, 1938)
Chingolo (Demare, 1940)
El día que me quieras (Reinhardt, 1935)
Dios se lo pague (Amadori, 1948)
Divorcio en Montevideo (Romero, 1939)
Don Quijote del Altillo (Romero, 1936)
Elvira Fernández, vendedora de tienda (Romero, 1942)
Gente bien (Romero, 1939)
La guerra gaucha (Demare, 1942)
Isabelita (Romero, 1940)
It Happened One Night (Capra, 1934)
Kilómetro 111 (Soffici, 1938)
La ley que olvidaron (Ferreyra, 1938)
Las luces de Buenos Aires (Millar, 1931)

Madreselva (Amadori, 1938)
Los mártes orquídeas (Múgica, 1941)
Mercado de abasto (Demare, 1955)
Los muchachos de antes no usaban gomina (Romero, 1937)
Mujeres que trabajan (Romero, 1938)
Nacha Regules (Amadori, 1950)
Navidad de los pobres (Romero, 1947)
Prisioneros de la tierra (Soffici, 1939)
Puente Alsina (Ferreyra, 1935)
Puerta cerrada (Saslavsky, 1939)
Riachuelo (Moglia Barth, 1934)
La rubia del camino (Romero, 1938)
Soñar no cuesta nada (Amadori, 1941)
Stella Dallas (Vidor, 1937)
¡Tango! (Moglia Barth, 1933)
Los tres berretines (1933)
La vida de Carlos Gardel (de Zavalía, 1939)

SELECTIVE DISCOGRAPHY

Much of the music discussed in this book has been reissued on the following compact discs:

Castillo, Alberto. *Soy porteño y soy barón.* El Bandoneón, EBCD 155 (2002).
Corsini, Ignacio. *El caballero cantor.* El Bandoneón, EBCD 37 (1994).
D'Arienzo, Juan. *King of Rhythm 1937–1944.* Harlequin, HQCD 71 (1996).
de Caro, Julio. *Julio de Caro 1926–1932.* Harlequin, HQCD 143 (1999).
———. "Bien Jaileife." EMI Reliquias (2002).
Gardel, Carlos. *100 por Carlos Gardel: Una exquisita selección de su obra.* EMI (2004).
Magaldi, Agustín. *Honor Gaucho: La voz sentimental de Buenos Aires 1925–1938.* El Bandoneón, EBCD 117 (2000).
Maizani, Azucena. *La ñata gaucha.* El Bandoneón, EBCD 27 (1991).
Various artists. *Before the Tango: Argentina's Folk Tradition, 1905–1936.* Harlequin, HQCD 114 (1998).
———. *Las damas del tango (1909–1946).* El Bandoneón, EBCD 93 (1998).
———. *Los 100 mejores tangos, milongas y valses del milenio.* El Bandoneón, EBCD 300–304 (2000).
———. *Las damas del tango, volumen 2 (1909–1946).* El Bandoneón, EBCD 113 (2000).

OTHER SOURCES

Adamovsky, Ezequiel. "Acerca de la relación entre el Radicalismo argentino y la 'clase media' (una vez más)." *Hispanic American Historical Review* 89, no. 2 (2009), 209–51.

———. *Historia de la clase media argentina: Apogeo y decadencia de una ilusión, 1919–2003*. Buenos Aires: Planeta, 2009.
Adelman, Jeremy. "The Political Economy of Labour in Argentina." *Essays in Argentine Labour History, 1870–1930*, 1–33. Basingstoke: Macmillan, 1992.
Adorno, Theodor, and Max Horkheimer. *Dialectic of Enlightenment*. London: Verso, 1979 [1947].
Agnew, Jean-Cristophe. "Coming Up for Air: Consumer Culture in Historical Perspective." *Consumption and the World of Goods*, ed. John Brewer and Roy Porter, 19–39. London: Routledge, 1993.
Alabarces, Pablo. *Entre gatos y violadores: El rock nacional en la cultura Argentina*. Buenos Aires: Colihue, 1993.
———. *Fútbol y patria: El fútbol y las narratives de la nación en la Argentina*. Buenos Aires: Prometeo, 2002.
Alberto, Paulina. "When Rio Was *Black*: Soul Music, National Culture, and the Politics of Racial Comparison in 1970s Brazil." *Hispanic American Historical Review* 89, no. 1 (2009), 3–39.
Alén Lascano, Luis C. "Homero Manzi: Poesía y política." *Todo es Historia* 46 (February 1971), 8–27.
———. "Cuando el folklore llegó a Buenos Aires." *Todo Es Historia* 5, no. 56 (December 1971), 64–75.
Almeida de Gargiulo, Hebe, Elsa de Yanzi, and Alda de Vera. *Buenaventura Luna: Su vida y su canto*. Buenos Aires: Senado de la Nación, 1985.
Amuchástegui, Irene. *Agustín Magaldi: La biografía*. Buenos Aires: Aguilar, 1998.
Andrews, George Reid. *The Afro-Argentines of Buenos Aires, 1800–1900*. Madison: University of Wisconsin Press, 1980.
Anuario "La Razón", 1928.
Appadurai, Arjun. *Modernity at Large: Cultural Dimensions of Globalization*. Minneapolis: University of Minnesota Press, 1996.
Archetti, Eduardo P. *Masculinities: Football, Polo and the Tango in Argentina*. Oxford: Berg, 1999.
Aresi, José Pedro. "Alberto Castillo, el cantor de los milongueros (El tango es danza de rango)," http://www.todotango.com/spanish/biblioteca/CRONICAS/acastillo.asp.
Arlt, Roberto. "Ayer ví ganar a los argentinos." *Nuevas aguafuertes porteñas*, 209–12. Buenos Aires: Hachette, 1960.
———. *Crónicas periodísticas* (www.elaleph.com).
———. *Notas sobre el cinematógrafo*, ed. Gastón Sebastián M. Gallo. Buenos Aires: Simurg, 1997.
Armus, Diego, ed. *Mundo urbano y cultura popular*. Buenos Aires: Sudamericana, 1990.
———. "Tango, Gender, and Tuberculosis in Buenos Aires, 1900–1940." *Disease in the History of Modern Latin America*, 101–29. Durham: Duke University Press, 2003.
Baily, Samuel L. "Marriage Patterns and Immigrant Assimilation in Buenos Aires, 1882–1923." *Hispanic American Historical Review* 60, no. 1 (1980), 32–48.

———. *Immigrants in the Lands of Promise: Italians in Buenos Aires and New York City, 1870–1914*. Ithaca: Cornell University Press, 1999.

Barnard, Tim, ed. *Argentine Cinema*. Toronto: Nightwood, 1986.

Barrese, Rodolfo, and Fernando Piana. "El último reportaje a Sebastián Piana: La vida como realidad de un deber cumplido." *Desmemoria Revista de Historia* 5 (October–December, 1994). Reprinted online at http://www.todotango.com/spanish/biblioteca/cronicas/entrevista_piana.asp.

Bates, Héctor, and Luis J. Bates. *La Historia del Tango*. Vol. 1. Buenos Aires: Fabril Financiera, 1936.

Bauer, Arnold J. *Goods, Power, History: Latin America's Material Culture*. Cambridge: Cambridge University Press, 2001.

Berhó, Deborah L. "Working Politics: Juan Domingo Perón's Creation of Positive Social Identity." *Rocky Mountain Review of Language and Literature* 54, no. 2 (2000), 65–76.

Bianchi, Susana, and Norma Sánchis. *El Partido Peronista Feminista*. Buenos Aires: Centro Editor de América Latina, 1987.

Bigenho, Michelle. *Sounding Indigenous: Authenticity in Bolivian Music Performance*. New York: Palgrave Macmillan, 2002.

Blomberg, Héctor Pedro, and Carlos Viale Paz. *Bajo la santa federación: Romances de la tiranía: novella radiotelefónica*. Buenos Aires: El Alma Que Canta.

Bordwell, David, Janet Staiger, and Kristin Thompson. *The Classical Hollywood Cinema: Film Style and Mode of Production to 1960*. New York: Columbia University Press, 1985.

Borges, Jorge Luis. *Evaristo Carriego*. Trans. Norman Thomas Di Giovanni. New York: E. P. Dutton, 1984.

Bourdieu, Pierre. *Distinction: A Critique of the Judgment of Taste*. Trans. Paul Patton. Cambridge: Harvard University Press, 1984.

Brennan, James P. *The Labor Wars in Córdoba, 1955–1976: Ideology, Work, and Labor Politics in an Argentine Industrial City*. Cambridge: Harvard University Press, 1994.

Brennan, James P., and Marcelo Rougier. *The Politics of National Capitalism: Peronism and the Argentine Bourgeoisie, 1946–1976*. University Park: Penn State University Press, 2009.

Brooks, Peter. *The Melodramatic Imagination: Balzac, Henry James, Melodrama, and the Mode of Excess*. New Haven, Conn.: Yale University Press, 1976.

Buchrucker, Cristián. *Nacionalismo y Peronismo: La Argentina en la crisis ideológica mundial, 1927–1955*. Buenos Aires: Sudamericana, 1987.

Caimari, Lila, and Mariano Ben Plotkin. *Pueblo contra antipueblo: La politización de identidades no-políticas en el Argentina peronista (1943–1955)*, Documento de Trabajo No. 3. Buenos Aires: INCIP, 1997.

Calistro, Mariano, et al., eds. *Reportaje al cine argentino: Los pioneros del sonoro*. Buenos Aires: ANESA, 1978.

Canaro, Francisco. *Mis bodas de oro con el tango y mis memorias, 1906–1956*. Buenos Aires: CESA, 1957.

Cane, James. *The Fourth Enemy: Journalism and Power in the Making of Peronist Argentina, 1930–1955.* University Park: Penn State University Press, 2012.
Cara-Walker, Ana. "Cocoliche: The Art of Assimilation and Dissimulation among Italians and Argentines." *Latin American Research Review* 22, no. 3 (1987), 37–67.
Carrera, Nicolás Iñigo. *La estrategia de la clase obrera—1936.* Buenos Aires: Madres de la Plaza de Mayo, 2004.
Castro, Donald S. *The Argentine Tango as Social History, 1880–1955: The Soul of the People.* Lewiston, N.Y.: Edwin Mellen, 1991.
———. "The Massification of the Tango: The Electronic Media, the Popular Theatre and the Cabaret from Contursi to Perón, 1917–1955." *Studies in Latin American Popular Culture* 18 (1999), 93–114.
———. "The Sainete Porteño, 1890–1935: The Image of Jews in the Argentine Popular Theater." *Studies in Latin American Popular Culture* 21 (2002), 29–57.
———. "The Image of the Creole Criminal in Argentine Popular Culture: 1880–1930." *Studies in Latin American Popular Culture* 25 (2006), 95–113.
Chamosa, Oscar. "Indigenous or Criollo: The Myth of White Argentina in Tucumán's Calchaquí Valley." *Hispanic American Historical Review* 88, no. 1 (February 2008), 71–106.
———. *The Argentine Folklore Movement: Sugar Elites, Criollo Workers, and the Politics of Cultural Nationalism, 1900–1950.* Tucson: University of Arizona Press, 2010.
———. "Criollo and Peronist: The Argentine Folklore Movement during the First Peronism 1943–1955." *The New Cultural History of Peronism,* ed. Karush and Chamosa, 113–42.
———. "The Folklore Movement in Tucumán, from Perón to the Revolución Libertadora 1945–1958." Paper presented to the American Historical Association, Boston, January 2011.
Chasteen, John Charles. *National Rhythms, African Roots: The Deep History of Latin American Popular Dance.* Albuquerque: University of New Mexico Press, 2004.
Ciria, Alberto. *Cultura y política popular: La Argentina peronista, 1946–1955.* Buenos Aires: Ediciones de la Flor, 1983.
Claxton, Robert Howard. *From Parsifal to Perón: Early Radio in Argentina, 1920–1944.* Tallahassee: University Press of Florida, 2007.
Cohen, Lizabeth. *Making a New Deal: Industrial Workers in Chicago, 1919–1939.* Cambridge: Cambridge University Press, 1990.
Collier, Simon. *The Life, Music, and Times of Carlos Gardel.* Pittsburgh: University of Pittsburgh Press, 1986.
———. "The Tango Is Born: 1880s–1920s." *Tango! The Dance, the Song, the Story,* by Collier et al., 18–64. London: Thames and Hudson, 1995.
Conti, Jorge. *Aguafuertes radials.* Santa Fe, Argentina: Universidad Nacional del Litoral, 2006.

Cooper, Artemis. "Tangomania in Europe and North America." *Tango! The Dance, the Song, the Story*, by Collier et al., 67–104.

Cosse, Isabella. "Relaciones de pareja a mediados de siglo en las representaciones de la radio porteña: Entre sueños románticos y visos de realidad." *Estudios Sociológicos* 25, no. 73 (2007), 131–53.

Couselo, Jorge Miguel. *El Negro Ferreyra: Un cine por instinto*. Buenos Aires: Freeland, 1969.

Dabove, Juan Pablo. *Nightmares of the Lettered City: Banditry and Literature in Latin America 1816–1929*. Pittsburgh: University of Pittsburgh Press, 2007.

D'Addario, Fernando. "Tita Merello." *Música argentina: La mirada de los críticos*, by Diego Fischerman et al., 49–51. Buenos Aires: Libros del Rojas, 2005.

de Caro, Julio. *El tango en mis recuerdos: Su evolución en la historia*. Buenos Aires: Centurión, 1964.

de Paoli, Pedro. *Función social de la radiotelefonía*. Buenos Aires: El Ateneo, 1943.

de Privitellio, Luciano. "Inventar el barrio: Boedo 1936–1942." *Cuadernos del CIESAL* 2 (1994), 113–28.

———. *Vecinos y ciudadanos: Política y sociedad en la Buenos Aires de entreguerras*. Buenos Aires: Siglo veintiuno, 2003.

del Monte, Juan. "Chispazos de tradición: Una emoción radiofónica." *Todo es historia* 155 (April 1980), 41–47.

Denning, Michael. *Mechanic Accents: Dime Novels and Working-Class Culture in America*. London: Verso, 1987.

Deutsch, Sandra McGee. *Las Derechas: The Extreme Right in Argentina, Brazil, and Chile, 1890–1939*. Stanford: Stanford University Press, 1999.

Devoto, Fernando. *Historia de los italianos en la Argentina*. Buenos Aires: Biblos, 2006.

Devoto, Fernando, and Alejandro Fernández. "Mutualismo étnico, liderazgo y participación política: Algunas hipótesis de trabajo." *Mundo urbano*, by Armus, 129–52.

Di Núbila, Domingo. *La época de oro: Historia del cine argentino I*. Buenos Aires: Ediciones del Jilguero, 1998 [1960].

———. *Historia del cine argentino II*. Buenos Aires: Cruz de Malta, 1960.

Dirección General de Correos y Telégrafos. *Reorganización de los servicios de radiodifusión*. 1939.

Discepolín. *¿A mí me la vas a contar?* Buenos Aires: Freeland, 1973.

Domínguez Zaldívar, Saúl. *La zamba: Historia, autores y letras*. Buenos Aires: GIDESA, 1998.

Durruty, Celia. *Clase obrera y peronismo*. Córdoba, Argentina: Pasado y Presente, 1969.

Ehrick, Christine T. " 'Savage Dissonance': Gender, Voice, and Women's Radio Speech in Argentina, 1930–1945." *Sound in the Era of Mechanical Reproduction*, ed. Susan Strasser and David Suisman, 69–94. Philadelphia: University of Pennsylvania Press, 2009.

Elena, Eduardo. "Peronist Consumer Politics and the Problem of Domesticating Markets in Argentina, 1943–1955." *Hispanic American Historical Review* 87, no. 1 (2007), 111–49.

———. "Peronism in 'Good Taste': Culture and Consumption in the Magazine *Argentina*." *The New Cultural History of Peronism*, ed. Karush and Chamosa, 209–37.

Elsaesser, Thomas. "Tales of Sound and Fury: Observations on the Family Melodrama" [1972]. In *Home Is Where the Heart Is: Studies in Melodrama and the Woman's Film*, ed. Christine Gledhill, 43–69. London: British Film Institute, 1987.

Erenberg, Lewis A. *Swingin' the Dream: Big Band Jazz and the Rebirth of American Culture*. Chicago: University of Chicago Press, 1998.

Escudé, Carlos. *Gran Bretaña, Estados Unidos, y la declinación Argentina*. Buenos Aires: Belgrano, 1988.

España, Claudio. *Luis César Amadori*. Buenos Aires: CEAL, 1993.

———. *Cine Argentino: Industria y clasicismo, 1933–1956*. Buenos Aires: Fondo Nacional de las Artes, 2000.

———. "El modelo institucional: Formas de representación en la edad de oro." *Cine Argentino*, vol. 1, 22–157.

———. "Los muchachos de antes no usaban gomina." *Cine Argentino*, vol. 1, 226–29.

España, Claudio, and Ricardo Manetti. "El cine argentino, una estética especular: Del orígen a los esquemas." *Nueva historia argentina: Arte, sociedad y política*, vol. 2, ed. José Emilio Borucúa, 235–78. Buenos Aires: Sudamericana, 1999.

Falcón, Ricardo. "Izquierdas, régimen político, cuestión étnica y cuestión social en Argentina 1890–1912." *Anuario, Escuela de Historia, Universidad Nacional de Rosario*, 12 (1987), 378–87.

Falicov, Tamara L. "Argentine Cinema and the Construction of National Popular Identity, 1930–1942." *Studies in Latin American Popular Culture* 17 (1998), 61–78.

———. "Hollywood's Rogue Neighbor: The Argentine Film Industry during the Good Neighbor Policy, 1939–1945." *Americas* 63, no. 2 (2006), 245–60.

———. *The Cinematic Tango: Contemporary Argentine Film*. London: Wallflower, 2007.

Félix-Didier, Paula. "Soñando con Hollywood: Los estudios Baires y la industria cinematográfica en Argentina." *Studies in Latin American Popular Culture* 21 (2002), 77–103.

Félix-Didier, Paula, and Andrés Levinson. "The Building of a Nation: *La guerra gaucha* as Historical Melodrama." *Latin American Melodrama*, ed. Darlene J. Sadlier, 50–63. Urbana: University of Illinois Press, 2009.

Finchelstein, Federico. *Transatlantic Fascism: Ideology, Violence, and the Sacred in Argentina and Italy, 1919–1945*. Durham: Duke University Press, 2010.

Finkielman, Jorge. *The Film Industry in Argentina: An Illustrated Cultural History*. Jefferson, N.C.: McFarland, 2004.

Ford, Aníbal. *Homero Manzi*. Buenos Aires: CEAL, 1971, 36–37.
Fox, Elizabeth. *Latin American Broadcasting: From Tango to Telenovela*. Luton, England: University of Luton Press, 1997.
Frank, Patrick. *Los Artistas del Pueblo: Prints and Workers' Culture in Buenos Aires, 1917–1935*. Albuquerque: University of New Mexico Press, 2006.
Frydenberg, Julio D. "Prácticas y valores en el proceso de popularización del fútbol, Buenos Aires, 1900–1910." *Entrepasados* 6, no. 12 (1997), 7–29.
Fürstenberger, Nathalie. "Güemes y los de abajo: Fabricación y alcance del heroismo en La guerra gaucha." *Revista Iberoamericana* 71, no. 213 (2005), 1109–19.
Gallo, Ricardo. *La radio: Ese mundo tan sonoro*. 2 vols. Buenos Aires: Corregidor, 1991.
Gálvez, Eduardo. "El tango en su época de gloria: ni prostibulario, ni orillero: Los bailes en los clubes sociales y deportivos de Buenos Aires 1938–1959." *Nuevo Mundo Mundos Nuevos*, http://nuevomundo.revues.org/55183 (2009).
García Canclini, Néstor. *Hybrid Cultures: Strategies for Entering and Leaving Modernity*. Minneapolis: University of Minnesota Press, 1995.
García Jiménez, Francisco. *Estampas de tango*. Buenos Aires: R. Alonso, 1968.
Garguin, Enrique. " 'Los Argentinos descendemos de los Barcos': The Racial Articulation of Middle-Class Identity in Argentina (1920–1960)." *Latin American and Caribbean Ethnic Studies* 2, no. 2 (2007), 161–84.
Garramuño, Florencia. *Modernidades primitivas: Tango, samba y nación*. Buenos Aires: Fondo de Cultura Económica, 2007.
Gené, Marcela. *Un mundo feliz: Imagines de los trabajadores en el primer peronismo, 1946–1955*. Buenos Aires: Universidad de San Andrés, 2005.
Germani, Gino. *Política y sociedad en una época de transición*. Buenos Aires: Paidós, 1962.
Gerstle, Gary. *American Crucible: Race and Nation in the Twentieth Century*. Princeton: Princeton University Press, 2001.
Gledhill, Christine. "The Melodramatic Field: An Investigation." *Home Is Where the Heart Is: Studies in Melodrama and the Woman's Film*, 5–39. London: British Film Institute, 1987.
Goldar, Ernesto. *Buenos Aires: Vida cotidiana en la década del 50*. Buenos Aires: Plus Ultra, 1980.
Golden, Nathan D. *Review of Foreign Film Markets during 1936*. Washington: U.S. Department of Commerce, 1937.
———. *Motion Picture Markets of Latin America*. Washington: U.S. Department of Commerce, 1944.
González Leandri, Ricardo. "Lo propio y lo ajeno: Actividades culturales y fomentismo en una asociación vecinal. Barrio Nazca (1925–1930)." *Mundo urbano y cultura popular*, ed. Armus, 91–128. Buenos Aires: Sudamericana, 1990.
———. "La nueva identidad de los sectores populares." *Nueva Historia Argentina*, vol. 7, ed. Alejandro Cattaruzza, 201–37. Buenos Aires: Sudamericana, 2001.
Gorelik, Adrián. *La grilla y el parque: Espacio público y cultura urbana en Buenos Aires, 1887–1936*. Buenos Aires: Universidad Nacional de Quilmes, 1998.

Göttling, Jorge. *Tango, melancólico testigo*. Buenos Aires: Corregidor, 1998.
Gramuglio, María Teresa. "La primera épica de Lugones." *Prismas* 1, no. 1 (1997), 157–63.
Grau, Luis M. *Los Pérez García y yo*. Buenos Aires: Ciordia and Rodríguez, n.d.
Gravano, Ariel. *El silencio y la porfía*. Buenos Aires: Corregidor, 1985.
Groppa, Carlos. *The Tango in the United States: A History*. Jefferson, N.C.: McFarland, 2003.
Gueñol, Zelmar. "Evocación del radioteatro." *Ensayos Argentinos*, 64–73. Buenos Aires: CEAL, 1971.
Gutiérrez, Leandro H., and Luis Alberto Romero. *Sectores populares, cultura y política: Buenos Aires en la entreguerra*. Buenos Aires: Sudamericana, 1995.
Gutiérrez, Leandro H., and Juan Suriano. "Workers' Housing in Buenos Aires, 1880–1930." *Essays in Argentine Labour History, 1870–1930*, ed. Jeremy Adelman, 35–51. Basingstoke: Macmillan, 1992.
Guy, Donna J. *Sex and Danger in Buenos Aires: Prostitution, Family, and Nation in Argentina*. Lincoln: University of Nebraska Press, 1990.
Habermas, Jürgen. *Legitimation Crisis*. Boston: Beacon, 1975.
Hall, Stuart. "Culture, Media and the 'Ideological Effect.'" In *Mass Communication and Society*, ed. James Curran, Michael Gurevitch, and Janet Woollacott, 315–48. Beverly Hills, Calif.: Sage, 1979.
———. "Encoding/Decoding." *Culture, Media, Language*, 128–38. London: Hutchinson, 1980.
Hansen, Miriam. *Babel and Babylon: Spectatorship in American Silent Film*. Cambridge: Harvard University Press, 1991.
———. "Fallen Women, Rising Stars, New Horizons: Shanghai Silent Film as Vernacular Modernism." *Film Quarterly* 54, no. 1 (2000), 10–22.
Hay, James. "Placing Cinema, Fascism, and the Nation in a Diagram of Italian Modernity." *Re-viewing Fascism: Italian Cinema, 1922–1943*, ed. Jacqueline Reich and Piero Garofalo, 115–37. Bloomington: Indiana University Press, 2002.
Hershfield, Joanne. *Imagining la Chica Moderna: Women, Nation, and Visual Culture in Mexico, 1917–1936*. Durham: Duke University Press, 2008.
Horowitz, Joel. *Argentine Unions, The State and the Rise of Perón*. Berkeley: Institute of International Studies, 1990.
———. *Argentina's Radical Party and Popular Mobilization, 1916–1930*. University Park: Penn State University Press, 2008.
Horvath, Ricardo. *Esos malditos tangos: Apuntes para la otra historia*. Buenos Aires: Biblos, 2006.
Insaurralde, Andrés. *Manuel Romero*. Buenos Aires: Centro Editor de América Latina, 1994.
James, Daniel. *Resistance and Integration: Peronism and the Argentine Working Class, 1946–1976*. Cambridge: Cambridge University Press, 1988.
———. *Doña María's Story: Life History, Memory, and Political Identity*. Durham: Duke University Press, 2000.

Johns, Michael. "The Urbanisation of a Secondary City: The Case of Rosario, Argentina, 1870–1920." *Journal of Latin American Studies* 23 (1991), 489–513.

Joseph, Gilbert M., Anne Rubenstein, and Eric Zolov. "Assembling the Fragments: Writing a Cultural History of Mexico Since 1940." *Fragments of a Golden Age: The Politics of Culture in Mexico since 1940*, 3–22. Durham: Duke University Press, 2001.

Kaplan, E. Ann. *Motherhood and Representation: The Mother in Popular Culture and Melodrama*. London: Routledge, 1992.

Karnick, Kristine Brunovska. "Comedy and Reaffirmation in Hollywood Romantic Comedy." *Classical Hollywood Comedy*, ed. Karnick and Jenkins, 123–46.

Karnick, Kristine Brunovska, and Henry Jenkins, eds. *Classical Hollywood Comedy*. New York: Routledge, 1995.

———. "Introduction: Comedy and the Social World." *Classical Hollywood Comedy*, 265–81.

Karush, Matthew B. *Workers or Citizens: Democracy and Identity in Rosario, Argentina (1912–1930)*. Albuquerque: University of New Mexico Press, 2002.

Karush, Matthew B., and Oscar Chamosa, eds. *The New Cultural History of Peronism: Power and Identity in Mid-Twentieth-Century Argentina*. Durham: Duke University Press, 2010.

Kenney, William Howland. *Recorded Music in American Life: The Phonograph and Popular Memory, 1890–1945*. New York: Oxford University Press, 1999.

Kohen, Héctor R. "Estudios Cinematográficos Argentinos SIDE: Sidetón, una herramienta eficaz." *Cine Argentino*, ed. España, vol. 1, 264–85.

Korzeniewicz, Roberto P. "The Labour Movement and the State in Argentina, 1887–1907." *Bulletin of Latin American Research* 8, no. 1 (1989), 25–45.

———. "The Labor Politics of Radicalism: The Santa Fe Crisis of 1928." *Hispanic American Historical Review* 73, no. 1 (1993), 1–32.

———. "Labor Unrest in Argentina, 1930–1943." *Latin American Research Review* 28, no. 1 (1993), 7–40.

Kriger, Clara. "El cine del peronismo, una reevaluación." *Archivos de la Filmoteca* 31 (February 1999), 136–55.

———. *Cine y peronismo: El estado en escena*. Buenos Aires: Siglo Veintiuno, 2009.

Labraña, Luis, and Ana Sebastián. *Tango: Una historia*. Buenos Aires: Corregidor, 1992.

Laclau, Ernesto. "Towards a Theory of Populism." *Politics and Ideology in Marxist Theory*, 143–89. London: NLB, 1977.

Lamarque, Libertad. *Libertad Lamarque*. Buenos Aires: Javier Vergara, 1986.

Lattes, Alfred E. "La dinámica de la población rural en la Argentina." *Cuadernos del CENEP* 9 (1979).

Leland, Christopher Towne. *The Last Happy Men: The Generation of 1922, Fiction, and the Argentine Reality*. Syracuse, N.Y.: Syracuse University Press, 1986.

Lent, Tina Olsin. "Romantic Love and Friendship: The Redefinition of Gender Relations in Screwball Comedy." *Classical Hollywood Comedy*, ed. Karnick and Jenkins, 314–31.

Levine, Lawrence W. "The Folklore of Industrial Society." *American Historical Review* 97, no. 5 (1992), 1369–99.

Lewis, Mollie. "Con Men, Cooks, and Cinema Kings: Popular Culture and Jewish Identities in Buenos Aires, 1905–1930." Ph.D. diss., Emory University, 2008.

Lipsitz, George. *Time Passages: Collective Memory and American Popular Culture*. Minneapolis: University of Minnesota Press, 1990.

Little, Walter. "The Social Origins of Peronism." *Argentina in the Twentieth Century*, ed. David Rock, 162–78. Pittsburgh: University of Pittsburgh Press, 1975.

Lobato, Mirta Zaida, María Damilakou, and Lizel Tornay. "Working-Class Beauty Queens under Peronism," trans. Beatrice D. Gurwitz. *The New Cultural History of Peronism*, ed. Karush and Chamosa, 171–207.

López, Ana M. " 'A Train of Shadows': Early Cinema and Modernity in Latin America." *Through the Kaleidoscope: The Experience of Modernity in Latin America*, ed. Vivian Schelling, 161–62. London: Verso, 2000.

Lugones, Leopoldo. *El Payador*. Buenos Aires: Centurión, 1961 [1916].

Lusnich, Ana Laura. *El drama social-folklórico: El universo rural en el cine argentino*. Buenos Aires: Biblos, 2007.

Mallimacci, Fortunato, and Irene Marrone, eds. *Cine e imaginario social*. Buenos Aires: Universidad de Buenos Aires, 1997.

Manetti, Ricardo. "Argentina Sono Film: Más estrellas que en el cielo." *Cine Argentino*, ed. España, vol. 1, 162–21.

Manrupe, Raúl, and María Alejandra Portela. *Un diccionario de films argentinos (1930–1995)*. Buenos Aires: Corregidor, 2001.

Manzano, Valeria. "Trabajadoras en la pantalla plateada: Representaciones de las trabajadoras en el cine argentino, 1938–1942." *La Ventana* 14 (2001), 267–89.

———. "The Blue Jean Generation: Youth, Gender, and Sexuality in Buenos Aires, 1958–1975." *Journal of Social History* 42, no. 3 (spring 2009), 657–76.

Manzi, Homero. *Sur: Barrio de tango "Letras para los hombres"*, ed. Acho Manzi. Buenos Aires: Corregidor, 2000.

Maranghello, César. "Cine y estado." *Cine Argentino*, ed. España, vol. 2, 24–159.

———. "El espacio de la recepción: Construcción del aparato crítico." *Cine Argentino*, ed. España, vol. 2, 524–67.

———. "Los exilios." *Cine Argentino*, ed. España, vol. 2, 170–72.

———. "Orígenes y evolución de la censura." *Cine Argentino*, ed. España, vol. 2, 160–83.

———. *Artistas argentinos asociados: La epopeya trunca*. Buenos Aires: Jilguero, 2002.

Marshall, Niní. *Las travesuras de Niní: Los mejores libretos de Catita, Cándida, Niña Jovita, y otras criaturas*. Buenos Aires: Planeta, 1994.

Marshall, Niní, and Salvador D. D'Anna. *Niní Marshall: Mis memorias*. Buenos Aires: Moreno, 1985.

Martín-Barbero, Jesús. *Communication, Culture and Hegemony: From the Media to Mediations*, trans. Elizabeth Fox and Robert A. White. London: Sage, 1993.

Martínez Estrada, Ezequiel. *La cabeza de Goliat*. Buenos Aires: Nova, 1956 [1940].

Mastrini, Guillermo. "Los orígenes de la televisión privada: Pantalla chica y política entre 1955 y 1965." *Todo es Historia* 411 (October 2001).
Matallana, Andrea. *"Locos por la radio": Una historia social de la radiofonía en la Argentina, 1923–1947*. Buenos Aires: Prometeo, 2006.
———. *Qué saben los pitucos: La experiencia del tango entre 1910 y 1940*. Buenos Aires: Prometeo, 2008.
Matamoro, Blas. *Ciudad del tango: Tango histórico y sociedad*. Buenos Aires: Galerna, 1982.
———. *El Tango*. Madrid: Acento, 1996.
May, Lary. *Screening Out the Past: The Birth of Mass Culture and the Motion Picture Industry*. Chicago: University of Chicago Press, 1983.
———. *The Big Tomorrow: Hollywood and the Politics of the American Way*. Chicago: University of Chicago Press, 2000.
Mazziotti, Nora. "Bambalinas: El Auge De Una Modalidad Teatral Periodística." *Mundo urbano y cultura popular: Estudios de historia social argentina*, ed. Armus, 69–89. Buenos Aires: Sudamericana, 1990.
McCann, Bryan. *Hello, Hello Brazil: Popular Music in the Making of Modern Brazil*. Durham: Duke University Press, 2004.
McCleary, Kristen. "Popular, Elite *and* Mass Culture? The Spanish Zarzuela in Buenos Aires, 1890–1900." *Studies in Latin American Popular Culture* 21 (2002), 1–27.
———. "Life Is a Cabaret? Recalibrating Gender Relations through Buenos Aires Stage Plays, 1919." Unpublished paper, 2009.
McGovern, Charles F. *Sold American: Consumption and Citizenship, 1890–1945*. Chapel Hill: University of North Carolina Press, 2006.
Míguez, Eduardo J. "Familias de clase media: La formación de un modelo." *Historia de la vida privada en la argentina*, vol. 2, ed. Fernando Devoto and María Madero, 21–45. Buenos Aires: Taurus, 1999.
Míguez, Eduardo José, María Elba Argeri, María Mónica Bjerg, and Hernán Otero. "Hasta que la Argentina nos una: Reconsiderando las pautas matrimoniales de los inmigrantes, el crisol de razas y el pluralismo cultural." *Hispanic American Historical Review* 71, no. 4 (1991), 781–808.
Milanesio, Natalia. "Peronists and *Cabecitas*: Stereotypes and Anxieties at the Peak of Social Change." *The New Cultural History of Peronism*, ed. Karush and Chamosa, 53–84.
Miller, Karl Hagstrom. *Segregating Sound: Inventing Folk and Pop Music in the Age of Jim Crow*. Durham: Duke University Press, 2010.
Miller, Nicola. *In the Shadow of the State: Intellectuals and the Quest for National Identity in Twentieth-Century Spanish America*. London: Verso, 1999.
Monsiváis, Carlos. "Se sufre, pero se aprende. (El melodrama y las reglas de la falta de límites)." *Archivos de la Filmoteca* 16 (1994), 7–19.
Moreno, Julio. *Yankee Don't Go Home! Mexican Nationalism, American Business Culture, and the Shaping of Modern Mexico, 1920–1950*. Chapel Hill: University of North Carolina Press, 2003.

Moya, José C. *Cousins and Strangers: Spanish Immigrants in Buenos Aires, 1850–1930*. Berkeley: University of California Press, 1998.
Moyano, María José. *Argentina's Lost Patrol: Armed Struggle, 1969–1979*. New Haven: Yale University Press, 1995.
Munck, Ronaldo, with Ricardo Falcón and Bernardo Galitelli. *Argentina: From Anarchism to Peronism: Workers, Unions and Politics, 1855–1985*. London: Zed, 1987.
Nudler, Julio. "La gran marcha." *Música argentina: La mirada de los críticos*, by Diego Fischerman et al., 52–54. Buenos Aires: Libros del Rojas, 2005.
———. "Julio De Caro: Tango y vanguardia." *Música argentina: La mirada de los críticos*, by Diego Fischerman et al., 45–48. Buenos Aires: Libros del Rojas, 2005.
———. "Osvaldo Fresedo," http://www.todotango.com.
O'Brien, Thomas F. *The Revolutionary Mission: American Enterprise in Latin America, 1900–1945*. Cambridge: Cambridge University Press, 1999.
O'Donnell, Guillermo. *Modernization and Bureaucratic-Authoritarianism: Studies in South American Politics*. Berkeley: University of California Press, 1973.
Office of Inter-American Affairs. *Data and Rates of Radio Stations in the Other American Republics and Puerto Rico*. New York: Koppel Printing, 1945.
Orlove, Benjamin, and Arnold J. Bauer. "Giving Importance to Imports." *The Allure of the Foreign: Imported Goods in Postcolonial Latin America*, 1–29. Ann Arbor: University of Michigan Press, 1997.
Oroz, Silvia. *Melodrama: El cine de lágrimas de América Latina*. Mexico City: UNAM, 1995.
Orquera, Yolanda F. "Marxismo, peronismo, indocriollismo: Atahualpa Yupanqui y el Norte Argentino." *Studies in Latin American Popular Culture* 27 (2008), 185–205.
Owensby, Brian P. *Intimate Ironies: Modernity and the Making of Middle-Class Lives in Brazil*. Stanford: Stanford University Press, 1999.
Paladino, Diana. "Libertad Lamarque, la reina de la lágrima." *Archivos de la filmoteca* 31 (February 1999), 61–75.
Paranaguá, Paulo Antonio. "Populismo y hibridación: *Dios se lo pague*, textos y contexto." *Revista Iberoamericana* 68, no. 199 (2002), 331–54.
Parker, David Stuart. *The Idea of the Middle Class: White-Collar Workers and Peruvian Society, 1900–1950*. University Park: Penn State University Press, 1998.
Pauls, Alan. *Lino Palacio La infancia de la risa*. Buenos Aires: Calpe, 1993.
Pellarolo, Silvia. *Sainete criollo/Democracia/Representación: El caso de Nemesio Trejo*. Buenos Aires: Corregidor, 1997.
Pellettieri, Osvaldo. *Cien años de teatro argentino (1886–1990): Del Moreira a Teatro Abierto*. Buenos Aires: Galerna, 1991.
———. *Historia del Teatro Argentino en Buenos Aires*. Vol. 2. Buenos Aires: Galerna, 2002.
———. "El ultimo actor popular: Luis Sandrini." *Cuadernos Hispanoamericanos* 644 (February 2004), 91–99.

Pérez, Louis. *On Becoming Cuban: Identity, Nationality and Culture*. Chapel Hill: University of North Carolina Press, 1999.
Perón, Eva. *My Mission in Life (La razón de mi vida)*, trans. Ethel Cherry. New York: Vintage, 1952.
Perón, Juan Domingo. *El pueblo quiere saber de qué se trata: Discursos sobre política social pronunciados por el secretario de Trabajo y Previsión durante el año 1944*. Buenos Aires: Freeland, 1973 [1944].
———. *Obras completas*. Vol. 8. Buenos Aires: Fundación pro Universitaria de la Producción y del Trabajo y Fundación Universidad a Distancia "Hernandarias," 1998.
Persello, Ana Virginia. *El Partido Radical: Gobierno y oposición 1916–1943*. Buenos Aires: Siglo 21, 2004.
Petit de Murat, Ulyses. *Este cine argentino*. Buenos Aires: Carro de Tespis, 1959.
Pinsón, Néstor. "Los concursos de Max Glücksmann," http://www.todotango.com.
———. "Rosita Quiroga," http://www.todotango.com/spanish/creadores/rquiroga.html.
Plotkin, Mariano Ben. *Mañana es San Perón*. Buenos Aires: Ariel, 1993.
Podalsky, Laura. "Disjointed Frames: Melodrama, Nationalism, and Representation in 1940s Mexico." *Studies in Latin American Popular Culture* 12 (1993), 57–71.
———. *Specular City: Transforming Culture, Consumption, and Space in Buenos Aires, 1955–1973*. Philadelphia: Temple University Press, 2004.
Posadas, Abel. *Niní Marshall: Desde un ayer lejano*. Buenos Aires: Colihue, 1993.
Potash, Robert A. *Perón y el GOU: Los documentos de una logia secreta*. Buenos Aires: Sudamericana, 1984.
Prieto, Adolfo. *El discurso criollista en la formación de la Argentina moderna*. Buenos Aires: Sudamericana, 1988.
Pujol, Sergio. *Jazz al sur: La música negra en la argentina*. Buenos Aires: Emecé, 1992.
———. *Valentino en Buenos Aires: Los años veinte y el espectáculo*. Buenos Aires: Emecé, 1994.
———. *Discépolo: Una biografía argentina*. Buenos Aires: Booket, 2006 [1996].
———. "El baile en la Argentina de los 40: Fiesta de tango." *Cuadernos Hispanoamericanos* 603 (2000), 75–84.
———. *La década rebelde: Los años 60 en la Argentina*. Buenos Aires: Emecé, 2002.
———. "Rebeldes y modernos: Una cultura de los jóvenes." *Nueva historia argentina*, vol. 9, ed. Daniel James, 281–328. Buenos Aires: Sudamericana, 2003.
Quattrocchi-Woisson, Diana. *Los males de la memoria: Historia y política en la Argentina*. Buenos Aires: Emecé, 1995.
Quinziano, Pascual. "La comedia: Un género impuro." *Cine Argentino: La otra historia*, ed. Sergio Wolf, 129–46. Buenos Aires: Letra Buena, 1992.
Ramacciotti, Karina, and Adriana Valobra, eds. *Generando el Peronismo: Estudios de cultura, política y género (1946–1955)*. Buenos Aires: Proyecto, 2004.

Rivero, Edmundo. *Una luz de almacén*. Buenos Aires: Emecé, 1982.
Rocchi, Fernando. "La americanización del consumo: Las batallas por el mercado argentino, 1920–1945." *Americanización: Estados Unidos y América Latina en el Siglo XX*, ed. María I. Barbero and Andrés M. Regalsky, 131–89. Buenos Aires: EDUNTREF, 2003.
———. *Chimneys in the Desert: Industrialization in Argentina during the Export Boom Years, 1870–1930*. Stanford: Stanford University Press, 2005.
Rock, David. *Politics in Argentina, 1890–1930: The Rise and Fall of Radicalism*. Cambridge: Cambridge University Press, 1975.
———. *Argentina 1516–1987: From Spanish Colonization to Alfonsín*. Berkeley: University of California Press, 1987.
Romano, Eduardo. "Apuntes sobre cultura popular y peronismo." *La cultura popular del peronismo*, by Norman Briski et al., 48–54. Buenos Aires: Cimarrón, 1973.
———, ed. *Las letras del Tango: Antología cronológica 1900–1980*. Rosario, Argentina: Fundación Ross, 1998.
Romero, Luis Alberto. *Breve historia contemporánea de la Argentina*. Buenos Aires: Fondo de Cultura Económica, 1994.
———. "Nueva Pompeya, libros y catecismo." Gutiérrez and Romero, *Sectores populares, cultura y política*, 173–93.
———. "El apogeo de la sociedad de masas." *Revista Digital* 8, no. 50 (2002), http://www.efdeportes.com/efd50/romero.htm.
Rosenzweig, Roy. *"Eight Hours for What We Will": Workers and Leisure in an Industrial City, 1870–1920*. Cambridge: Cambridge University Press, 1983.
Ross, Steven J. *Working-Class Hollywood: Silent Film and the Shaping of Class in America*. Princeton: Princeton University Press, 1998.
Saítta, Sylvia. *Regueros de tinta: El diario Crítica en la década de 1920*. Buenos Aires: Sudamericana, 1998.
———. "Entre la cultura y la política: Los escritores de izquierda." *Nueva historia Argentina*, vol. 7, ed. Alejandro Cattaruzza, 383–428. Buenos Aires: Sudamericana, 2001.
Salas, Horacio. "Relaciones tango y política." *Tango tuyo, mío y nuestro*, ed. Ercilia Moreno Chá. Buenos Aires: Instituto Nacional de Antropología y Pensamiento Latinoamericano, 1995.
———. *El tango*. Buenos Aires: Planeta, 1995.
———. *Homero Manzi y su tiempo*. Buenos Aires: Javier Vergara, 2001.
Salvatore, Ricardo D. "Yankee Advertising in Buenos Aires." *Interventions* 7, no. 2 (2005), 216–35.
Sarlo, Beatriz. *El imperio de los sentimientos*. Buenos Aires: Norma, 2000 [1985].
———. *Una modernidad periférica: Buenos Aires 1920 y 1930*. Buenos Aires: Nueva Visión, 1988.
———. *La imaginación técnica: Sueños modernos de la cultura argentina*. Buenos Aires: Nueva Visión, 1992.
Sarmiento, Domingo Faustino. *Facundo: Civilization and Barbarism: The First*

Complete English Translation, trans. Kathleen Ross. Berkeley: University of California Press, 2003.

Savigliano, Marta. *Tango and the Political Economy of Passion*. Boulder: Westview, 1995.

Schnitman, Jorge Alberto. "The Argentine Film Industry: A Contextual Study." Ph.D. diss., Stanford University, 1979.

Schroeder Rodríguez, Paul A. "Latin American Silent Cinema: Triangulation and the Politics of Criollo Aesthetics." *Latin American Research Review* 43, no. 3 (2008), 36.

Schwoch, James. *The American Radio Industry and Its Latin American Activities, 1900–1939*. Urbana: University of Illinois Press, 1990.

Scobie, James R. *Buenos Aires: Plaza to Suburb, 1870–1910*. New York: Oxford University Press, 1974.

Seigel, Micol. "Cocoliche's Romp: Fun with Nationalism at Argentina's Carnival." *Drama Review* 44, no. 2 (2000), 56–83.

———. *Uneven Encounters: Making Race and Nation in Brazil and the United States*. Durham: Duke University Press, 2009.

Seveso, César. "Political Emotions and the Origins of the Peronist Resistance." *The New Cultural History of Peronsim*, ed. Karush and Chamosa, 239–70.

Sheinin, David. *Argentina and the United States: An Alliance Contained*. Athens: University of Georgia Press, 2006.

Shipley, Robert E. "On the Outside Looking In: A Social History of the Porteño Worker during the Golden Age of Argentine Development." Ph.D. diss., Rutgers University, 1977.

Sierra, Luis Adolfo. *Historia de la orquesta típica: Evolución instrumental del tango*. Buenos Aires: Corregidor, 1985.

Sigal, Silvia, and Eliseo Verón. *Perón o muerte: Los fundamentos discursivos del fenómeno peronista*. Buenos Aires: EUDEBA, 2003 [1986].

Silvestri, Graciela, and Adrián Gorelik. "San Cristóbal Sur entre el Matadero y el Parque: Acción municipal, conformación barrial y crecimiento urbano en Buenos Aires, 1895–1915." *Boletín del Instituto de Historia Argentina y Americana Dr. E. Ravignani* 3 (1991), 81–107.

Simari, Tomás. *Mi historia la escribo yo*. Buenos Aires: A. Ruiz, 1956.

Singer, Ben. *Melodrama and Modernity: Early Sensational Cinema and Its Contents*. New York: Columbia University Press, 2001.

Sirvén, Pablo. *Perón y los medios de comunicación (1943–1955)*. Buenos Aires: CEAL, 1984.

Sklar, Robert. *Movie-Made America: A Cultural History of American Movies*. New York: Vintage, 1994 [1975].

Slatta, Richard W. *Gauchos and the Vanishing Frontier*. Lincoln: University of Nebraska Press, 1992.

Sommer, Doris. *Foundational Fictions: The National Romances of Latin America*. Berkeley: University of California Press, 1991.

Spektorowski, Alberto. *The Origins of Argentina's Revolution of the Right*. Notre Dame: University of Notre Dame Press, 2003.

Starr, Paul. *The Creation of the Media: Political Origins of Modern Communications*. New York: Basic Books, 2004.

Stern, Steve J. "Between Tragedy and Promise: The Politics of Writing Latin American History in the Late Twentieth Century." *Reclaiming the Political in Latin American History: Essays from the North*, ed. Gilbert Joseph, 32–77. Durham: Duke University Press, 2001.

Storey, John. *Inventing Popular Culture*. Malden, Mass.: Blackwell, 2003.

Stowe, David W. *Swing Changes: Big-Band Jazz in New Deal America*. Cambridge: Harvard University Press, 1994.

Sublette, Ned. *Cuba and Its Music: From the First Drum to the Mambo*. Chicago: Chicago Review, 2004.

Suriano, Juan. *Anarquistas*. Buenos Aires: Manantial, 2001.

Susman, Warren. *Culture as History: The Transformation of American Culture in the Twentieth Century*. New York: Pantheon, 1984.

Szmetan, Ricardo. "Enigmas sobre aspectos de la vida, y la relación con su obra, de Almafuerte." *Journal of Humanities* 11 (1998), 219–30.

Szuchman, Mark. "The Limits of the Melting Pot in Urban Argentina: Marriage and Integration in Córdoba, 1869–1909." *Hispanic American Historical Review* 57, no. 1 (1977), 24–50.

Tamarin, David. *The Argentine Labor Movement, 1930–1945*. Albuquerque: University of New Mexico Press.

Thompson, Kristin. *Exporting Entertainment: America in the World Film Market, 1907–34*. London: British Film Institute, 1985.

Thompson, Robert Farris. *Tango: The Art History of Love*. New York: Pantheon, 2005.

Thompson, Ruth. "The Limitations of Ideology in the Early Argentine Labour Movement: Anarchism in the Trade Unions, 1890–1920." *Journal of Latin American Studies* 16 (1984), 81–99.

Tormo, Antonio. "Chamamé de sobrepaso, charla entre Antonio Tormo y León Gieco." Liner notes to the album *20 y 20*. Buenos Aires: Cañada Discos, 1996.

Torre, Juan Carlos. *La vieja guardia sindical y Perón: Sobre los orígenes del peronismo*. Buenos Aires: Sudamericana, 1990.

Tranchini, Elina. "El Cine Argentino y la construcción de un imaginario criollista 1915–1945." *Entrepasados* 9, nos. 18–19 (2000), 113–41.

Turino, Thomas. "Nationalism and Latin American Music: Selected Case Studies and Theoretical Considerations." *Latin American Music Review* 24, no. 2 (2003), 169–209.

Ulanovsky, Carlos, et al. *Días de radio: 1920–1959*. Buenos Aires: Emecé, 2004.

Ulanovsky, Carlos, Silvia Itkin, and Pablo Sirvén. *Estamos en el aire: Una historia de la televisión en la Argentina*. Buenos Aires: Planeta, 1999.

Ulla, Noemí. *Tango, rebelión y nostalgia*. Buenos Aires: Jorge Alvarez, 1967.

U.S. Department of Commerce. *Motion Pictures in Argentina and Brazil* (1929).
———. *World Radio Markets: Argentina* (July 23, 1940), 25–32.
Valdez, María. "Luis Sandrini." *Cine Argentino*, ed. España, vol. 1, 44–45.
———. "El reino de la comedia: Un terreno escurridizo y ambiguo." *Cine Argentino*, ed. España, vol. 2, 270–345.
Velázquez, Marco, and Mary Kay Vaughan. "*Mestizaje* and Musical Nationalism in Mexico." *The Eagle and the Virgin: Nation and Cultural Revolution in Mexico, 1920–1940*, ed. Mary Kay Vaughan and Stephen E. Lewis, 95–118. Durham: Duke University Press, 2006.
Vianna, Hermano. *The Mystery of Samba: Popular Music and National Identity in Brazil*. Trans. John Chasteen. Chapel Hill: University of North Carolina Press, 1999.
Vila, Pablo. "Tango to Folk: Hegemony Construction and Popular Identities in Argentina." *Studies in Latin American Popular Culture* 10 (1991), 107–39.
Viladrich, Anahí. "Neither Virgins nor Whores: Tango Lyrics and Gender Representations in the Tango World." *Journal of Popular Culture* 39, no. 2 (April 2006), 272–93.
Vitale, Cristian. "Fui vocero de los cabecitas." *Página 12* (September 16, 2002).
Walkowitz, Judith R. *City of Dreadful Delight: Narratives of Sexual Danger in Late Victorian London*. Chicago: University of Chicago Press, 1992.
Walter, Richard J. *Politics and Urban Growth in Buenos Aires: 1910–1942*. Cambridge: Cambridge University Press, 1993.
Weinstein, Barbara. " 'They Don't Even Look like Women Workers': Femininity and Class in Twentieth-Century Latin America." *International Labor and Working-Class History* 69, no. 1 (2006), 161–76.
Williams, Linda. " 'Something Else Besides a Mother': *Stella Dallas* and the Maternal Melodrama." *Home Is Where the Heart Is: Studies in Melodrama and the Woman's Film*, ed. Christine Gledhill, 299–325. London: British Film Institute, 1987.
Yrigoyen, Hipólito. *Mi vida y mi doctrina*. Buenos Aires: Leviatan, 1981.
Zanatta, Loris. *Del estado liberal a la nación católica: Iglesia y ejército en los orígenes del peronismo*. Buenos Aires: Universidad Nacional de Quilmes, 1996.
Zolov, Eric. *Refried Elvis: The Rise of the Mexican Counterculture*. Berkeley: University of California Press, 1999.
Zucchi, Oscar. *El tango, el bandoneón, y sus intérpretes*. Vol. 1. Buenos Aires: Corregidor, 1998.

INDEX

Advertising, 8, 15, 33, 37, 38; nationalism in, 7, 226 n. 15; on radio, 63–65, 69–71, 142, 185; for records, 231 n. 8; tango in, 50–51; upward mobility depicted in, 34–35, 87, 92
Afro-Argentines, 106; milonga and, 146–47; origins of the tango and, 52, 54, 153; as symbols of the past, 147–48; as tango musicians, 49
Almafuerte [pseud. for Pedro Palacios], 89, 92, 151
Alton, John, 75–76, 235 n. 113
Alvear, Marcelo T. de, 112
Amadori, Luis César, 102, 111, 120, 131–32, 188, 189, 217
Americanization. *See* United States
Anarchism, 2, 15, 24, 37–39, 89, 136, 151
Antena, 66, 138, 142–43, 149, 152, 162, 164–65
Apold, Raúl Alejandro, 184, 186–89, 198–99, 246 n. 23
Argentina Sono Film, 74–76, 80, 82, 107–8, 110–12, 184, 187, 189

Arlt, Roberto, 1–2, 15–16, 79, 116
Arrabales, 54, 56, 78, 109–10, 112, 136, 148, 175, 239 n. 50
Artistas Argentinas Asociadas, 155–56
Authenticity: cinema and, 76, 113–14, 116, 132, 159, 166, 168, 174; folk music and, 160–66, 195; immigrants and, 25; in mass culture, 9–10, 42, 44, 84, 175; in Peronist discourse, 178, 205, 207–8, 213–14; radio and, 61, 66, 69, 192; tango and, 11, 53, 58–59, 92, 98–99, 139–54

Bajo la Santa Federación (Blomberg and Viale Paz), 67, 147–48
Bandoneón, 48, 50, 155; introduced in Argentina, 52; as symbol of tango, 103, 150
Barrio associations, 29–32, 41
Barrios: class composition of, 35, 38–41, 85; consumerism in, 33; expansion of, 15, 22, 26–29; in film, 19, 79; mass cultural audience in, 14, 42,

Barrios (cont.)
66, 77, 92, 129; movie theaters in, 81–83; in poetry, 89–90; politics in, 34–35; in popular fiction, 104–5, 210; in tango lyrics, 11, 99, 101, 199. See also Boedo; La Boca

Bayón Herrera, Luis, 55, 125, 137

Blacklists, 187, 197, 217

Blomberg, Héctor Pedro, 67, 161

Boedo: barrio, 36; tango song, 240 n. 6; writers' group, 151

Borges, Jorge Luis, 91–92, 94, 151

Botana, Natalio, 40, 155, 180. See also *Crítica*

Cadícamo, Enrique, 94, 198

Calki [pseud. for Raimundo Calcagno], 78, 159, 244 n. 105

Canaro, Francisco, 47, 53, 98, 101, 144

Candombe, 146–47, 153

Capra, Frank, 11, 213, 227 n. 28. See also *It Happened One Night*

Carabelli, Adolfo, 48

Carriego, Evaristo, 89–92, 95, 98, 106

Castillo, Alberto, 197–98, 201, 212, 217, 247 n. 53

Castillo, Ramón, 161, 179, 181, 202

Catholic nationalism, 78, 134, 184–85, 206

Censorship: in the 1930s, 63, 78, 180–81, 245 n. 9; after 1943, 178, 184–87, 192, 198–99

Chazarreta, Andrés, 160, 162, 195

Chingolo (Demare), 120–23, 125, 159

Chispazos de Tradición (González Pulido), 66–67, 70, 126, 133, 152, 157, 161, 192

Cinema: as alternative modernism, 8, 44, 75–77, 80, 83, 106; audience for, 81–82; classism of, 16; comedy in, 116–32, 167–75; criticisms of, 77–79, 135, 167; foreign, 21; melodrama in, 86, 105–16; Mexican, 182–83; Perón-era, 183–84, 188–91; promotes integration, 2–3; rural settings in, 155–60; silent, 5, 45, 71–74. See also Hollywood

Class pride, 99, 125–26, 130, 132, 179, 209

Cobián, Juan Carlos, 50, 231 n. 21

Cocoliche, 25, 65, 88

Commercialism, 135, 142–43, 153–54, 166

Communism, 1, 15–16, 39–41, 127, 164, 179, 225 n. 1

Compadrito, 91–92, 94, 96, 102, 110, 139, 148, 247 n. 53

Contursi, Pascual, 90–93, 101, 137, 198

Conventillos, 27, 91, 93, 108–10, 118, 125

Corsini, Ignacio, 52–53, 56, 65, 153, 157, 160

Cortázar, Julio, 198

Criollismo: in cinema, 72–73, 157–61, 190; in radio programs, 65–66, 192; tango influenced by, 53–54, 90–91, 96, 113, 155; in theater, 88–89. See also *Chispazos de Tradición*

Crítica, 15, 40–41, 58, 78, 116, 151, 160–61, 180

D'Arienzo, Juan, 148–50, 154, 163, 166, 196, 198, 242 n. 50

De Caro, Julio, 50–51, 83, 136–37, 143–50, 153, 164–66, 242 n. 50

De Los Ríos, Martha, 65, 162

Del Carril, Hugo, 99, 111, 187–88, 190, 197, 217

Del Ponte, Enrique, 68–69

Demare, Lucas, 120, 156, 188, 191. See also *Chingolo*; *La guerra gaucha*

Demare, Lucio, 146–47

Discépolo, Enrique Santos, 58, 96–97, 100, 102, 151, 168, 186, 198–200

Discos Nacional, 46–47

Disney, Walt, 11

Divitos, 197, 247 n. 53

Ellington, Duke, 227 n. 1, 231 n. 7, 231 n. 18
Envy: mass culture expresses, 132, 159, 208; Peronism validates, 179, 209–10, 212

Ferreyra, José Agustín, 105–11, 115, 118, 131, 147, 158, 188
Filiberto, Juan de Dios, 68, 98, 141
Firpo, Luis, 48, 61–62, 64
Firpo, Roberto, 46–48
Flores, Celedonio, 93–97, 99–100, 103, 137, 198, 205
Folk music: after Peronism, 217–19, 222; in cinema, 160; as national symbol, 9, 135, 150, 153, 213; Peronism and, 194–96, 201, 212; on radio, 61, 65–67, 161–64, 185; tango and, 46, 52–56, 143–47, 157, 164–66
FORJA, 152, 155–56
Franceschi, Monsignor Gustavo, 184–85
Fresedo, Osvaldo, 48, 50, 144, 149–50, 232 n. 36, 242 n. 50
Frondizi, Arturo, 219–20, 222

Gardel, Carlos, 46–47, 59, 101, 104, 145, 192, 198, 205; begins career as folksinger, 52–54, 157, 160–61; film career, 55–56, 72, 75–76, 83, 108–11, 137, 167; as national symbol, 56–57, 79, 152–53; on radio, 60; and rags-to-riches fantasy, 97–99, 136, 208, 210; tango boom and, 90–91
Gauchos, 9, 53, 56, 66, 80, 133, 145, 156–57, 164, 207, 243 n. 77
Glücksmann, Max, 45–47, 49, 53, 64–66, 70–71, 75, 90
González Castillo, José, 46, 75, 90–91, 109–10
González Pulido, José Andrés, 66. See also *Chispazos de Tradición*
González Tuñón, Enrique, 151
Greco, Vicente, 52

Hansen, Miriam, 5, 8, 44, 84, 237 n. 19
Hollywood, 2–3, 7–8, 10–11, 44, 55, 64–65, 70, 73–84, 87, 105–6, 111, 115–17, 122, 131, 159, 181–82, 192, 213, 223, 227 n. 28, 236 n. 127. See also *It Happened One Night*

Immigrants, 12, 134, 175; assimilation of, 23–26, 81, 88, 153, 163; children of, 2, 15, 35, 65, 123, 138, 144; in cinema, 19–22, 76, 78, 107, 172, 219; criollismo and, 53; labor movement and, 37–38, 229 n. 59; as mass culture entrepreneurs, 17, 64, 74–75; mobility of, 28; radio programs for, 67; tango and, 52; in United States, 5
It Happened One Night (Capra), 168–75

Jauretche, Arturo, 152, 155
Jazz, 11, 187, 200, 223; in cinema, 19; influence on tango, 7–8, 44, 47–50, 59, 72, 75, 143, 146, 150; on radio, 61, 65, 67–71, 84, 142, 162; tango competes with, 3, 10, 50–54, 56, 58, 80, 92, 97, 136, 161, 201, 207
Juan Moreira, 25, 53, 88–90, 92, 158, 161
Justo, Agustín P., 78, 180

Karstulovic, Emilio, 138. See also *Sintonía*
Kordon, Bernardo, 141, 146
Korn, Julio, 138. See also *Radiolandia*

La Boca, 27, 80–81, 98, 104, 118
La Canción Moderna. See *Radiolandia*
La guerra gaucha (Demare), 156–59, 163–64
La rubia del camino (Romero), 168–75, 244 n. 108, 245 n. 112
Laclau, Ernesto, 14–15, 212
Lamarque, Libertad: in cinema, 83, 108–18, 122–23, 129–30, 148, 205, 210, 213, 239 n. 50, 245 n. 114; feuds with Eva Perón, 187; on radio, 65

INDEX | 271

Las luces de Buenos Aires (Millar), 55–56, 72, 75, 109, 137, 157, 167
Le Pera, Alfredo, 137, 139, 153–54, 241 n. 18
Legrand, Mirtha, 131, 240 n. 83
Linnig, Samuel, 91, 94
Linyera, Dante [pseud. for Francisco Bautista Rímoli], 32, 136, 138, 240 n. 6
Los Pérez García, 192–94, 219–21
Los tres berretines, 19–22, 25, 28, 37, 42, 76, 78, 80, 107, 117–18, 219, 227 n. 2, 230 n. 73, 239 n. 62
Lugones, Leopoldo, 56, 156–57
Lumiton, 74–76, 82, 107–8, 118, 126–27, 167
Luna, Buenaventura [pseud. for Eusebio Dojorti], 163–64, 166, 194
Lunfardo, 42; in tango lyrics, 9, 21, 114, 136–41, 150, 154, 166, 175, 178, 186, 196–97; in theater, 91

Maffia, Pedro, 47, 241 n. 39
Magaldi, Agustín, 52–53, 65, 100–101
Maizani, Azucena, 56, 59, 68, 101–4, 109, 166, 210
Manzi, Homero, 166–67, 243 n. 67; as cultural critic, 152–54; Peronism and, 188; as radio scriptwriter, 161; as screenwriter, 155–57; as tango lyricist, 102, 145–46, 154–55, 160, 163–64, 198–99, 218
Marshall, Niní [pseud. for Marina Esther Traverso]: in cinema, 117, 126–31, 133, 167, 192, 198, 210, 216, 239 n. 75; criticized, 133; on radio, 123–26; Peronism and, 186–87, 190; after Peronism, 217
Martínez Estrada, Ezequiel, 134–35
Materialism: folk culture rejects, 164–66, 175, 213; Peronism and, 206, 209–10; of the rich, 172; of working-class women, 129, 216
Melodrama: in cinema, 83, 106–31, 157–58, 168–74, 188–92, 230 n. 73, 237 n. 6; classism of, 3, 10, 16, 85–87, 132, 134, 136, 167, 175, 210, 216, 219; in Peronist rhetoric, 178, 202, 205–8, 211–13; in poetry, 89–90; in popular fiction, 104–5; on radio, 44, 66, 147–48; in tango lyrics, 91–103; in theater, 53, 87–89; in United States, 77
Mentasti, Angel, 74–76. *See also* Argentina Sono Film
Merello, Tita, 188, 191–93, 196, 201, 217, 239 n. 50
Middle class, 53, 144; in 1920s and 1930s, 2–3, 33, 36–37, 41, 82, 109, 138; after Peronism, 218–24; under Peronism, 188, 193–98, 200, 209, 212–14, 216; in United States, 49; values ascribed to, 16–17, 20, 22, 35, 42, 132
Military coup (1930), 34, 39, 180
Military coup (1943), 16, 177, 179–80, 183–84, 194, 206
Milonga: in cinema, 102, 191–92; folk music and, 196; revival of, 145–48, 153–55, 160, 166, 199, 218, 241 n. 38; in theater, 53, 89
Milonguita, 90–91, 94–96, 99–100, 107, 109–11, 129, 151, 191, 205, 210
Modernity: associated with United States, 3, 7, 17, 44, 49–51, 81, 177, 201; peripheral, 6, 10; resistance to, 42, 132, 163; symbolized by technology, 69–70, 72, 80, 221; in tension with tradition, 8, 45, 54, 56–59, 84, 150, 166, 174–75, 207
Moglia Barth, Luis, 75, 80, 118

National identity. *See* Authenticity
Nationalism: cultural, 9; economic, 207; Mexican, 7; popular, 152, 156, 199; rural symbols of, 159, 163
Navarro, Fanny, 186–88, 217
Néstor [pseud. for Miguel Paulino Tato], 78, 189, 235 n. 123

Nobleza gaucha (Cairo), 72, 80, 157, 171
Nostalgia, 6, 17, 42, 145, 150, 154–55, 160, 163, 199–200, 207, 218

Ochoa, Fernando, 161–63, 192
Office of the Coordinator of Inter-American Affairs (OCIAA), 181–84
Ortiz, Roberto, 63, 67, 78, 184

Palacio, Lino, 124
Perón, Eva, 1, 14, 18, 185, 200, 202, 216; acting career of, 188, 206; anti-elitism of, 190, 213; attacked, 211; blacklists and, 187; influence on women workers, 208–10
Perón, Juan: fall of, 216–18, 220, 223; followers of, 14–15, 196–200; gains power, 9, 180; media policies of, 64, 178, 183–88, 192, 194, 201; rhetoric of, 16, 178–79, 202–14
Petit de Murat, Ulyses, 78, 156–57, 186, 188
Piana, Sebastián, 145–48, 153, 242 n. 45
Piazzolla, Astor, 200
Podestá brothers, 25, 53, 88–89, 92
Populism: definition of, 14; mass cultural, 10, 16–17, 22, 40–42, 68, 116–17, 123, 126, 130–36, 151–52, 168, 174–75, 177–78, 197–98, 201, 206–7, 211–12; Peronist, 1–2, 179–80, 189, 196, 210, 213–14, 224
Prisioneros de la tierra (Soffici), 158–59, 163, 190, 243 n. 80
Propaganda, 178, 180–81, 186, 188, 200–201, 206
Puerta cerrada (Saslavsky), 112–15, 148, 245 n. 114

Quiroga, Rosita, 101, 103

Radical Party, 15, 34–35, 38, 41, 152
Radio: as alternative modernism, 44, 61, 70; audience for, 22, 37, 60, 179; classism of, 16, 42, 177, 211–12; criticism of, 142–43, 152, 161; networks, 14, 71; after Peronism, 217–20; under Peronism, 192, 194–96, 200–201, 206; programs on, 8, 48, 50–51, 58–59, 65–70, 101, 104, 108–9, 123–27, 134–35, 145–46, 162–64; promotes integration, 2–3; state intervenes in, 10, 62–64, 178, 180, 184–88. See also *individual radio stations*; Radio theater
Radio Belgrano, 64–70, 84, 133, 138, 140–42, 144, 161, 185, 188
Radio El Mundo, 68–69, 71, 123, 129, 138, 142, 148, 161, 164, 185, 192, 219
Radio Splendid (formerly Radio Grand Splendid), 46, 49, 64, 68, 71, 109, 142
Radio theater, 86–87, 115, 147, 157, 161, 185, 192, 224. See also *Bajo la Santa Federación*; *Chispazos de Tradición*
Radiolandia (formerly *La Canción Moderna*), 65, 70, 80, 138–41, 143–47
Recording industry, 7–8, 44, 90–91, 101, 109; audience for, 60, 71; constructs alternative modernism, 51–54, 134–36, 145, 157, 194–95, 217–18; North American influence in, 45–49
Revolución Libertadora, 216–17, 219, 222
Rivero, Edmundo, 41–42, 196–97
Romero, Manuel, 55, 75, 119, 126–27, 137, 150, 167–75, 188, 190, 205, 213, 245 n. 114
Rosas, Juan Manuel de, 67, 147–48, 153
Rossi, Vicente, 146, 153

Sainete, 25, 76, 78, 87–91, 106, 108, 123, 219, 230 n. 73
Sandrini, Luis, 20–21, 117–23, 125, 130–31, 158–59, 167, 192, 205, 227 n. 2, 239 n. 62

INDEX | 273

Sarlo, Beatriz, 6, 105
Saslavsky, Luis, 112, 187. See also *Puerta cerrada*
Scalabrini Ortiz, Raúl, 134, 152
Scolatti Almeyda, Félix, 66–67, 161
Simari, Tomás, 65–66
Simone, Mercedes, 58, 65, 101
Singerman, Paulina, 168–70, 174, 187
Sintonía, 48, 51, 58–59, 66, 79, 98, 104, 126, 129, 138, 141–43, 146, 148–49, 159, 161
Socialism, 1, 30–32, 34–35, 39–40, 89, 151, 156, 187, 219, 229 n. 49
Sociedades de fomento. *See* Barrio associations
Soffici, Mario, 109–10, 158–61, 164, 166, 187–88, 190
Susini, Enrique, 75

Tango: Afro-Argentine origins, 145–48; as alternative modernism, 8, 51, 59, 92, 136, 201; attempts to improve, 137–45; in cinema, 20–21, 25, 55, 75–76, 78–79, 83, 106–16, 118, 168, 174; female singers of, 101–4, 191; folk music competes with, 161–66, 194, 196; as national symbol, 9, 84, 152–55; Peronism and, 197–201, 217; on radio, 61–62, 64–71; state regulation of, 133, 185–86; in theater, 89–91. *See also individual musicians, composers, and lyricists*; Jazz: influence on tango; Jazz: tango competes with; Melodrama: in tango lyrics; Recording industry
¡*Tango!* (Moglia Barth), 75, 83, 102, 107, 145, 148
Tania [pseud. for Ana Luciano Divis], 139
Television, 5, 219–21, 224
Theater, 71, 86, 92, 101, 105, 189. *See also* Sainete
Thorry, Juan Carlos, 125, 129

Tormo, Antonio, 194–95, 198, 201, 212, 217, 247 n. 47
Troilo, Aníbal, 196, 198
Tropilla de Huachi-Pampa, 163–64, 194

United States, 5; Argentina compared to, 10–11, 63, 71, 77, 82, 99, 200–201; Argentine government opposed by, 179, 181–82, 188; companies based in, 45, 47, 55, 61, 220; mass culture imported from, 2, 8, 43–44, 73, 76, 83–84, 106, 147, 221. *See also* Modernity: associated with United States
Upward mobility: advertising promises, 22, 33–34; barrio residents pursue, 15–16, 28, 30–31, 35; mass culture sells fantasy of, 3, 18, 42, 97, 116, 179, 200, 216, 220; melodrama warns against, 87, 90, 96, 99–101, 104–5, 111–12, 115, 119, 123, 129, 132, 166, 189, 207, 212; as middle-class value, 36–39; Peronism and, 208

Vaccarezza, Alberto, 91, 108
Valentino, Rudolph, 1–2, 55, 74, 80
Valle, Pablo Osvaldo, 69, 123, 141
Vera, Virginia, 162, 164–66, 172
Viale Paz, Carlos, 67, 161
Victor Talking Machine Company (later, RCA Victor), 7, 45–50, 60, 101, 108, 195, 221
Villoldo, Angel, 90, 113–14, 198, 232 n. 30

White telephone films, 131, 188, 240 n. 81
Whiteman, Paul, 47, 49–51, 83, 231 n. 7
Women: as audience for mass culture, 5, 79–80, 125–27; as consumers, 19; in melodrama, 17, 86, 90, 92–95,

101–16, 129, 173–74; in Perón-era cinema, 191–92; Peronism and, 208–10, 213; in workforce, 28–29, 37, 89. *See also* Milonguita

Working class, 40, 89, 104, 136; as audience for mass culture, 77; in barrios, 35; consciousness of, 1–2, 4, 151; depicted in mass culture, 107–8, 131, 159, 188; Peronism and, 180, 195, 202–3, 221; values ascribed to, 99–101

Yankelevich, Jaime, 64–71, 75, 138, 162, 185

Yrigoyen, Hipólito, 14, 34–35, 38, 62, 152, 180, 199

Yupanqui, Atahualpa [pseud. for Héctor Chavero], 164, 218, 222

MATTHEW B. KARUSH is an associate professor of history at George Mason University. He is the author of *Workers or Citizens: Democracy and Identity in Rosario, Argentina (1912–1930)* (2002) and the coeditor of *The New Cultural History of Peronism: Power and Identity in Mid-Twentieth-Century Argentina* (2010).

Library of Congress Cataloging-in-Publication Data

Karush, Matthew B. (Matthew Benjamin), 1968–
Culture of class : radio and cinema in the making of a divided Argentina, 1920–1946 / Matthew B. Karush.
p. cm.
Includes bibliographical references and index.
ISBN 978-0-8223-5243-3 (cloth : alk. paper)
ISBN 978-0-8223-5264-8 (pbk. : alk. paper)
1. Social classes—Argentina—History—20th century.
2. Popular culture—Argentina—History—20th century.
3. Motion pictures—Argentina—History—20th century.
4. Radio broadcasting—Argentina—History—
20th century. I. Title.
HN270.Z9S6444 2012
305.50982—dc23   2011041903

www.ingramcontent.com/pod-product-compliance
Lightning Source LLC
Chambersburg PA
CBHW070755230426
43665CB00017B/2373